VIOLENCE AND VICTIMS

VIOLENCE AND VICTIMS

Edited by

Stefan A. Pasternack, M.D.
Georgetown University School of Medicine
Washington, D.C.

SP

S P Books Division of
SPECTRUM PUBLICATIONS, INC.
New York

Distributed by Halsted Press
A Division of John Wiley & Sons

New York   Toronto   London   Sydney

Copyright © 1975 by Spectrum Pulbications, Inc.

Grateful acknowledgement is made to the following publishers for permission to reprint material presented in this book:

The American Psychiatric Association
Simon & Schuster
The American Medical Association
Grune & Stratton, Inc.

Full copyright information for reprinted articles is given on the first page of each reprinted chapter.

Spectrum Publications, Inc.
86-19 Sancho Street, Holliswood, New York 11423

Distributed solely by the Halsted Press Division of John Wiley & Sons, Inc., New York.

Library of Congress Cataloging in Publication Data

Pasternack, Stefan A
    Violence and victims.

    1. Personality, Disorders of. 2. Violence.
3. Victims of crime. I. Title
RC554.P37   616.8'58   74-14971
ISBN 0-470-66921-7

Printed in the United States of America
123456789

Contributors

Richard Boucher, Administrative Assistant, Treatment Center, Correctional Institution, Bridgewater, Mass.

Murray L. Cohen, Ph.D. Consultant Psychologist, Treatment Center, Correctional Institution, Bridgewater, Mass.

Ralph Garofalo, M.A. Deputy Director, Treatment Center, Correctional Institution, Bridgewater, Massachusetts.

William Barry Gault, M.D. Instructor in Psychiatry, Harvard Medical School, Psychiatrist, Massachusetts Mental Health Center.

Roderick Gorney, M.D. Director, Program on Psychosocial Adaptation and the Future, Department of Psychiatry, School of Medicine, University of California, Los Angeles, California.

Arthur Green, M.D. Clinical Assistant Professor of Psychiatry, Division of Child and Adolescent Psychiatry, Box 32, Downstate Medical Center, Brooklyn, New York.

Sarah Haley, M.S.W., Clinical Social Worker, Veterans Administration Outpatient Clinic, Boston, Massachusetts.

Harry Kozol, M.D. Director, Treatment Center, Bridgewater Correctional Institution, Bridgewater, Mass.

John Lion, M.D. Associate Professor of Psychiatry, University of Maryland, Department of Human Behavior and Director Violence Clinic, Baltimore, Maryland.

Carl P. Malmquist, M.D., Professor, Institute of Child Development, and of Criminal Justice, University of Minnesota, Minneapolis, Minn.

Stefan A. Pasternack, M.D. Assistant Professor of Psychiatry and Director Psychiatric In-Patient Service, Georgetown University Hospital, Washington, D.C.

Albert Rothenberg, M.D. Associate Professor of Psychiatry, Yale University School of Medicine, New Haven, Conn.

Bernard Rubin, M.D. Professorial lecturer, Department of Psychiatry, University of Chicago, Pritzker School of Medicine, Chicago, Illinois

Theoharis Seghorn, Ph.D. Staff Psychologist, Treatment Center, Correctional Institution, Bridgewater, Mass.

Martin Symonds, M.D. Assistant Dean, American Institute of Psycho-Analysis, Adjunct Associate Professor of Psychiatry, John Jay College of Criminal Justice, New York, and Consultant Police Department, New York City.

Sherwyn Woods, M.D. Associate Professor, Department of Psychiatry, University of Southern California School of Medicine, Los Angeles, California.

Preface

I have brought together in this book material regarding the clinical evaluation and treatment of violent persons and the victims of violent crime. I was motivated to do this by my contact with many mental health professions who sought such information during a course I offered on Violent Persons through the Metropolitan Mental Health Skills Center of the Washington School of Psychiatry, Washington, D.C. I was impressed by the urgent need of those who saw potentially dangerous persons within traveler's aide stations, court clinics, mental hospitals, schools, rape crisis centers and child protective agencies. Dr. Richard Steinbach, Professor and Chairman of the Department of Psychiatry Georgetown University School of Medicine encouraged me to organize a Symposium on Violence. With the aide of Dr. Steinbach and Dr. Henry Lederer, a symposium was convened at Georgetown Medical Center on October 24th and 25th, 1973. There was great enthusiasm among the participants for a volume of the papers presented. I was thus motivated to organize a publication. It seemed valuable to supplement the Symposium material with other important works relating to evaluation and treatment of various types of dangerous persons.

I wish to thank Dr. Steinbach and Dr. Lederer for their support in these endeavors and am greatly indebted to the staff of the Department of Psychiatry for their steadfast assistance in making the Symposium a success. Elsie Fuller, our Department Assistant was exceptionally helpful. I was also aided greatly by my wife, Gail, who encouraged me to get the book together, who read much of the material, and aided me in composing my editorial comments. We will be richly rewarded if this volume makes work with violent patients a bit easier.

Oct. 1974   Stefan A. Pasternack

Introduction

If we stop to think about violence in our time we will realize that violence has come a lot closer to our lives than we ever imagined. This is especially true living in or near a major metropolitan area where one is likely to be a victim of robbery, assault or rape or where one's home is a likely target for burglary. Most of us probably know someone who has been mugged and we are likely to have witnessed a violent act of some kind. This was simply not true 15-20 years ago. We would never have thought we might be in danger of a violent assault in our lifetimes. Violence in the minds of most Americans was something that happened "across the tracks," in "crime ridden areas," but not in our own communities. Then we witnessed the assassination of President Kennedy, the murder of Lee Harvey Oswald, the killing of Martin Luther King, and Robert Kennedy. Years of campus discord, race riots, anti-war protests with disruption of businesses and daily activities, bombings, kidnappings, and prison revolts, have now conditioned us to a daily fare of violence. We now find ourselves trying to adapt to unprecedented violence, trying to conduct our lives in spite of it. It is a very definite change in our society. We can not fully explain the complex causes for the steady acceleration of violence nor can we reverse the trend. It is going to be "around" for a while.

Recent events have brought the problem into the minds of every citizen. Armed gunmen wander the streets and shoot down innocent citizens for no apparent reason. No one knows why such evil occurs, but these "random killings" are on the rise as the dramatic "Zebra" case in San Francisco highlighted. Prior to that case few persons realized that in many major cities police officials have reported many such random slayings. Such homicides are impossible to predict; they are often impossible to solve. They strike terror into everyone. We go about our daily lives with new fear and vigilance for potential assailants. Those who fly, fear skyjackers and fantasize repeatedly how they might overpower, persuade, or otherwise control potential captors. Insurance companies offer "kidnap" programs for high risk executives who seem the likely targets for rapidly increasing extortion attempts. Other frightening incidents have occurred: a demented man captures a plane and attempts to crash into the White House; Mass killings are discovered in Texas and California. Cannibalism is reported in the death of a traveler in Oregon. Dismembered bodies of missing persons are found in car trunks. The tales are grisly and the message unmistakeable: we must be careful. There is not only more violence, but it is savage.

The way we live has been affected and our life space narrowed. Some inner city areas are "no man's lands" where criminals stalk their prey with impunity. Downtown theater, stores, and restaurants report substantial loss of revenue as a frightened clientele seek safety in the suburbs. Police mount "offensives" to "recapture" streets with improved lighting and increased foot patrols. A war is now waged for control of the streets. Shoppers are careful where they park and some garages and lots offer escort services after dark. In many homes and apartments residents stock weapons, tear gas pellets, attack-canines, not only to protect against robbers but to discourage sadistic killers. Physicians fear to enter certain city areas while other doctors carry handguns for protection. Police lecturers offer advice on "how to avoid rape," or "how to protect against robbery," while urging defensive living. The "greening" of America has been surpassed by the "mugging" of America. Safety consciousness and security measures are now predominant. We hide behind an increasing array of sophisticated locks, burglar alarms, sonic alarms and hired guards. In one ironic and tragic episode two security guards at a well-known university had a dispute and solved it with a gun duel. When the smoke cleared one was dead, the other seriously injured. In another incredible case it appears that a university guard stood by while a co-ed was raped. There is a growing fear of the men who wear the guns, even if they are in uniform. "Who can one trust?" is a frequent question. Some cities are relaxing laws regulating the wearing of sidearms. Could the days of the wild west with pistol packing return to our streets? It is no longer an outlandish possibility. History can and does repeat itself, but now the frontier is the inner city. In some schools principals have advocated that teachers bring side arms with them;

in others police guards are now routine. Police muscle is needed to keep peace in our public schools! Rape and theft, once thought only to occur in the city are now reported frequently on college campuses. The steady spread of violence into hitherto "safe areas," has touched off a new wave of handgun sales which have now passed the 25 million mark for the last ten years. Too often guns bought "in case of need," are used recklessly by persons ill prepared to use them. Many impulsive gunbuyers seeking a kind of "home insurance" do not appreciate the awesome firepower of handguns. Even the National Rifle Association seems unable to persuade many handgun buyers to undertake enough training in their safe use and storage. Home handgun accidents have risen sharply.

There is not only more danger on the streets, but recent evidences suggests that there is more violence within the family life of American families. Witness the serious child abuse problem and one is aware of the struggle to contain violent feelings which many parents must endure. It is also surprising to recognize the diversity of persons concerned with losing control of their violent impulses. Among patients seen in an outpatient clinic were the following: a rookie policeman who feared he would take out his hatreds by shooting the persons he was charged to arrest; a hospital technician who felt he had to compensate for his violent outbursts in which he had previously injured a fiancee and sister; an attorney who feared he would kill his wife; a bus driver who wished to drive his bus over a gorge. The spectrum of persons deeply troubled by violent fantasies and violent deeds indicates that these phemomena is not limited to criminal types. In fact the homicide problem brings some interesting facts to light.

The public, and many professionals as well, is under the misconception that murder is the work of criminal masterminds who kill to achieve power and profit. The psychiatric study of homicide reveals the exact opposite to be true. Homicide is a simple-minded deed. Most murders are not associated with the commission of felonious crimes. Most murders are not the result of Mafia type contracts perpetrated in the name of criminal organizations.

In 1972 as in years past over 70 percent of all homicides were committed by relatives of the victim or by the victims close personal acquaintances. It is therefore startling to realize that if all known criminals were immediately imprisoned we would continue to witness an increase in murder. The majority of murders occur in private homes within social circumstances and thus homicide is according to FBI interpretation a "national social problem beyond police prevention." While a significant number of homicides are committed by usually law-abiding citizens who are not consciously intent upon murder, such persons inadvertently become killers when, during a temporary explosion of anger, they utilize a dangerous weapon as means of expressing hostility.

The dynamics of homicide has been studied by many, and research clearly shows that any person, even without serious predisposing factors can be caught in the crushing existential trap from which he may seek escape by homicide. For most persons when under sufficient stress may revert to primitive thinking patterns characterized by inordinate fear of attack, feelings of vulnerability, and increasing anxiety. All too often an unwitting victim or a victim unconsciously seeking injury continues to provoke the person who is on the verge of explosion. Sadomasochistic pairing of would-be victim and would-be assailant has been documented in homicide studies. Victimology reveals that some victims actually desire injury as the price of a greater glory. Murder has been associated with a wide variety of clinical states, but murder by acutely psychotic persons is rare. The clinical state most often discovered in someone who has committed a homicide not in conjunction with a felonious crime is variously described as a dissociative homicide. This reflects the sudden breakdown of emotional controls and the uncontrolled expression of murderous rage. Too often such transient disruption is facilitated by drugs or alcohol, provoked by passion and followed by remorse. In most instances the murderer only sought to hurt his victim and killing represents an ego dystonic act.

It seems that there are many factors which would erode our mastery of violent urges and that a cult of violence exists within our society. Social scientists agree that our national heritage and our way of contemporary life encourage violent solutions to life's vexing problems. The report of the National Commission on the Causes and Prevention of Violence is the most comprehensive investigation of the subject yet undertaken. Unfortunately the report has been largely ignored. Violence thrives in the media and many scientists believe that increasingly sadistic portrayal's of man's inhumanity to man may be taking their toll. There is an upswing in the readiness to strike out vengefully. Quick-draw street quarrels have led the District of Columbia Homicide Chief to say.

"We do not want to panic people but they should be aware if they get into an altercation with a stranger there is a distinct possibility he may be carrying a gun. You can get shot if you simply get out of your car to settle a minor driving accident."

At this critical moment in our national life our public officials have been debating a national crime strategy but given only conflicting advice. There is no overall program to stem the rising tide of media productions which incite violence through their glory examples. We have no responsible fire-arms control legislation: existing statues are, in the opinion of Police Chief Jerry Wilson of Washington, D.C. "a farce." The ambitious "new cities" plans have not had enough time to influence terrible conditions within our larger cities. A dreadful inflation has brought spiralling costs, undermining many welfare efforts and adding to the agonies of the poor above all. We can not predict what new bitterness these societal catastrophies may engender, but more violence can certainly be expected.

How then can the mental health profession mount an effort to ameliorate the violence in our society? We can begin first by recognizing that this is an area about which we must be professionally not just personally concerned. Too often, violent persons are simply shunted off to state hospitals to receive custodial care rather than treatment. Too often such persons are denied treatment from which they could realistically benefit. A second point of intervention derives from our relative ignorance about human motivations towards violence. We know that hopelessness is likely to spur desperate actions and that dehumanized attitudes towards persons makes it easy for a desperate person to act violently. There is reason to be hopeful. Work with self-referred violent patients and other categories of "dangerous persons" reveals that such patients can acquire new repertoires of personal styles. It is much more difficult to "humanize" our society. But another point of intervention could be professional pressure for laws which would effectively reduce the availability of handguns, the predominant weapon for murder. The new generation of mental helath professionals guided by the experience of the past will have to tackle the problem of violence and do what it can to discover new treatment methods, new preventive techniques, and new predictive criteria.

All this violence does not mean that we are about to succomb to a new age of barbarism, a new "dark age." It does mean that we have to cope with dangers in our lives which we have never before encountered on such a scale. It means that our lives and the lives of our loved ones are less secure. Our civilization is less able to protect us. We must now make wise and forceful use of existing resources lest the next generation face even greater danger from man's greatest enemy: other men.

Table of Contents

EVALUATION OF DANGEROUS PERSONS

A man was committed to a mental hospital because he "was dangerous to himself and to others." His case was never reviewed. During the next twenty years of confinement in an old state hospital he received little treatment. Life passed him by before he was finally released as "no longer dangerous." A gross miscarriage of justice and of psychiatric treatment had been committed, all because he was once considered "dangerous." Was he really dangerous? Are there other "dangerous persons" languishing in hospitals because their cases have not been adequately evaluated and because the usual review procedures have failed?

Another man was enraged at his wife and shot at her. He was arrested for misusing a firearm and then released on bail. No one bothered to determine his reason for shooting at his wife or to determine if he would do so again. He went home and killed her. Could this homicide have been prevented?

In another case a violent sex offender was convicted of sordid rape assaults. He was sent to prison for 15 years. He received no treatment, never regretted his misdeeds, and never knew the grief he had caused to his victims. Once set free his pathological impulses resurged and he struck again. The outraged community protested but had no means to improve the situation. Community officials helplessly pondered the shortcomings of the penal system. Others called for the death penalty. All recognized the

1

difficulty in dealing with dangerous sex offenders and the dramatic need for viable treatment alternatives. The mental health profession now stands at a fascinating but difficult juncture with its credibility as well as its capability under scrutiny. It is being asked to determine before the act whether or not a given individual might at some future point become dangerous. The profession is being challenged to render safe those persons declared dangerous and to prevent others from becoming dangerous should they show violent proensities. We must speak so clearly that no one can misunderstand nor misrepresent the realistic limitations of treatment. Overzealous statement of psychiatric ability could lead to public disillusionment; understatement could lead to missed opportunities. Meanwhile many civil libertarians express concern that the collaboration of mental health professionals with law enforcement agencies could help produce a police state. These fears are given credence when one considers the daily invasions of privacy, violations of civil rights, and police excesses reported in the news media. Psychosurgery has made a dramatic return and some scientists vigorously propose to control violent persons by destroying parts of their brains. An ambitious California project "to reduce violence" was publicly assailed as unethical, racist, and inhumane. The controversy in that matter still rages. More persons are needed to continue research into violent behavior. There is a need for more data on which to base testable hypothesis regarding treatment approaches. In this context the work of several investigators is noteworthy.

Dr. Harry Kozol reports on his extensive experience with dangerous sex offenders at the Bridgewater Center for the Treatment of Dangerous Persons. He makes it clear that there are no pat answers. The diagnosis of dangerousness must be arrived at carefully after a detailed clinical examination in which the patient, the circumstances, and all other factors are weighed. Dr. Rubin reviews the literature on the prediction of dangerousness in mentally ill criminals. He cautions us to be conservative and to recognize that such predictions are extremely difficult to validate. Dr. Carl Malmquist reports on his clinical experiences with youths who murdered and suggests premonitory signs which any clinical investigator might monitor.

I.

The Diagnosis
of Dangerousness*

Karry Kozol

Society has sought to cope with the problem of the dangerous offenders in its midst from time immemorial. Much of this effort appears to have been futile. Neither extreme punishment nor great indulgence appears to have had an appreciable effect in reducing the incidence of crime. The rise of interest in the criminal as a person rather than the crime as an act parallels the rise and development of dynamic psychiatry in this century. The individualization of the offender was the proclaimed objective and much has been contributed. Nevertheless, traditional jurisprudence and penology have tended to resist experimentation with new proposals and to persist in a policy of punishment as a principal instrument of deterrence. The failure of such policy is manifest in the increasing incidence of primary crimes and recidivism. The obvious alternative was to draft another discipline, namely, psychiatry. The failure of traditional penal retribution had incited a search for more effective preventive measures. Nearly 15 years ago the Commonwealth of Massachusetts embarked on a sociological experiment in which a special class of criminals was delegated to the primary jurisdiction of psychiatry rather than penology. The legislation imposed upon psychiatry the task of diagnostically identifying from among a special

*This paper was presented at the Georgetown University Medical Center Symposium on Violence, October 26, 1973.

3

class of offenders those who were "dangerous." It further imposed upon psychiatry the responsibility for treatment of those so designated. Authority to recommend the conditional discharge of those patients whose dangerous assaultive potential appeared to have been dissipated was also given to psychiatry. In a sense this was a program where the treatment, not the punishment, would fit the criminal and not the crime. This innovation was philosophically and legally based on a concept of preventive medicine. The offender is looked upon as a menace to the health and well-being of his potential victims. Accordingly he is quarantined from society, by detention, and treated, until such time as he is considered free of his dangerous potential and thus is no longer a threat to the welfare of others. Recidivism is the plague of penology, and the ultimate objective of treatment is identical with that of punishment, namely, to modify the potential of the offender so that he will not repeat his offenses. All communities have witnessed the tragic repetition of vicious and even murderous offenses by persons who had been released from prison after having served long sentences for identical crimes. The decision of the legislature to delegate this responsibility to psychiatry reflected a loss of confidence in the effectiveness of traditional penal methods. There was of course no assurance that psychiatry would or could do any better than penology. Only time could provide an answer. This is a report of our experience.

In essence the law established a new disease entity "the dangerous person" and provided for psychiatric examination for a convicted offender in order to determine whether or not he is dangerous. The law was specifically related to offenses in which sex was an element—even if only incidental. The law provided that any person diagnosed as "dangerous" would become subject to lifelong detention under a special mental health commitment, and the law further provided that such persons receive "treatment." Persons so committed and treated could be released and returned to the community once it was decided that they were no longer dangerous.

The rising tide of violent crime in our times has sharpened the apprehensions of all and has stimulated an avalanche of proposals for its containment ranging from preventive detention (in this jurisdiction) to the death penalty. Much of the legislation proclaims the desirability of special programs of treatment and rehabilitation but few jurisdictions have gone beyond such lip service. I wish to report the experience of *one* jurisdiction where such a statute was taken seriously.

The Massachusetts statute was enacted in 1957, but it took 2 years before it could be implemented. The statute came about in this way. In

June of 1957 a young man was returned to the community after serving nearly 10 years for a teenage sadistic, sexual assault on a little boy followed by repeated stabbings of the victim through the back of the chest. Seven weeks to the day after discharge from prison he murdered two little brothers aged eight and ten and then made a bonfire of their bodies. This case was a tragic demonstration of the futility of contemporary sentencing practices, most of which call for return to the community at the termination of the sentence regardless of the menace which the subject may pose to others. Clearly, so long as sentences are fixed and terminate, the whole philosophy of penology in practice must be looked upon as retributive since it surely can not be looked upon as predicated on the test of whether or not the subject is fit to be free in a community where he may again do harm to others.

Our facility is a mental health institution in law and in fact, despite its location within the confines of a large maximum security correctional institution. Both responsibility and authority are vested in the clinical organization, and the assigned security officers are subordinate to and under the control of the clinical authority. Such an approach is rare if not unique in the history of criminology in that it delegates primary authority and responsibility to psychiatry rather than to penology. It is a sociological experiment in the broadest and most compelling sense. Only time will tell whether or not psychiatry will do better or, for that matter, worse than penology.

Our first problem was to define the subject with which we were supposed to be dealing. The legislature had ordered psychiatry to *diagnose* dangerousness. The statutory definition was somewhat vague and it remained for us to conceptualize a definition. In doing so we looked to the tragic case out of which this entire program derived. In general terms dangerousness means a potential for doing harm to others. The criminal law tends to limit the term to acts which may result in serious physical injury to others although some jurisdictions include psychological injury on a more tenuous basis. The word "dangerous" does not appear in the common law which deals with narrowly specified crimes: treason, murder, rape, robbery, and so forth. Nor does it appear in the statutory codifications of the criminal law. However, spearheaded by the National Council on Crime and Delinquency (1963) there has been a rising tide of concern about the *theme* of dangerousness which runs through all crimes involving personal violence or the threat of such. (Violence is looked upon as one instrument of the dangerous potential.) More than half the jurisdictions in this country have enacted specific laws relating to dangerous behavior collateral to specifically designated crimes. This legislation superimposes special measures for dealing with the convicted offender such as particularly long sentences or detention in special facilities. Regrettably, Massachusetts in common with a number of other states requires that a sex offense appear in the subject's criminal history or in the instant offense. This is a curious expression of society's paradoxical ambivalence toward and fascination with all things sexual. It is our hypothesis that there is no difference between the man who kills to rob and the man who kills to rape. The important thing is the *harm* that is done to the victim.

Since the literature of psychiatry was virtually silent on these issues, and we had neither precepts nor precedence to guide us, it devolved upon us to establish our own criteria of dangerousness, to devise a diagnostic modus operandi, and to conceptualize an effective treatment plan.

This report updates previous reports of our work. It covers an experience extending over 12 years. Our case material is derived from a total of over 3,000 convicted offenders most of whom were screened by psychiatrists from our consulting staff. Of this group we have made diagnostic studies of 981. We concluded that 285 of these men were dangerous and recommended their commitment to our facility. The courts rejected our recommendations in 31 cases but committed 254 for a period of a day to life. In these 12 years we have recommended the discharge of 103 patients after varying periods of treatment, the average being 47 months. Of those patients whom *we* recommended for return to the community following this average 47-month period of treatment the recidivism rate stands at 5.8%, for repetition of dangerous offenses, after an average period of freedom (at risk) of 59 months—nearly 5 years. This figure closely approximates the recidivism rates in those patients whom we initially excluded from the diagnosis of dangerousness and who were ultimately released into the community. Forty-nine patients who were released into the community against our advice by judges who rejected our recommendations had a recidivism rate of 34.7%. Twenty-nine of these 49 patients had been committed to and studied by us in the earliest years of our program—all within the first 5 years of its inception at a time when our experience was limited. A case history study reveals that at least 14 of these patients would not have been diagnosed as dangerous in the latter years of our study. Exclusion of these 14 cases leaves us with a more accurate recidivism rate derived from the fact that 17 out of 35 patients who were released against our advice committed dangerous offenses—a recidivism rate of 48.6 %.

As we have just noted, the first years of our venture were ones of trial and error in which we sought to develop criteria and to test them over the succeeding years. Out of our trial and error we developed our concept of the dangerous person as contrasted with the safe person.

DEFINITION OF DANGEROUS PERSON

We conceive the *dangerous person* as one who has actually inflicted or attempted to inflict serious physical injury on another person; harbors anger, hostility, and resentment; enjoys witnessing or inflicting suffering; lacks altruistic and compassionate concern for others; sees himself as a victim rather than as an aggressor; resents or rejects authority; is primarily concerned with his own discomfort; is intolerant of frustration or delay of satisfaction; lacks control of his own impulses; has immature attitudes toward social responsibility; lacks insight into his own psychological structure; and distorts his perception of reality in accordance with his own wishes and needs.

DEFINITION OF A SAFE PERSON

We conceive of the *safe person* as one who has generally mature attitudes toward social responsibility, has developed a compassionate concern for the welfare and interests of others, has divested himself of hostilities and resentments, is relatively free of gross distortion of reality, has developed insight into his own nature, appears to have developed strong conditioning against repetition of his original offensive behavior, and specifically recognizes that freedom in the community involves responsibility as well as gratification.

SPECTRUM

No one is totally primitive—concerned only with the immediate satisfaction of limited goals—or totally mature—maintaining judicious control of all impulses. The dangerous potential may be fixed and habitual, episodic, or sporadic. People cannot be divided into the dangerous and the nondangerous—the bad guys and the good guys. The spectrum is wide, with the extremely dangerous at one end and the absolutely nondangerous at the other. The ability to measure dangerousness and the factors that contribute to it is limited by our clinical judgement and experience.

HOW DO WE MAKE THE DIAGNOSIS?

Dangerousness seems to be a resultant of multiple forces. It cannot be attributed to a single factor, and it is not detectable through routine psychiatric examination. There is no single test for it. We doubt that any tests or methods of examination, in and of themselves, are subtle enough to evaluate the delicate balance between those impulsive elements that lead to dangerous behavior and those self-controlling elements that inhibit it.

The diagnosis of dangerousness is based on inquiry and examinations that extensively pursue areas of concern not fully dealt with in routine psychiatric assessment. There are no rigid criteria of dangerousness; there are only clues gleaned from a meticulous inquiry into multiple aspects of the personality. We have developed these clues out of painstaking years of trial and error, in the course of which we have developed frames of references for investigation of the personality. Out of these investigations emerges our clinical prediction as to the patient's future behavior. Our frames of reference are not fixed nor are they proposed as a rigid schema for examination; rather, they are a guide for the clinician who is charged with the responsibility of advising the court as to the person's potential.

How Do We Make the Diagnosis of Dangerousness?

How do we use all this material? Our final diagnosis is based on an estimate of the relative quantity and intensity of dangerous elements contrasted with the safe ones. Our clinical judgment of the comparative weight of these elements determines the final diagnosis. We make the diagnosis when the total study clearly places the patient within our concept of the dangerous person.

THE ACT

Of paramount importance is a meticulous description of the actual assault. The potential for violent assaultiveness is the core of our diagnostic problem, and the description of the aggressor in action is often the most valuable single source of information. The patient's version is compared with the victim's version. In many cases we interview the victim ourselves. Our most serious errors in diagnosis have been made when we ignored the details in the description of the assault. No one can predict dangerous behavior in an individual with no history of dangerous acting out.

FRAMES OF REFERENCE

In each study we explore the regions of the personality that we consider relevant. Since multiple forces and experiences influence the personality, we seek information on themes and experiences in the patient's history. We have developed wide frames of references and lines of inquiry designed to reveal and give in depth dimension to the structure and dynamic potential of the personality we are studying. In practice, we pose a series of questions of ourselves. These reflect some but not all of our frames of reference and lines of inquiry. They do not constitute a check list, and they are not complete or final. They are suggestions and reminders to us, not a questionnaire put to the patient. A series of these questions follows.

With respect to the use of force and violence

Was he aggressively and wantonly cruel?

Did he enjoy inflicting pain?

What was his affect or emotional state at the time he perpetrated his crime?

Did he have any identification with his victim?

Was he angry?

With his victim?

With whom, or at what?

Since when?

Was he angry at the world or specifically angry with a person or a class?

Was the anger realistic and justified or unrealistic and disproportionate?

What was the fate of this anger?

Did his anger persist or evaporate?

Is he cruel toward himself?

Does he enjoy suffering?

How has he reacted to frustration or delay of satisfaction?

With violence?

With anger?

With both?

Must he have immediate satisfaction?

Has there been any expression of violence in his drawings,

Has there been any expression of violence in his drawings, writings, statements, fantasies, dreams?

What is the subject's view of himself?

How does he feel about what he sees in himself?

What does he like best about himself?

What does he like least about himself?

What is his conception of an ideal person?

Whom does he admire?

Whom is he for?

Who are his heroes?

Whose exploits does he applaud?

Whom does he tend to imitate in speech and manner? Why?

What is the subject's views of others?

Are they his potential enemies and he their potential victim?

Are they his potential prey?

Are they nonexistent as persons and seen only as objects that he may use or exploit?

Does he confuse their identity?

How does he relate to others?

Is he a social isolate, either alienated from othe persons or never affiliated with them?

Does he have sympathetic identification with others?

What is his view of his prospects for the future?

Is he optimistic or pessimistic?

Is he hopeful or discouraged?

Is he depressed?

Does life hold any meaning for him? What?

What was his view of himself vis-a-vis the general community?

How has he related to other persons?

How has he dealt with authority figures?

Did he have difficulty in school and work adjustments?

How did he get along with his peers?

Did he feel that he belonged?

Or was he a loner?

Did he feel dependent on his peers?

Did he crave their recognition and respect?

Was he concerned about his status in the eyes of others?

Was he embittered?

Did he feel frustrated, rejected, discriminated against, deprived, unrecognized, mistreated, abused, in short, victimized?

Did he feel threatened and persecuted?

Did he have a sense of longing and hunger with a concomitant sense of despair about ever dissipating this hunger?

How did he relate to his family?

Was the family constellation meaningful? In what way?

Was there conflict with parents? With siblings?

Did the patient feel loved, supported, encouraged by either or both parents?

Did he feel threatened, disdained, rejected?

We are interested in the patient's general life style. Was he conventional and socially conformative and responsible, was he unconventional, and irresponsible, or was he unconventional, irresponsible, and opposed to social standards? We are interested in the nature and amount of control that he asserted in his life pattern of behavior. Has control been by repression or sublimation? What has been the result?

There is nothing unique about the content of these diagnostic areas of inquiry. They are familiar to all students of human nature. Our selectivity and emphasis, arrived at by arduous trial and error, are what determine the consistency and uniformity of our diagnostic procedure.

PSYCHOLOGICAL TESTS

Psychological testing supplements our total diagnostic procedure. To our knowledge, there is no single test or combination of tests that can predict dangerous acting out. None of our testing is routine. It is specifically designed for each case according to the particular history and clinical findings.

THE TOTAL PERSONALITY

In assessing the personality, we seek information about the patient's assets, the safe elements in the personality, as well as his liabilities. No one is totally and exclusively safe or dangerous. Safeness is the complement of dangerousness. Its determination is at least as difficult as that of dangerousness. Releasing an offender from sentence or other commitment requires at least as much expertise as determining that an offender is dangerous. Release procedures endorse the safeness of a person and should be carried out by a competent aggregate of experts. We conceive of the safe person as one who has generally mature attitudes toward social responsibility, has developed a compassionate concern for the welfare and interests of others, has divested himself of hostilities and resentments, is relatively free of gross distortion of reality, has developed insight into his own nature, appears to have developed strong conditioning against repetition of his original offensive behavior, and specifically recognizes that freedom in the community involves responsibility as well as gratification.

Treatment

Individualization is the essence of treatment. On admission, a therapeutic plan is formulated for each patient, and this plan is regularly reviewed and modified. Individualization does not necessarily mean individual therapy, which is not necessarily the best treatment for every patient or a guarantee of success and early release. Individual treatment not only failed to modify some patients' potential but seemed to reinforce an exclusive interest in themselves. In our opinion a *combination* of individual and group psychotherapy offers the greatest promise for the largest number. Each group therapist is responsible for each patient in his group as an individual and sees each patient individually at varying intervals. This has multiple value: It assures the patient that there is a specific continuing interest in him, it gives him an opportunity to say things that he might be reluctant to say in the group, and it allows the therapist to focus all his attention on the individual patient. In our opinion group therapy without individualization is specious. It is the individual who is held accountable by criminal conviction, not the group, and it is the individual, not the group, who will be considered for release.

Our treatment is based on contemporary psychiatry and psychology. We have no dogmatic bias and no therapeutic ax to grind. Out of necessity and ignorance, our approach is experimental. We have no firm answers and we doubt that others have, but we do have some emerging hypotheses which we are constantly testing. The ultimate test of these hypotheses will come when our patients are returned to the community.

Neither drugs and hormones nor any other chemical or physical modalities play any part in our basic program of treatment. Dangerousness is too subtle to be materially modified or affected by any specious modalities of treatment. Neuroanatomical and neurophysiological research has not progressed to the point where simple extirpation of brain centers or pharmacological intervention can be generally applied. Nor do we use so-called conditioning therapies or behavior modification techniques. We are skeptical of the duration of any possible effect of such procedures and would neither exploit our patients nor jeopardize the security of the community by experimenting with such a dubious modality of treatment.

In group and individual psychotherapy, we distinguish between intensive and supportive treatment. We try not to lecture to our patients and prefer that they make discoveries for themselves. However, we cannot simply try to outwait them. Some patients would long outlive us without uttering a meaningful word.

For the small group of patients who suffer from developmental retardation or psychological regression and therefore cannot be helped by conventional therapy, we seek to effect benefit through repetitive social conditioning. Treatment for them is didactic and prescriptive.

SOCIAL REMONSTRANCE AND VIOLENCE

We do not equate dangerousness with contemporary patterns of social remonstrance and violence, although the latter may be perceived as dangerous by target establishments. We define dangerousness as a pathological self-serving potential for violence. An individual participant in mass violence may or may not be dangerous, depending on whether his motivation is essentially altruistic (based on a compassionate identification with others) or egoistic (concerned primarily with venting personal rage). Altruism and egoism reflect polar levels of maturity. The presence of anger in a participant is not pathognomonic of a dangerous potential if it reflects a primary concern for other. Rage at oppression has been considered righteous from time immemorial. In the context of history, when the absence of alternatives has engendered desperation, extreme violence resulting in injury to property and persons has been socially acceptable. Primary insistence on violence when alternatives do exist and without benevolent regard for the consequences to others is another thing. As history has shown, leaders of great nations may be infinitely more dangerous than the most depraved lone killer. The dynamics are identical; only the scope and magnitude of their crimes are different.

REGARDING TREATMENT AND SOCIAL BACKGROUND

Individualization of the offender requires consideration of the world from whence he came and the world to which he will return.

The correlation between criminal incidence and backgrounds of deprivation, discrimination, exploitation, frustration, and desperation is self-evident. Man's collective inhumanity to man surpasses in evil anything that one man as an individual may do to another man. May not our labors in dealing with the individual offender be wasted and futile if we return him from prison or hospital to a world which is no better, and probably worse, than the one from whence he came?

May not *crime* be the *law* for the embittered?

II.

Prediction of Dangerousness in Mentally Ill Criminals*

Bernard Rubin

The belief in the psychiatrist's ability to predict the likely dangerousness of a patient's future behavior is almost universally held, yet it lacks empirical support. This paper is an attempt to organize the problem of prediction of dangerousness. Recent empirical studies which begin to isolate the characteristics of danger as well as supporting data from the psychiatric, sociologic, and legal literature are detailed. The histories of a group of mentally ill criminals recently released from prison, which I have followed over time, are examined in terms of possible determinants of their dangerousness, and predictions are made and compared to those made by others.

Indications are that social factors have primacy, while psychologic and biologic factors require further study.

Treatment interventions depend on predictions of the likely consequences of such interventions. Such predictions are unavoidable for the psychiatrist, as indeed they are for anyone who proposes to treat another's illness. There is, however, another type of prediction, that of the likely dangerousness of a patient's future behavior. This prediction is expected of the psychiatrist—and psychiatrists acquiesce daily. This belief in the psy-

*Reprinted from the *Archives of General Psychiatry* Vol 27, pp 297-407, Sept. 1972. © American Medical Association, 1972.

chiatrist's capacity to make such predictions is firmly held and constantly relied upon, in spite of a lack of empirical support.

The law requires, in Illinois as in other states, that the civil commitment of a mentally ill patient depend on psychiatric testimony. The patient must be in need of mental treatment and dangerous to himself or others.

Similarly, relevant commitment and release laws concerning psychologically disturbed criminals accused or "convicted" of a serious crime, depend upon psychiatric testimony as to the likely recurrence of serious crime.

The problem is not a small one. Although the number of civil commitments to mental hospitals have been markedly reduced in the past ten years, approximately 50,000 mentally ill persons per year are predicted to be dangerous and preventively detained for society's and their protection as well as their treatment. In addition about 5% (2% and 28%) of the total mental hospital population of the United States (approximately 337,000) are kept in maximum security sections on assessment of their potential dangerousness. Of the approximately 600,000 (1968 — 598,660) persons who will be apprehended and accused of index crimes against persons (homicide, aggravated assault, forcible rape, and robbery) in a year, about 5% to 10% will be examined (pretrial or presentence) to advise the court about their potential future dangerousness and associated questions of appropriate intervention (prison vs hospital, etc.). Lastly about 10,000 persons designated as mentally ill offenders will be admitted in a year (1967 — 11,840 admissions—estimate 10,000 persons), two-thirds of whom will be in special hospitals for the criminally insane, one-sixth in ordinary mental hospitals, and one-sixth in correctional institutions. These include persons who are: (1) charged with a crime, and held pending determination of their competency trial. (2) Charged with a crime and found incompetent to stand trial. (3) Found not guilty by reason of insanity. (4) Convicted of a crime and found mentally ill at the time of sentencing. (5) Found to be mentally ill while serving a sentence. (6) Sex offenders not included in the above. Of this group, those in the last five categories require yearly or more frequent examinations or reviews to determine whether the state of predicted dangerousness has altered, modified, or disappeared.[1,2] Szasz has compellingly written[3] that the behavioral sciences have not yet been able to solve simple and operational definitions of eccentricity and dangerousness, and because of that he feels[4] that psychiatrists have been motivated in large part to be counter-aggressive to very provocative patients. Such aggressiveness can be related to the psychiatrist's identification with prevailing societal sanctions regarding certain deviant behavior, to an unwillingness by the psychiatrist to share deviant power, and to the psychiatrist's personal readiness to respond to provocative behavior. Szasz's answer is to reject the concept of dangerousness and to argue that the psychiatrist, in the conflict between the patient's and society's rights, should always side with the patient. As Szasz notes correctly,[5] few people are dangerous and psychiatrists may serve as a bearer of society's guilty decision to punish. But what about the "few" who are dangerous?

For some investigators concerned with prediction there is no serious problem. It matters only that the right diagnostic test be done to isolate a particular brain-damaged population at risk.[6,7] For others,[8,9] certain toxins are implicated as the predictive cause of violent behavior. Subcultures are described[10 13] and those descriptive qualities are dealt with as predictive of violent behavior. Careful clinical study[14 17] is done and thought to provide sufficient data for prediction.

This naive certainty has not been supported by empirical studies nor by the few evaluations of the results of such prediction. Even in the most careful, painstaking, laborious, and lengthy clinical approach to the prediction of dangerousness, false positives may be at a minimum of 60% to 70%.[18]

In addition to the area of civil commitment, Morris and Hawkins[19] note that the American Law Institute's Model Penal Code provides that criminal sentence may be extended if the person is a "dangerous mentally abnormal person," and in the Model Sentencing Act of the Advisory Council of Judges of the National Council on Crime and Delinquency, dangerous offenders are defined as those who have committed or attempted certain crimes of physical violence and who are found to be "suffering from a severe personality disorder indicating a propensity toward criminal activity." The Durham decision in the District of Columbia has led to the commitment of those acquitted by reason of insanity until (1) their sanity is recovered and (2) they will not in the reasonable future be dangerous to themselves or others. The authors insist that the above require psychiatric definitions of an operable concept of dangerousness and they correctly conclude that not until such predictions can be made can the policy questions concerning what degree of risk should the community bear and how many false positives are acceptable be answered.

To be able to predict dangerousness is related to the basic capacity to understand disordered behavior, and to intervene in those circumstances where the result is an increase in social good, where society's members are reasonably protected, and where effective rehabilitative efforts can be made.

A myth and misconception stand between the problem and its possible solution. The myth is that of individual clinical judgement which demands that each case be taken in its own right. Nevertheless many authors[16][18][20][21] who can recognize a need for the prediction of dangerousness insist on individual clinical judgment, intuition, and unexplained hunches. Spiegel[22] who deplores a lack of research in the development of techniques for intervention, ignores prediction even though it underpins intervention.

The misconception is that particular psychiatric disorders are per se dangerous which is encouraged by certain mental disorders being characterized by some kind of confused, bizzare, agitated, threatening, frightened, panicked, paranoid, or impulsive behavior. That and the view that impulse (ie, ideation) and action are interchangeable support the belief that all mental disorder must of necessity lead to inappropriate, antisocial, or dangerous actions. In a staff report to the Commission on the Causes and Prevention of Violence, Erwin and Lion [16] note that "violence refers to assaultive or destructive acts or ideations. The term ideation is included because patients with fears and fantasies of violence sometimes act them out." Later they make a very doubtful unsubstantiated statement connecting violence with psychological disorder: " . . . our impression has been that the largest group of patients complaining of violence fall into the classification of 'borderline' or 'schizoid' personality types."[16] (p.1187) Another author, Muller[23] while arguing that "more specific criteria need to be established for imposing involuntary mental hospitalization," and the "degree of likely damage must be great," then states his criteria: "These are the psychoses, both functional and organic, and conditions in which there is permanent or temporary impairment of cerebral cortical functioning so that, at the time, the person is not considered fully responsible for his own behavior." Thus, the author confuses psychosis and/or the absence of responsibility with dangerousness. The argument is not very compelling. The criteria remain vague and inaccurate. Part of the problem may be that psychiatrists use mental disease as a concept which relates to treatment as Shah noted[24] and labeling of deviancy as mental illness or predicting dangerousness is just a convention to get someone to treatment. Once in treatment the concept of dangerousness is forgotten. It is a device which enlarges and thereby confuses the apparent size of the problem. The confusion of serious psychological impairment and dangerousness and the dialogue of misunderstanding between the law and psychiatry about this is best illustrated by the following exchange (Hough[7][16] vs United States, 217 F2d, 458 (1959)):

(Dr. Karpman): I urged her father to hospitalize her; but of course he wouldn't do it. I predicted, I told him personally that we never can tell what measures of what a person of this type of psychosis might do. It may be something very drastic. But I didn't think of murder, because I am not an astrologer and I couldn't predict in advance; but I said something drastic might happen.

Q: You thought she had a psychosis at that time?
A: Yes.
Q: What psychosis?
A: Paranoid schizophrenia.
Q: In your opinion, is Edith L. Hough the aggressive type of paranoid?
A: Yes, she is the aggressive type—as evidenced by the fact that she took measures of her own in killing the man. That is aggressiveness.
Q: In your opinion, is an aggressive paranoid potentially dangerous?
A: It is conceded universally an aggressive paranoid is dangerous. I would say that universally we think that any paranoid schizophrenic is potentially dangerous, because one can never tell them the meekness and sub-missiveness may suddenly turn around and become aggressive.
Q: Would you say the Edith L. Hough at this time is dangerous because she has schizophrenia, paranoid type?
A: I would rather not answer this question directly. Ask me whether a paranoid schizophrenic is potentially dangerous and I would say yes.
Q: You would say yes?
A: Yes.

In his testimony the psychiatrist states he can, and yet he cannot predict dangerousness.

Arguments about dangerousness are frequently circular, and so before proceeding there should be some agreement about what kinds of behavior are sufficiently threatening and damaging to be called dangerous. The National Commission on the Causes and Prevention of Violence defined violence as "overtly threatened or overtly accomplished application of force which results in the trying or destruction of persons or property or reputation or the illegal appropriation of property."[25] Katz and Goldstein[26] attempt to list the kinds of violence that might be subsumed under the heading of such injury to persons:

1. Crime for which defense of insanity invoked
2. All crime
3. Felonies
4. Crime for which maximum sentence given

   5. Crimes categorized as violent
   6. Crimes that are harmful, physical or psychological
   7. Any conduct, harmful or threatening
   8. Conduct provoking retaliation
   9. Violence toward self
   10. Any combination of the above

This list does not exhaust the possibilities. While too broadly inclusive, this begins to define the possible boundaries. For my purposes I would limit the concept to that of actual injury and destruction of persons. These will be considered to include four index crimes against persons: (1) criminal homicide, (2) forcible rape, (3) robbery, and (4) aggravated assault.

I have excluded auto fatalities, the leading cause of accidental death. While the violent results of organized crime are included in the above categories, prediction in those cases relates to other factors than will be dealt with in this paper. Disorderly conduct, assault and battery, and fighting are excluded unless they lead to serious harm. All of these are excluded because the dangerousness is not clearly defined or, as for example the problem of auto fatalities and organized crime, require examination in their own right. Suicide has also been excluded because I wanted to deal only with dangerousness to others, knowing that the problem of suicide is not so easily isolated from doing harm to others. The four index crimes are defined clear categories in which undeniable serious harm is brought to another person. Having then reduced the scope to dangerousness to the violence toward others subsumed under the crimes noted, we can ask—with what degree of certainty can we establish the likelihood of that behavior occurring within a certain time.[19] [26] In a series of cases concerning the dangerously mentally ill, both in relation to civil commitment and persons accused or found guilty of "violent" crimes, considered in the United States Court of Appeals, District of Columbia Circuit, the character of danger has been refined from 1958 to 1969. First the concept of reasonable foreseeability (Rosenfield vs Overholser 262 F2d, 34 (1958)). That is, the dangerous act must occur in "the community in the reasonably foreseeable future." Not only must the dangerousness occur soon, but it must be based on a "high probability of substantial injury (Millard vs Harris 406 F2d, 964 (1968) and Cross vs Harris 418 F2d, 1095 (1969)). Thus, the term dangerous to others cannot be simply a way of singling out anyone whom we would prefer not to meet on the streets. Possibility of injury is not enough, it must be likely, and the threatened harm must be substantial (refer to the three cases cited above). Thus, the psychiatrist must define "likely" as meaning "virtual certainty," (as in the cases cited above) rather than mere chance.

What information is available about such dangerous behavior and its genesis that might be helpful in making predictions about its (re)occurrence with some validity within these definitions of dangerousness? What are the characteristics of danger and what are their relative weights in assessing the probabilities of such behavior? Unfortunately the literature is sparse, disorganized, and impressionistic.

Violent crime is primarily a phenomenon of larger cities by youths, who are for the most part male, uneducated, and black. There are certainly criminogenic forces such as poverty, inadequate housing, overcrowded living conditions, poor employment opportunities, reduced family functions, and broken homes which can be implicated as forces in that particular population at risk. Yet these demographic characteristics, while indicating some direction that can be pursued to reduce or remove criminogenic factors, do not help in developing subpopulations in which predictions of dangerousness (as defined above) have any reliability much less validity. Sociological concepts such as criminal subcultures, opportunity, deviant role models, and a lack of "stake" just as anthropological explanations related to territoriality and the frustration-rage continuum have no predictive value. Violence is a form of social interaction, and attitudes to it are learned. For that reason culture provides the triggering mechanism in human aggressive response to frustration, just as it provides inhibiting mechanisms.[10] [27] The data[13] that the United States has a culture that appears to celebrate violence may help explain the comparatively larger numbers of violent crimes in this country, but in itself has no predictive value.

The reported association of violent crimes with biologic defects has not been persuasive. Episodic dyscontrol with violent behavior has been associated with minimal brain damage[6] and temporal lobe disorder and seizures.[7] [16] Chromosomal defects (XYY) and even testosterone overproduction have been implicated.[16] In these cases the presence of these defects in known criminals has no predictive value in their possible future violent behavior and at best can be found in from 10% to 50% of the known (apprehended and found guilty) criminal population samples studied. The prior crime of robbery by an individual is more predictive of the reoccurence of that crime than any of the biological factors.

Psychiatry and psychiatry and psychoanalytic theory and studies have given very conflicting evidence[25] [28] [32] having no predictive value. Hypotheses concerning a "destructive drive" are used as to develop models to explain human development, particularly the effect of fantasy on conflict and resultant inhibition rather than action. Notions such as "destructiveness is probably at its most perfect in early childhood and all later manifestations are, for most people, dilutions or mitigations,"[30] which describe the theoretical civilizing of destructive impulses, and ". . . there is one representative of the destructive instincts that is accessible to observation, mainly sadism,"[29] as well as "the destructive instinct appears most clearly in negativism"[29] seems to be describing either violent fantasy or action which is not truly violent. Glover, in his collection of psychoanalytic studies of crime, states[28] (pp349-350) ". . . the potentially anti-social and violent child is one of the most easily detected educational problems," and "Although so far it is not possible to predict exactly the form of delinquency it will take, a fair estimate as to whether crimes of violence were likely to occur could be arrived at . . ." Again "destructive" is used more in its ideational sense rather than as describing action. From that an unwarranted connection is made between such ideas and possible delinquency; after which delinquency and violence are equated.

The nature of innate aggressivity in man, if it exists, has yet to be fully explored, and the vicissitudes of such a drive and its possible relation to violence has yet to be described and understood. Operational relationships between the concepts of anger, hate, rage, and violence are poorly differentiated. In a recent article attempting to do just that, Rothenberg[33] states "regardless of the explanation it is a consistent observation that the most truly violent people are those who have difficulty dealing with angry feeling," and then states predictively that "Therefore, there are predispositions to anxiety and anger in relation to particular situations and persons or classes of situations and persons. Such predispositions are so constant and predictable that they may be considered to be structural features of the personality that tend to instigate violence."

It is repeatedly noted that violence and violent crimes are associated with childhood familial brutality and violence.[6 15 34 36] Duncan and Duncan[15] feel it has predictive value stating, "a history of parental violence remains a significant consideration in evaluating homicidal risks," and they then go even further in predicting that should the hated brutal patient be killed and the offender be sane and immediately apprehended, he would be "minimally" expected to kill again. A number of authors[35 37] have reported that the triad of enuresis, fire setting, and cruelty to animals in children is predictive of adult crime. In one study of 84 prisoners, three fourths (75%) of 31 charged with aggressive crimes (felonies) had the triad, while of 53 charged with misdemeanors and minor felonies 28% had the triad. While the difference is significant within a prisoner population, its predictive value seems minor at best, and what of the nonprisoner population with this triad?

The abuse of alcohol[19] [16] [34] and drugs (amphetamines[8] [16] [3] [4] in particular) have been implicated in violent behavior, and some have sought to prove that those particular drugs are the cause of violent crime. While their use may be associated with persons who engage in violence and violent crime, it is more likely[8] that a particular predisposing personality is necessary. The nature of that personality and what triggers violence is unknown. Blum,[38] in a compelling study of drugs and violence in a Staff report to the Commission on the Causes and Prevention of Violence, finds that one cannot link amphetamines to crimes of violence, sexual crimes, or accidents. Drugs do act as releasers or facilitators and in that sense can trigger violence in a person predisposed to it. Megargee[25] in a critical review of theories of violence shows that, as seen above, few studies test theories of human violence. Empirical studies do not test such theories. When such theories are tested they often focus on milder aggressive behavior or use infrahuman subjects. An exception is the work of Palmer[39] in which he did an empirical study of a prediction from a deduction of a theory of aggression. He interviewed the mothers of convicted murderers and discovered that for them the incidence of childhood frustration was significantly higher as compared to their next older brothers. A small start. It would be helpful if many such studies were attempted and more data collected. Nevertheless what is strikingly clear is that there is no unidimensional topology of violence.

What about the possible relationship between mental illness and violent acts? Certainly a strong relationship is implied. Nevertheless, epidemiological data indicate that (1) the major mental illness rates are not comparable to violence rates and (2) the distribution of major mental illness is not the same as the distribution of violence. Szasz[5] [40] goes further stating " . . . there is no evidence that mental patients are a greater source of danger than nonmental patients, . . . and that (the) myth lingers partly because of our tendency to ascribe mental illness to individuals who have engaged in aggressive or destructive acts." Szasz's solution is an administrative one—"Lawbreakers, irrespective of their mental health, ought to be treated as offenders." Thus by calling them a different name, the issue of mental illness and dangerousness is side stepped. Much of the psychiatric literature prior to 1950[41] indicated that mental patients were less of a risk for violence than the general population. Most recently, Ekblom,[42] in a book published in 1970, took the position that the evidence in Sweden was that risk injury to others from mental patients was less than in industrial employment. Three recent studies[43] [45] in 1965 through 1967 in the United States, take a very different view. Rappeport and Lassen[44] in a study of two cohorts of male patients discharged from all Maryland psychiatric hospitals—708 in fiscal 1974 and 2,152 in fiscal 1957, challenge the findings of early studies. In comparing the rate of arrest for their patients five years prior to and subsequent to hospital admission, they found the patients' arrest rate equal to, and for some crimes (notably robbery), greater than that of equivalent years for general population of Maryland. A parallel report[45] of data for two cohorts of released women showed a particularly high rate of aggravated assault, as opposed to the high incidence of robbery which characterized men. Giovannoni and Gurel[43] followed 1,142 released male psychiatric patients (out of hospital for at least 30 consecutive days and alive four years after admission) from Veterans Administration hospitals in California and found that of that group, 156 expatients were involved in a total of 192 incidents of socially disruptive behavior with the expatient rates for homicide, aggravated assault, and robbery exceeding the general population 20, 3, and 1.5 times, respectively. What of the threat of violence as made by mentally ill patients who have not committed crimes? The difficulty in the prediction of dangerousness is immeasureably increased when the subject has never actually performed an assaultive act. This is particularly relevant to involuntary mental hospitalization and to proposals for preventive detention without bail of persons accused but not convicted of crime.[46] [47] Macdonald[35] in a study of 100 patients who had made homicidal threats, 21 months after the study began and when all of the patients were released, knew of only one former patient who had committed murder. The idea of incarcerating 99 in order to prevent the one murder seems a very high price to pay in the prevention of violence. These negative data support Morris and Hawkins[19] who correctly state "at present there is no operable concept of dangerousness, and when it is used it usually is for retributive purposes." For our purposes then we will not attempt to consider dangerousness in persons mentally ill who have not committed an act of violence. Can we start with the mentally ill criminal? If we can make such predictions, it has importance in the criminal justice system in relation to distinguishing different kinds of criminal problems, so that rather than the indiscriminate mixing of different populations in prisons, rehabilitation can occur in relation to appropriate prison subpopulations.[48] It has significance for civil liberties insofar as present methods of defining dangerousness consist of mixes of discretion in sentencing and paroling, habitual and dangerous offender laws, and sexual psychopath laws, all of which do not successfully distinguish the dangerous from the social nuisances and keep people in prisons for excessive periods of time. The individual and social costs are high and the policy issues relating to civil liberties and what degree of risk the community can accept are never met.

The question of where to begin was answered in part by two events: one, in New York, when the United States Supreme Court decided (Baxstrom vs Herold, 383 US, 107 (1966) Feb 23, 1966, that 650 mentally ill criminals in the Dannermora and Matteawan Hospitals for the Criminally Insane had been denied their equal rights as guaranteed by the 14th Amendment to the US Constitution. All of these mentally ill had been kept beyond the expiration of their sentences. All had been accused and/or found guilty of defined violent crime, and all were predicted as being dangerous if released. That was the reason for their continued incarceration beyond their imposed sentences. After that court decision, many were sent to civil mental hospitals from which they were released to the open community. A report[49] on 72 men sent to the Central Islip State Hospital (New York) indicates that as a group they presented no different problems than "regular" mental patients. Also, "the data showed that the diagnosis of psychosis is neither necessary nor sufficient reason to anticipate destructive behavior."[49] The natural history of these men, over 200 of whom have been in the open community for the past two years, will serve as data about a large population of diagnosed dangerous mentally ill criminals many of whom now are living in the open community and whose behavior can be observed, violent or not. These empirical findings, when correlated to personality factors and precipitating circumstances will be the first quantitative data of a significant subpopulation at risk of engaging in violent behavior.

The second was in Illinois where a number of prisoners were found to have been retained in the Illinois penitentiary system by "administrative error" beyond the time, after 1941 through 1943, when they were to be transferred from prison to the mental health system.

Some of the legislative background is as follows. The Psychiatric Division of the Illinois Penitentiary system, located on the grounds of the Menard Branch of the State Penitentiary near Chester, Ill., was created in 1933 by an act of the State Legislature which consolidated and reorganized the state penitentiary system. Prior to this reorganization, the mentally ill within the prison system were referred to the Illinois Asylum for Insane Criminals, also at Chester, Ill. The asylum, established by the State Board of Charities in 1889, housed dangerous mental hospital patients, mentally ill convicts from the prison system, persons found incompetent to stand trial, and persons found to have become insane after a verdict of guilty but before judgment or sentencing were also transferred to the psychiatric division.

The asylum building was turned over to the predecessor of the Department of Mental Health; and the name of the facility was changed to the Illinois Security Hospital. (In 1933, the state agency responsible for care and treatment of the mentally ill was the Department of Public Welfare. This department has since been reorganized and the responsibility for the mentally ill in Illinois now lies with the Department of Mental Health. In this paper, for convenience, this change in name will be ignored. Throughout, the Department of Mental Health will be cited as the responsible agency. Likewise, although in 1933 the state prisons were the charge of the Department of Public Safety, the currently responsible agency, the Department of Corrections will be cited in this paper.) This new facility was to treat two classes of persons: dangerous mental hospital patients already housed in the asylum or subsequently transferred from state hospitals, and those persons found incompetent to stand trial.

This initial scheme was operative until 1937 when the State Legislature amended section 12 of Division II of the Criminal Code and provided that those persons found by a jury to be not guilty of a crime by reason of insanity be committed to the custody of the Department of Mental Health. In 1941 this section was amended again to require that such persons be housed in the Illinois Security Hospital. In 1943, the section was amended once more to make the change retroactive, requiring all persons found not guilty by reason insanity but confined to the Psychiatric Division to be transferred to the Illinois Security Hospital.

In 1968 it was discovered that the required relocations had not been carried out in several cases—"the Menard 18." The details of the original assignment errors are clear from the following discussion of 17 of these transferred inmates. It appears that one person found incompetent to stand trial prior to the 1933 reorganization was wrongly transferred from the Asylum to the Psychiatric Division in 1933. Six others found incompetent after 1933 were incorrectly assigned to the Psychiatric Division rather than to the Illinois Security Hospital. Six persons found not guilty by reason of insanity before 1937 and correctly assigned to the psychiatric division were not transferred to the Department of Mental Health as required by the 1943 amendments to the Criminal Code. And three persons found not guilty by reason of insanity were mistakenly assigned to the psychiatric division after the 1943 amendment. (It has been informally reported that this situation was made known to a former director of the Department of

Public Safety some time ago. But, according to this report, he was reluctant to order the necessary transfers because of the reorganization of the Department of Mental Health and the voting on the bond issue in process at the time.)

Explanations for these oversights have never been offered, but one source of misunderstanding may have been the statutes themselves. Although the amendments of the Criminal Code requiring assignment or transfer of persons found not guilty by reason of insanity to the Department of Mental Health were quite clear, the corresponding changes in the Penitentiary Act were somewhat confusing. In 1933, section 111 of the Penitentiary Act listed persons found by a jury to be not guilty by reason of insanity among those to be confined in the psychiatric division. When the provisions of the Criminal Code were changed, this section of the Penitentiary Act was amended to include, as it does today, "all persons committed to the Department of Corrections as having committed a criminal act while lunatic or insane." Section 113 repeats this language, stating that such inmates will be released when recovered. Although it is not clear exactly to what class of persons these provisions refer, it is easily seen that they may have been misinterpreted to justify continued placement of persons found not guilty by reason of insanity in spite of the clear requirements of the criminal code.

With subsequent investigations and cooperation between the Department of Mental Health and the Department of Corrections, these 17 inmates were transferred to the Department of Mental Health. I had the opportunity to see these "17" men while still in prison and to follow them for 2½ years after their leaving the Psychiatric Division of Menard Penitentiary. It is a somewhat distressing fact that in spite of the administrative misplacement of 18 men, I have never seen or heard of more than 17. A summary of my contact with each of the "Menard (18 minus 1) 17" is given in the table.

COMMENT
The Men

The 17 men spent a cumulative 425 years in prison, after legislative remedy should have resulted in their being placed in treatment or community settings. This was based in part on some inconsistencies in the law but more likely on the stereotypes of dangerousness with which they had been labeled and which had been consistently reaffirmed by their examiners. Shah[24] has indicated that there are many problems in the defining and labeling of deviant behavior—mental illness and dangerousness are both

Case No.	Age, Race, Marital Status	Crime	Event	Status
1	64 N Single	Aggravated assault	Struck and cut two women with knife	Not guilty insane, 1924
2	62 W Single	Robbery		Not guilty insane, 1929
3	75 N Single	Assault to rape	Pushed white girl to ground	Not guilty insane, 1927
4	46 N Single	Murder	Apprehended in vicinity of murder	Unable to execute insane, 1939
5	46 N Single	Murder	Apprehended in vicinity of murder	Incompetent to stand trial, 1942
6	64 W Single	Incedent liberties with a child	Seen with 4-year-old girl	Not guilty insane, 1938
7	72 W Married	Aggravated assault	Shot wife three times	Incompetent to stand trial, 1939
8	55 W Single	Arson	Set fires, masturbated	Incompetent to stand trial, 1938
9	85 W Married	Murder	Killed (shot) physician	Not guilty insane, 1917
10	61 W Single	Aggravated assault	Attacked neighbor woman with knife	Not guilty insane, 1929
11	77 W Unknown	Murder	Unknown	Incompetent to stand trial, 1941
12	82 W Married	Aggravated assault	Shot policeman in foot	Incompetent to stand trial, 1930
13	60 W Single	Murder	Killed mother (who was a mental patient)	Incompetent to stand trial, 1937
14	66 W Married	Murder	Shot and killed fellow worker	Incompetent to serve sentence, 1944
15	54 W Married	Murder	Shot and killed fellow worker	Incompetent to stand trial, 1939
16	79 W Married	Assault to rape	Attempted robbery and rape, woman	Not guilty insane, 1932
17	48 W Single	Robbery	Gas station $31	Sentenced 1-20 yr. vacated not guilty insane, 1941

Admission Prison Diagnosis	Final Prison Diagnosis	My Diagnosis	Disposition
Borderline mental disease, dementia preacox, paranoid type	Chronic dementia praecox	Mental deficiency moderate-severe	Chicago State Hospital and then a Nursing Home
Psychosis with epilepsy	Chronic brain syndrome with psychotic behavior	Chronic brain syndrome with seizures and partial deafness	Chicago State Hospital
Psychosis with mental deficiency	Mental retardation	Mental deficiency, moderate	Dixon State Training School for the Mentally Retarded Died 7/26/69: death due to gastric carcinoma
Benign catatonic stupor manic-depressive psychosis depressed type	Psychosis, atypical type	Chronic undifferentiated schizophrenia	Tinley Park Mental Health Center sent home, and then sent to Manteno State Hospital
Dementia praecox, paranoid type	Schizophrenia, hebephrenic type	1. Schizophrenia, paranoid type 2. Phenothaizine toxicity	Manteno State Hospital Died 10/26/70: death due to coronary occlusion
Mental deficiency with criminal tendencies	Mental deficiency psychopathic tendencies	Mental deficiency severe	Lincoln State Training School for the Mentally Retarded then sent to Kankakee State Hospital Died 2/16/70: death due to gastric carcinoma
Dementia praecox, paranoid type	Dementia praecox, hebephrenic type	Paranoid psychotic reaction	Chicago State Hospital then sent to Elgin State Hospital Died 9/18/69
Dementia praecox, hebephrenic type	Dementia praecox	Schizoid character disorder	Manteno State Hospital
Dementia praecox, paranoid type	Chronic brain syndrome with paranoid state	Paranoid state in remission	Manteno State Hospital
Catatonic stupor	Schizophrenia, catatonic type	Schizophrenia, catatonic type	Chicago State Hospital
Paranoid praecox with CNS disease	Chronic brain syndrome, left hemiplegia	Severe brain damage: cause unknown	Chicago State Hospital Died 10/11/68: death due to pneumonia
Dementia praecox, paranoid type	Paranoid psychosis amputation of left leg	Schizophrenia, paranoid type partial remission	Manteno State Hospital then sent to the Danville (III) VA Hospital
Dementia praecox, hebephrenic type	Dementia praecox, hebephrenic type	Chronic undifferentiated schizophrenia	Manteno State Hospital
Psychosis, paranoid type	Paranoid state	1. Paranoia in remission 2. Phenothiazine toxicity	Illinois Security Hospital then Elgin State Hospital: after a trial 4/18/70 he was placed in a nursing home
1. Paranoid state 2. Inadequate personality	Schizophrenia, paranoid type	Possible psychotic reaction in remission	Alton State Hospital then sent home
Dementia praecox, hebephrenic type	1. Chronic brain syndrome 2. Bilateral cataracts	1. Senescence 2. Bilateral cataracts	Chicago State Hospital then a nursing home
Dementia praecox, catatonic type	Dementia praecox, hebephrenic type	Chronic undifferentiated schizophrenia, partial remission	Peoria State Hospital

seen under certain circumstances as deviant in our society; and their definitions are often more dependent on social rather than other contingencies. But, in addition, violence is accompanied by our evaluation of that act of violence because "violence is a form of social interaction on which some sort of damage is inflicted on a party by another."[10] Thus in retrospect, two of the men engaged in activity which, because of its nature, required a violent response. One, a 34-year-old black man with moderate mental deficiency, knocked down a 10- or 12-year-old white girl on a busy street during the day in 1927 and was charged with assault to rape. The other, a 34-year-old white man with severe mental deficiency, played with a four-year-old girl in 1938 and was charged with assault to rape. A black man touched a white girl and a white man questionably molested a child. Both activities, at the time, considered very deviant and about which there were strong mores and sanctions. Both men were to be punished, but psychiatry offered the myth of treatment and mitigation of that punishment as they both are found not guilty by reason of insanity. Given both men and the circumstances, neither could be defined as mentally ill or dangerous.

Two of the men were convicted of robbery and murder, respectively, the details of which are not available. Yet neither was mentally ill at the time of their crimes. One had a seizure disorder and the other had a significant brain injury. The one with the seizure disorder was found not guilty by reason of insanity and served for 39 years; while the brain injured man was found incompetent to stand trial for murder in 1941. He certainly was competent in 1968 when I saw him just prior to his release and almost immediate death due to pneumonia.

The elderly man who had committed assault to rape and who at the age of 79, spoke freely of his crime and still felt remorse 37 years after the crime had been committed, was not mentally ill when I examined him. From the data, he was likely not psychotic or dangerous within a few years after his finding of not guilty by reason of insanity. Of all these men, he was the one who most likely recovered. That is, his mental illness was in remission within a few years of his imprisonment. He certainly was punished, insofar as he suffered for his crime, and was aware of the significance of that distress. Better than that, he recovered. Yet the system had no capacity to respond to that reality. What seems more likely is that the system redefines society's judgement of badness and continues to predict dangerousness in order to support that continuing definition.

Another of the men was sentenced to from one to 20 years for an armed robbery in which he took $31. Unluckily for him, he was found not guilty by reason of insanity and spent 27 years in a prison hospital. He was surely psychotic then but when I examined him there was evidence of the psychotic process being in partial remission. How dangerous he was at the time of the commission of the crime or from a time after imprisonment cannot be determined. However, in this case it is clear that had he been given the opportunity for treatment and employment, he would not have been dangerous and most certainly would have been more socially competent than he is today. Evidence for present dangerousness is minimal. Evidence for anxiety is extensive.

One of the 17 made the mistake of killing a doctor. Insofar as he had to be examined by a physician in order tó gain release and since the examining doctor became afraid of him, something abundantly clear from the clinical records, he remained in prison. This suggests that examinations and reviews without the examiner's knowledge of the prior crime can be a device for minimizing the social response to that crime which tends to contaminate the diagnostic process.

The man of this group considered most dangerous while in prison was so categorized because, infuriated by platitudes and being put off for 22 years about his wishes to be considered for release, he struck an assistant warden. After that he remained in handcuffs for three years and was overdosed with phenothiazine medication until the toxicity (dyskinesia) was apparent to any observer. After release from prison in 1969, he, who had been found incompetent to be sentenced in 1943, was found competent in 1970. His lawyer argued the novel idea that he had the right to elect whether the sentencing procedure would be governed by the laws in effect in 1943 or the present code. He chose to be governed by the latter. This avoided the problem posed by the 1944 jury recommendation that he be sentenced to life in prison. Sentenced to a term of 14 to 27 years for the murder committed on Oct. 4, 1943, he was credited for time already served and released. His designation of dangerousness was conditioned more by his aggressive response to 22 years of being frustrated and patronized and the fact that the object of his aggressiveness was a prison official, than the nature of his prior crime, murder.

A young man set fires which destroyed property and potentially endangered lives. He was 25 years old when found incompetent to stand trial. It is not clear how dangerous he would have been if released but there is no doubt he could have stood trial sometime within the 31 years he spent in prison and that during imprisonment he was prevented from receiving any treatment that might have helped.

Four of the men had been and remained psychotic in striking ways, in spite of forceful although intermittent therapeutic interventions. One was no longer dangerous by virtue of his aging and other organic factors (he subsequently died on release). A second was probably never dangerous. It is uncertain that he committed the crime for which he was found guilty. Given his interested family he could have returned home and also been treated as an out-patient long before 1969 when he was released. That release was complicated because of the execution being postponed by reason of insanity in 1939. His status in relation to the courts is not yet resolved. Two of these men's behavior was difficult to predict because of their inaccessibility to examination and treatment. One of them assaulted a physician after his admission to a mental hospital in 1969. The other has settled into a quiet, almost somnolent existence in another state hospital. What is the difference if any between these two men? Both committed violent crimes, and both remained relatively inaccessible to examination throughout their imprisonment. That data inform us little of their dangerousness except that one or both may become dangerous if pressed too vigorously to recover by some psychological therapy. The relationship between prior violent behavior and the assault (the physician was pushed down) required further examination with the patient over considerable time in order to be understood. The behavior of the second patient, who has sunk into a torpor, does not mean that intervention would be hopeless or dangerous, but rather that it should be appropriate to the man and his problems and be correctly timed in its application.

What then about the prediction of dangerousness in this group of mentally ill who had "committed" crimes? Do we have a predictive capacity given this particular group of persons? First, from the data, it is not possible to establish a connection between mental illness and the nature of the crime committed. The relationship to dangerousness in the mentally ill is even more tenuous. If a mentally ill person is involved in or found near a violent crime, he is likely to be accused of it as well as found guilty. This is because of pervasive notion that the mentally ill person is more likely to be dangerous and once so labeled, to remain dangerous. All subsequent examinations to predict dangerousness in the "Menard 17" were based on an original accusation of a violent crime, a stereotype of dangerousness, and a reaffirmation of the stereotype rather than data from the examinations. Dangerousness then is over-predicted in the presence of mental illness, and/or by the nature of the "crime." Even the diagnosis of schizophrenia (dementia praecox) may be conditioned by the circumstances of the person's contact with the examiner, i.e., having been found guilty of a prior violent crime. Seven of the 17 men were diagnosed as having severe and dangerous mental illness without much evidence. Upon separation from prison, three of these have been rediagnosed as nonpsychotic by prison physicians. The diagnosis in this circumstance is related to the condition of anticipated discharge rather than the prisoner's mental status. Aging certainly affects criminality, as do the pernicious effects of prolonged institutionalization. Crippling a man may certainly change a propensity for dangerousness—if he was dangerous in the first place. The method, however, seems unusually cruel. But in addition, in the cases of two of the 17, the imprisonment prolonged the illness, increased the disability, and possibly continued the dangerousness, if it existed, or conditioned its appearance if it had not existed at the onset.

What about the number of mental retardates in this group? It is hard to assess. Mental retardation may exist concomitantly with mental illness or alone. The retardation may be the peculiar social variety superimposed on the mentally ill by living in a total institution with little or no concern with care or expectation of the maintenance of social skills. Those persons who are mental retardates have evidence of both primary and secondary social causes. Another reason they may be overrepresented in this study is that the mental retardate mounts a poor defense and is more likely to be caught (whether guilty or not) and sentenced. The retardate is then the beneficiary of a double benevolence. First, segregated for "treatment," and then kept in prison for their protection because in the free community they would fall prey to persons who would "use them."

Three of these men were never dangerous and probably had not committed any crime. Of these, one was psychotic and two were mentally retarded. Four had never been psychotic. Of that four, two, as noted, were mentally retarded and were not dangerous. The other two had both been involved in dangerous crimes, arson and armed robbery. Both could have served sentences directly, and in addition, treatment could have been instituted quickly and vigorously; in the former, psychological, and in the latter, medical. Two men were severely brain damaged, both were not dangerous since their first contact with the corrections system. Given some kind of sheltered setting they would have done better than in the many years they spent in prison. Both died shortly after leaving prison. Five of these men had their psychotic symptoms partially remit in prison, and this trend accelerated upon release given the opportunity to be part of a more therapeutic setting. Five remained psychotic, two inaccessibly so. Of the 17, one may have been dangerous on release because of the inaccessibility and the catatonic features of his psychosis. At the time of release from prison, he was the only one possibly in that category. Of the rest who actually had committed a dangerous crime, there is little evidence in any of them to support continued dangerousness after two years of imprisonment.

The Problem

In a sense, we have come full circle. We have viewed in microcosm, society's way of labeling some mentally ill criminals, overpredicting violence, and then acting on that prediction to exact retributive costs. From the data it seems likely that the poor, the mentally incompetent, the drifter, and the black are more likely to be labeled in this way for social reasons unrelated to any violent behavior but rather to society's need to find objects who represent projections of its own violence, or who can be scapegoated for a number of reasons. Scheff[50] has written persuasively about the labeling of deviants, and indicates that this process of categorizing is the single most important cause of a "career of residual deviance." Whether for reasons of anger, punishment, benevolence, or just chance, a number of social forces are set into motion which tend to not only support that label but in effect to shape the behavior of the labeled person so as to indicate the correctness of the original diagnosis and prediction. Other investigators[51,53] have shown that this occurs by controlling the amount and kind of information available for orientation to the labeled person. By so doing he can be led to embrace the attitudes which were entirely foreign to his original ways of thinking. In addition, social communications are used to define internal stimuli and the nature of communication to the labeled dangerous deviant is that he has little but dangerous wishes which require external control. Lastly, self-control is not automatic, but rather is determined in a large part by one's image of one's self. It requires propitious circumstances to operate effectively. Nevertheless in the circumstances of labeled dangerous deviance, eventually our self-image and the resultant self-control can function at low levels at best.

Given the present reality[17,54,55] it is unlikely that dangerousness can be predicted in a person who has not acted in a dangerous or violent way. From a preventive point of view,[55] it has been shown that gun control could reduce the number of fatalities resulting from acts of violence, but no body of knowledge about human behavior gives us the information to make predictions about potential initial violence. In fact, given the above work of Scheff, Blake, Mouton, Schachter, Singer, and Shibutani, social forces are set into motion once labeling has occurred which are powerful enough to support the label of dangerousness, whether the original facts support it or not. Therefore, prior prediction seems to have dangers that outweigh its usefulness. Then what of the labeled deviant, the person who has presumably commited a violent act? It is critical that we develop methods to predict future dangerousness. What is there in the data collected as well as what data can we continue to collect that will allow us to systematically determine dangerousness?

First we must be able to predict as much as possible free of the social system which has labeled the deviant behavior as dangerous and the social system which task it is to maintain the "residual deviance." We are part of the larger social system and cannot be free of it[10] nevertheless whenever possible predictions should be made by persons not within or supported by correctional, mental health, or criminally insane institutions, given their present roles in maintaining "residual deviance." It becomes clear that in dealing with the problem of prediction of violence, that as already has been known, the culture's view of, acceptance of, or sanctions against violence cannot be ignored, as the nature of society's institutional agencies for the custody, punishment, and rehabilitation must be taken into account.

Second, enough of the predicted violent as well as non-violent must be free to enter the open community in order that we can truly evaluate not only the correctness of our predictions but the factors that enter into the reoccurrence of or absence of a violent act, within a reasonable time after release from custody. Macdonald's data[35] should make us more willing to take that chance. What then are the factors and problems in predictions of future violent behavior? It is known that those who commit crimes of violence are associated with lower parole violations. Glazer et al[11] in a study of the violent offender and difficulties of parole prediction noted that homicide offenders have a 0.4% recidivism. Those with sex offenses have 2.9% and those with assault 3.6%. The highest sex offense recidivism is for the nonviolent type. All of which means that the reoccurrence of individual violence is a relatively rare event, and the difficulty of predicting such an event is great. Eighty percent predictive accuracy is the greatest precision that has been demonstrated when applied to a cross-section of all prisoners who are considered for parole. How then can one begin to identify the less than 5% of potential parolees who may commit another violent act? Glazer et al [11] support the notion that prediction must be made before release and that long-term tabulations occur which relate the relevance of those predictions to post-release behavior. Also, he feels that his calls for the experimentation with the release of randomly selected prisoners. The accumulating evidence resulting from the Baxstrom vs Herold decision and the clinical data from the Menard 17 would support earlier release and further testing of predictive capacity. It is clear that the present response to violence or anticipated violence is a kind of societal "overkill."

What about the factors that may be implicated in the capacity to predict the reoccurrence of violent behavior? How can we weigh the respective forces of biological determinants, such as XYY chromosomes, temporal lobe disorder, and certain mental retardations, given the vectors of certain demographic characteristics? While more work is required to determine the extent and relationship of these disorders in normal populations, it now seems likely that this may be a very small, special, and exotic population. It is critical to be able to distinguish such individuals and provide those who can benefit with the special techniques available for their treatment. However, it is also likely that many persons who do not have these disorders are lumped into this group. The most extensive work on the subject[7] does not clearly separate the characteristics of episodic dyscontrol from episodic reaction, but rather forces distinctions, which do not exist as for example:

> What appears at times to be hypochondriasis may be the result of somatic auras or episodic psychophysiologic reactions. Also there is mounting evidence that many of the bizarre, and at least superficially appearing motivationless aggressive acts, may be related to this "excessive neuronal discharge" or the potentiality for such.[7] (175)

How can we determine the strengths of impulse vs the degress of control, and the particular social circumstances which inhibit or facilitate one or another or both? Studies, by weighted questionnaire, to examine various aspects of impulse and impulsiveness are required. Then both experimental and natural settings (release to the open community) can be used to test and measure the degree of reactivity as related to the measured impulsivity.

What role does frustration play in aggression? Can it be measured? The work of Palmer[39] is a small beginning. More studies of both normal, criminal, and mentally ill populations are required. Then rating scales of emotional experiences, particularly on the frustration-aggression axis. need development and testing with each of the three populations noted.

Given certain possible outcomes of the relationships of the above to one another, how much alcohol and what kinds of dosages of drugs will act as sufficient facilitators? What about accidental factors? How much and what kinds of infant and child abuse are predictive of adult crime, and under what circumstances? The kinds of parents given to child abusing are reasonably well known,[56] and may give data useful in the prevention of such violence toward children. It is also known that adult child abusers were raised in ways similar to those that they have recreated with their own children. The necessary information still related to the question of how much and what kind of abuse to children leads to their adult violent behavior?

What is the predictive value of the childhood triad of firesetting, enuresis, and cruelty to animals? What weights to give to each alone and together? What feelings should one have for others, how much? What forms of mental illness in what settings result in violence? It should be clear by now that unlike the belief of some authors[57] criminality and mental illness are not the reciprocals of one another nor does one necessarily follow the other. Both can exist somewhat independently of one another in the same person, or in varied degrees of interdependence. The relationship of emotion or its absence to criminality and mental illness has yet to be charted.

What subpopulations of mentally ill are more prone to violence, and under what circumstances? How important is a violent fantasy—a threat? It may be that fantasy, as reported, or a threat, as uttered, may have little or no connection with acts of violence, at least not statistically. Again, more study is required. Except for the small study by Macdonald[35] the literature is barren.

What does the commission of a violent crime do to change the possible weightings given above, and in what direction? What kind of interventions, how much, and for how long affect the weightings and in what way? Perhaps given the empirical studies, and the isolation of various subpopulations with various characteristics of danger, we can begin to design morbidity—experience—prediction tables which can be tested by others. Then perhaps the percent chance of an event reoccuring can be stated with some certainty, and then and only then can we responsibly face the difficult moral issue.

This study was made possible in part through funds provided by the Center for Studies in Criminal Justice, the Law School, University of Chicago, and the encouragement of Prof. Norval Morris.

References

1. Scheidemandel PL, Kanno CK: *The Mentally Ill Offender: A Survey of Treatment Programs*. Washington, DC, Joint Information Service, American Psychiatric Association and National Association of Mental Health, 1969.

2. Hall J: Psychiatry and criminal responsibility. *Yale Law J* 65:761-785, 1956.
3. Szasz TS: Civil liberties and mental illness:Some observations of the case of Miss Edith L. Hough, *J Nerv Ment Dis* 131:58-63, 1960.
4. Szasz TS: Commitment of the mentally ill: "Treatment" or social restraint. *J Nerv Ment Dis* 125:293-307, 1957.
5. Szasz TS: *Law, Liberty and Psychiatry.* New York, Collier Books, 1968, pp 91-108, 131-145, 199-207.
6. Bach-Y-Rita G, et al.: Episodic dyscontrol: A study of 130 violent patients. *Amer J Psychiat* 127:1473-1478, 1971.
7. Monroe RR: *Episodic Behavioral Disorders.* Cambridge, Mass, Harvard University Press, 1970.
8. Ellinwood EH Jr: Assault and homicide associated with amphetamine abuse. *Amer J Psychiat* 127:1170-1175, 1971.
9. Guze S, et al: Psychiatric illness and crime with particular reference to alcoholism: A study of 223 criminals. *J Nerv Ment Dis* 134-512-521, 1962.
10. Bohannan P: Cross-cultural comparison of aggression and violence, in Mulvihill D, Tumin M (eds): *Crimes of Violence: Staff Report to the National Commission on the Causes and Prevention of Violence.* Government Printing Office, 1969, vol 13, appendix 25, pp 1189-1239.
11. Glazer D, Kenefick D, O'Leary V: *The Violent Offender: Parole Decision Making.* Department of Health Education and Welfare, Office of Juvenile Delinquency and Youth Development, Government Printing Office, 1966.
12. Gorney R: Interpersonal intensity, competition and synergy: Determinants of achievement, aggression, and mental disease. *Amer J Psychiat* 128:436-445, 1971.
13. Graham HD, Gurr TR (eds): *Violence in America: Historical and Comparative Perspectives: Staff Report to the National Commission on the Causes and Prevention of Violence,* Government Printing Office, 1969, vol 1 and 2.
14. Dession GH, et al: Drug-induced revelation and criminal investigation. *Yale Law J* 62:315-347, 1953.
15. Duncan JW, Duncan GM: Murder in the family: A study of some homicidal adolescents. *Amer J Psychiat* 127:1498-1501, 1971.
16. Erwin FR, Lion JR: Clinical evaluation of the violent patient, in *Staff Report to the National Commission on the Causes and Prevention of Violence.* Government Printing Office, 1969, vol 13, appendix 24, pp 1163-1188.
17. Helleck SL: *Psychiatry and the Dilemmas of Crime.* New York: Harper & Row Publishers Inc, 1969, pp 301-318.
18. Kozal HL, Boucher RJ, Garofalo RF: The diagnosis of dangerousness. Read before the annual meeting of the Psychiatric Association, San Francisco, May 13, 1970.
19. Morris N, Hawkins G: *The Honest Politician's Guide to Crime Control.* Chicago, University of Chicago Press, 1970, pp 185-192.
20. Davidson HA: *Forensic Psychiatry.* New York: Ronald Press, 1952.
21. Guttmacher MD, Weihofen H: *Psychiatry and the Law.* New York, WW Norton & Co Inc, 1952.
22. Spiegel J: Aggression and violence, editorial. *Amer J Psychiat* 128:473-474, 1971.
23. Muller DJ: Involuntary mental hospitalization. *Compr Psychiat* 9:187-193, 1968.
24. Shah SA: Crime and mental illness: Some problems in defining and labeling deviant behavior. *Ment Hyg* 53:21-33, 1969.
25. Megargee EI: A critical review of theories of violence, in *Staff Report to the National*

Commission on the Causes and Prevention of violence. Government Printing Office 1969, vol 13, appendix 22 pp 1037-1115.

26. Katz J, Goldstein J: Dangerousness and mental illness. *J Nerv Dis* 131:404-413, 1960.
27. Wooten B: *Social Science and Social Pathology.* London, George Allen & Unwin, 1955.
28. Glover E: *The Roots of Crime.* New York: International Universities Press, 1970, pp 347-351.
29. Nunberg H: *Principles of Psychoanalysis.* New York; International Universities Press, 1962, pp 84-88, 218.
30. Waelder R: Psychiatry and the problem of criminal responsibility. *Univ Pennsylvania Law Rev* 101:385-390, 1952.
31. Redlich FC, Freedman DX: *The Theory and Practice of Psychiatry.* New York, Basic Books Inc Publishers, 1966, pp 778-798.
32. Waelder R: *Basic Theory of Psychoanalysis.* New York, Schocken Books, 1966, p 151.
33. Rothenberg A: On anger. *Amer J Psychiat* 128:454-460, 1971
34. Mulvihill D, Tumin M (eds): *Crimes of Violence, Staff Report to the National Commission on the Causes and Prevention of Violence.* Government Printing Office, 1969, pp xxv-xxxviii, 3-11, 43-46, 444-448, 451, 453-466.
35. Macdonald JM: The threat to kill. *Amer J Psychiat* 120:125-130, 1963.
36. Wertham F: *Dark Legend.* New York, Duell Sloan & Pearce, 1941.
37. Hellman DS, Blackman N: Enuresis, firesetting and cruelty to animals: A triad predictive of adult crime. *Amer J Psychiat* 122:1431-1435, 1966.
38. Blum R: *Drugs and violence: Staff Report to the National Commission on the Causes and Prevention of Violence.* Government Printing Office, 1969, vol 13 appendix 32, pp 1461-1523.
39. Palmer S: *A Study of Murder.* New York, Thomas Y Crowell, 1960.
40. Szasz TS: Some observations on the relationship between psychiatry and the law. *Arch Neurol Psychiat* 75:297-315, 1956.
41. Pollack HM: Is the paroled patient a menace to the community? *Psychiat Quart* 12:236-244, 1938.
42. Ekblom B: *Acts of Violence by Patients in Mental Hospitals.* Uppsala, Sweden, Svenska Bokforleget, 1970.
43. Giovannoni J, Gurel L: Socially disruptive behavior of ex-mental patients. *Arch Gen Psychiat* 17:146-153, 1967.
44. Rappeport J, Lassen G: Dangerousness: Arrest rate comparisons of discharged patients and the general population. *Amer J Psychiat* 121:776-783, 1965.
45. Rappeport J, Lassen G: The dangerousness of female patients: A comparison of the arrest rate of discharged psychiatric patients and the general population. *Amer J Psychiat* 123:413-419, 1966.
46. Dershowitz AM: On preventive detention. *New York Review of Books,* March 13, 1969, p 22.
47. Katz J, Goldstein J, Dershowitz AM: *Psychoanalysis Psychiatry and Law,* New York: Free Press of Glencoe Inc, 1967, pp 503-632.
48. Macdonald JM: *Psychiatry and the Criminal.* Springfield, Ill, Charles C Thomas Publishers, 1958.
49. White L, Krumholz WV, Fink L: The adjustment of criminally insane patients to a civil mental hospital. *Ment Hyg* 53:34-40, 1969.
50. Scheff TJ: The role of the mentally ill and the dynamics of mental disorder, *Sociometry* 26:436-453, 1963.

51. Blake RR, Mouton JS: Conformity, resistance and conversion, in Berg IA, Bass BM (eds): *Conformity and Deviation,* New York, Harper & Row Publishers Inc, 1961, pp 1-2.
52. Schachter S, Singer JE: Cognitive, social and physiological determinants of emotional states. *Psycho Rev* 69:379-399, 1962.
53. Shibutani T: *Society and Personality.* Englewood Cliffs, NJ, Prentice-Hall Inc, 1961, pp 80, 94-110, 193-233.
54. Daniels DN, Gilula MF, Ochsberg FM: Violence and the struggle for existence. Boston, Little Brown & Co Inc, 1970.
55. Tanay E: Psychiatric aspects of homicide prevention. *Amer J Psychiat* 128:805-818, 1972.
56. Steele BF, Pollock CB: A psychiatric study of parents who abuse infants and children, in Helfer RE, Kempe CH (eds): *The Battered Child.* Chicago, University of Chicago Press, 1968, pp 103-147.
57. Roche PQ: Criminality and mental illness: Two faces of the same coin. *Univ Chicago Law Rev* 22:320-324, 1955.

III.

Premonitory Signs of Homicidal Aggression in Juveniles*

Carl P. Malmquist*

This article delineates some of the clinical features observed in juveniles who have committed a homicide. Prodromal signs before the act was committed included behavioral changes, "cries for help," use of drugs, object losses, threats to manhood, somatization, an emotional crescendo, and homosexual threats. The author believes the homocide can serve the illusory function of saving one's self and ego from destruction by displacing onto someone else the focus for aggressive discharge.

For psychiatrists who deal with adolescents, the prediction of certain types of violent behavior and the consequent need to intervene therapeutically are uncommon. A specific type of potential violence pertains to the proneness to homicide. Unfortunately, the predictive indicators of when an actual act might occur are poorly defined for all who are homicidally prone, but especially for the adolescent group. This forces us to rely on subjective impressions in our appraisals. Our recommendations may then be made on relatively arbitrary grounds with a low reliability. When dealing with the multifarious nature of aggression in adolescents—

*Reprinted from the *American Journal of Psychiatry*, 128, 93-97, 1971. Copyright, *American Journal of Psychiatry*, 1971.

especially when it is of homicidal proportions—diagnostic signs and clues become of great assistance.

Emphases vary within different theoretical frameworks as to the crucial predisposing variables that make a person actually act out his aggression. These might be biological variability, certain psychodynamic aspects dealing with aggression or hostility, a high rate of exposure to violence in one's community, or a generally adverse environmental setting. This article delineates some of the clinical factors present in juveniles who have committed a homicide. It is a retrospective study based on those who have "successfully" completed such an act. Several questions were raised:

1. What are the most conspicuous signs indicating a vulnerability to homicide in a juvenile?

2. Is any commonality present in the signs between different juveniles?

3. Is it likely that a prediction can be made of who such adolescents are within a population?

4. Are any preventive measures against juvenile homicide possible?

Descriptive Aspects

Twenty adolescents charged with murder in some degree were personally evaluated by me. They were appraised in terms of their behavior and mental state preceding the act; my purpose was to try to formulate postdictive predictions from this group that could be applied to other juveniles with such potential. All but three were certified to an adult criminal court after a waiver hearing in the juvenile court. The criteria used for waiver are themselves vague and uncertain. The leading case, Kent vs. U.S., merely set forth certain procedural standards, since at the time (1966) many states did not even have a requirement for a hearing before a juvenile was transferred to an adult court.[1] A juvenile judge still has great discretion since he need only give his reasons for certifying—e.g., the juvenile's not being amenable to treatment by juvenile authorities.

Not all adolescents who commit homicide are seen for psychiatric evaluation. Some are waived without being seen under juvenile auspices. Once they are in an adult court, unless a specific motion is entered for a psychiatric evaluation there is no requirement that such an evaluation be performed.

Nor need this take place as part of the presentence examination. A juvenile may be convicted and sentenced without any appraisal of the act beyond the evidence needed to secure a criminal conviction. The group reported on here was seen because of my position as psychiatric consultant to the district court; those charged with juvenile homicide are not routinely seen by a psychiatrist in this court.

Certain premonitory signs and symptoms culminating in a homicide appeared consistently. But a major difficulty is the prevalence of similar signs and symptoms in people who never commit a violent act. The homicides were individual acts of violence in which one or more individuals were killed, in contrast to the violence perpetrated by youths in groups and gangs as described in a staff report to the National Commission on the Causes and Prevention of Violence.[2] A more exhaustive study would utilize a large population of children and preadolescents who had never committed such an act and make predictions of future murderers from psychosocial variables. For such a group deterrence has obviously failed. More than the usual citations on race, social class, and urban area predispositions are needed since their lack of specificity offers as little aid to the clinician in contact with these youths as it does to police officers directly on the scene. Empirical results are reported from psychiatric interviews with juvenile defendants, relatives, and witnesses. Psychological testing was available (Minnesota Multiphasic Personality Inventories, IQs, and Rorschachs). The object was to determine the presence of danger signs during the hours or days before the eruption. Police records and material in the file of the district attorney were available. Elimination of false positive and false negative signs—all too prevalent in these situations—would be a hoped-for by-product.

Seventeen of the patients were males and three females; four of the males were black. The age range was 13 to 18 years. With the exception of one girl, none of the subjects was in a retarded category on individually administered IQ tests. Four of the boys and none of the girls were married. Sexual offenses that resulted in a homicide or related charge of aggravated assault had been previously eliminated. Past delinquencies were either property offenses such as petty thefts or juvenile offenses such as truancy or absenting. None of the 20 had committed an offense against a person, although one had been witness to a homicide by a friend a year earlier. Diagnoses were: schizophrenia, three; depressive disorders, ten; and personality disorders, seven. All social classes were represented in contrast to the lower-class bias found in juvenile court records. Only five of the group were from the lowest social class in terms of parental occupation, education, or residence. Hence I do not offer the hypothesis that this behavior represents a type of psychopathology linked to social class. The focus is rather on adolescent ego functioning leading to homicide.

Findings

A prodromal period of events was delineated between the time of a beginning psychological shift and the homicidal act. For purposes of brevity these events are summarized with accompanying commentary.

1. Behavioral changes took diverse forms but the juvenile (and those in close contact with him) could approximate within 48 hours the time when his behavior had changed. The changes usually related to shifts in mood or cognitive reflections. Most noticeable was a deep pessimism about themselves or their predicament. In contrast to adults, who showed more evidence of impairment in work or relating to others, the juvenile shifted into a period of brooding where his already defective self-criticism gained ascendancy. Self-hate did not need to be confined to silent brooding but was often verbalized among peers. It was impossible to predict who among the juveniles with this diathesis would act out his hate in a homicide.

2. A "call for help" was muted and often not perceived by those in daily contact beforehand; for many it was not perceived even afterward. When a behavioral change was sensed, denial was prominent among family members. If the probability estimates for the individual from the past are employed, it appears that the cognitive appraisal of the situation by parents or friends takes the following form: Since he (and many other people we know) has snapped out of it in the past and did not commit a violent act, why should such an unexpected event occur now? When contact had been made with mental health facilities, this same type of appraisal operated. The psychopathology and unconscious determinants of "victimology" are relevant. A course of events, seen in retrospect, can be formulated in terms of the involvement of a victim in an entanglement of sadomasochistic relationships. The victim was customarily a friend or parent whose own personality needs and role had led him to permit the patient to gain self-esteem through him. A threat, however subtle, that this other person might not be so obliging acted as a precipitant.

One juvenile precipitously shot a man he had never seen outside his home while the man pleaded for mercy. A few weeks earlier he had called for an ambulance requesting admission to a psychiatric ward because of "strange feelings—I'm somewhere outside myself." Hospitalization was refused, but his irrational talk, coupled with a beer smell, led to a recommendation that he be detained overnight as a juvenile delinquent. In some cases a parent accentuated the skepticism of the adolescent by comments about his laziness, ineffectiveness, or his being a "bum" or "hippie" because of what he had done in the past.

3. Use of druqs occurred in two ways. Barbiturates and tranquilizers

were used to contain impulses and affects. This was not very effective. Five of the juveniles had been taking at least one such drug, and they had increased their intake prior to the incident to two or three times the prescribed dosages. This was done on their own initiative and can be taken as a measure of their personal distress.

A second usage involved amphetamines and psychotomimetics, with or without marijuana. Four of the juveniles had been using amphetamines irregularly; this use corroborates impressions of clinicians and correctional personnel that speed may indeed kill.[3] Only in one case did a homicide occur while the juvenile was under the active influence of a psychedelic drug:

Case 1. A 15-year-old had been involved in "pot" parties that occasionally also involved LSD. On the evening of the homicide he took mescaline for the first time; this was added to LSD and marijuana over a period of seven to eight hours. After he returned home at 2 a.m., a favorite uncle who lived with the boy and his grandmother asked the boy to get his cigarettes from a coat in the hallway. On reaching for the cigarettes, the boy discovered a gun. He stood and debated suicide for an unknown period. Instead of suicide he shot several slugs into his seated uncle. This appeared to be a result of unresolved difficulties in the realm of separation—individuation from his uncle and lack of clear ego boundaries.

Complex legal questions under tests for criminal responsibility arise in such cases. The impact of drugs on a homicidal act—presuming that evidence establishes the ingestion of the drugs—is a situation that will be seen with increasing frequency.

4. Object losses that appeared related to homicide involved lovers or mothers. These people were involved in complex relationships. For some the situation could best be described as "wild therapy," in which all the intensities of unsupervised therapy took place and were accentuated by the actual attachments involved. A quasi-therapeutic relationship with a friend led to the friend's being caught in a demand for help, yet incapable of giving it. The friend was likely to have dependency conflicts similar to the patient's. An abandonment or a situation experienced as a rejection from someone in an official role at a clinic or agency was another type of contributory loss. The capacity to tolerate separation—let alone master it—proved insufferable to many of those adolescents. Their minimal tolerance for painful affect led to both drive and ego regressions.

Case 2. One married teenage couple had separated; the victims were the separated wife and an unknown boy found with her. The perpetrator had been on the receiving end for months from his own mother, who was demanding that her son get his father to leave a young girl with whom he was living. Feeling helpless to carry out this mandate, the boy had spent months as an ineffectual intermediary between his parents; he drove his mother by the apartment where his father resided and allowed her to spend an hour a day on the phone with him asking for information about his father. After the homicides, he worried about his mother's unresolved difficulties. His obsessional delimma was seen as he sat contemplating suicide with a last bullet while the police were on the telephone with him from an apartment lobby. The act not only punished a deserting wife but resolved his helplessness concerning his mother by taking him away from her— although leaving guilt residues from this betrayal.

   5. Threats to manhood. A provocative incitement by teenage girls was their urging boys or gangs to fight. These possibilities are acted out in the context of sadomasochistic balances in which threats to the boy elicit an aggressive response to "put her down." Hitting or beating her may be a forerunner to this type of marriage. Subtle flirtations may precipitate a fight between two boys. In some cases a direct instigation to homicide occurs.

Case 3. A 15-year-old boy with an IQ of 135 on the Wechsler Adult Intelligence Scale and with legs crippled from polio had developed a close relationship with a girl of the same age. He lived at her house when her divorced mother was absent for two- or three-day periods. Although physically strong in the upper extremities, he was restricted in locomotion and used half-crutches. The couple decided to obtain money for a vacation by holding up a cab driver. The plan was to tell the cabbie to stop and hand over his money. Instead, the cabbie sped down the street while the girl screamed at the boy: "Shoot! Kill him! Don't be yellow, you weakling!" He briefly hesitated but then shot the man in the back. When the car crashed, the girl ran while he attempted to crawl away.

Case 4. A variant of the foregoing was seen when a 15-year-old boy shot and killed his stepfather. The boy had been witness to a series of beatings when the father was intoxicated. On the occasion of the homicide, the father had gone outside mumbling he wanted a piece of wood with which to beat his wife. During his brief absence, the boy's mother sat down next to him on a couch and, laying a pistol down between them, stated: "I know you're big enough to protect me now."

6. Somatization, hypochondriasis, or a recurrent medical problem occurred in ten cases. Headaches of increasing severity, persistent physical aches, and in two cases somatic delusions that a certain organ was diseased were among the patterns. No adolescent had a florid delusion such as those seen in psychotic adults, although states of guilt, self-depreciation, and worthlessness abounded. Again, somatic concerns were present in many anxious adolescents. General practitioners, family service agencies, mental health centers, school counselors, and clergy had all been involved; proprietary medications were sometimes implicated. The complaints were more typically chronic than occurring for the first time, although during the prodromal period an intensification of concerns occurred.

7. An emotional crescendo appeared in the form of an increasing buildup of agitation and energy, accompanied by motor restlessness and distrubed sleeping and eating patterns. For some, restless pacing and talking to themselves in an incomprehensible and unintelligible manner appeared in the prodromal period. Acute anxiety, panic, or a presaging of catatonic excitement were in the clinical pictures. A manic solution when he emerged from a depressed state was present in one boy; lucid intervals during which those who observed the boy reported nothing unusual were interspersed. Even observers who had contact with one of these adolescents the day of the homicide were rarely aware of the degree of internal turmoil. The same people, an hour or two later, were stunned to witness the fragmentation. Witnesses who saw an individual in a wildly agitated state or even making a suicidal attempt by shooting himself were still unable to accept the behavior as "real"; some believed it was faked to escape responsibility. When reintegrated, the adolescents themselves sought to deny they could have done such a thing. This was blatantly incongruous in view of the fact that the acts were witnessed. Depersonalization or ego-splitting, rather than dissimulation, appear to be better explanations.

A breakdown of ego control over affective discharge was evidenced in crying and sobbing spells and moody preoccupation. An hour preceding a homicidal outburst one mother had observed her son huddled over a chair convulsively sobbing. She was not sure at the time if he was laughing or crying. He subsequently dashed outside and shot an unknown passerby. In another case, after a night of restless pacing a juvenile fired a bullet through the head of the family cat. He accompanied this with wild laughter, which gave him a temporary feeling of relief. Within an hour he brutally assaulted a repair man working in the building.

8. Homosexual threats—overt or covert—raised the homicidal index. A boy of 16, involved with his stepfather in an incestuous homosexual relationship, plunged a knife into him when he realized "there was no other way out." In another case, an overt homosexual relationship existed between two schoolmates in which one performed fellatio and received physical beatings. This schoolmate obtained a gun, which he kept hidden under a mattress for months. Following a denial of oral intercourse one morning, his roommate came toward him and "to save my life I got the gun and shot him." He went to an airport and, although he had had only four hours of flying lessons, he took a plane up alone. He was eventually forced into landing by means of patrol planes buzzing him from the rear of his plane; he complained of severe rectal pain during the course of the chase.

A group of adolescents, two 15 years old and one 16 years old, would visit a single, 40-year-old bachelor who gave them beer. On one occasion the man displayed an overt interest in one of the boys by putting his arm around him as they were drinking. The intent of the boys preceding that visit was to rob the man, using his own gun, which they knew was in a drawer. After the display of affection the boy felt nauseous and faint. He went to another room and sat with his head in his hands in an effort to avoid passing out. When the man appeared in the doorway, he began shooting with the man's gun, which he had taken. Most interesting was the committing of a homicide by one of the other boys exactly one year to the day later. The "anniversary" was celebrated by the boy's shooting his mother's common-law husband.

Discussion

What is the final "breaking point" in individuals predisposed to this type of decompensation? Halleck holds that an ultimate feeling of helplessness and hopelessness is the predisposing factor that culminates in an act of violence.[4] I have been impressed by an additional specific component. A deep state of mourning may have brought the adolescent to a point of no return because of the seeming hopelessness of relief. It is as though an irretrievable blow or insult had been delivered to his integrity from which repair seemed impossible. Relationships between depression and acts of violence have been detailed by Cormier.[5]

This theme overlaps several diagnostic categories. Mourning need not involve a literal loss but can reflect an affective state attendant upon a sense of disappointment. The disappointment may be an accumulation of aca-

demic or vocational failures, social disappointments, failures in love relationships, heterosexual or homosexual disillusionment, or a feeling that
someone has betrayed one or has been dishonest. A brief moratorium may
intervene. In some cases episodes like this had occurred previously in
which grief work commenced, but repetitive self-defeating patterns were
later established.

The closeness of the homicide-suicide phenomenon corresponds to
the observations of West in England.[6] Fifteen of his patients had suicidal
preoccupations during the week of the homicidal episode. In some it
seemed an option in the immediate hours before the homicide. Again, this
preoccupation had been present in the past. The combination and weight-
ing of variables that pass the breaking point for an ego rupture may largely
be unknown. The homicide can serve the illusory function of saving one's
self and ego from a disintegration by displacing onto someone else the focus
for aggressive discharge. It may be a last desperate effort to survive. A
lesser evil is then "chosen" in preference to the greater one of self-
dissolution.[7] Could one go so far as to hypothesize juvenile homicide as a
miscarried triumph based on a continuing desire to live rather than to die?

References

1. Kent v United States, 383 US 541 (1966).
2. *A Staff Report to the National Commission on Causes and Prevention of Violence: Youth and violence,* in *Crimes of Violence,* vol 12. Washington, D.C. , US Government Printing Office, 1969, pp 603-637.
3. Ellinwood EH Jr: Assault and homicide associated with amphetamine abuse. *Amer J psychiat* 127:1170-1175, 1971.
4. Halleck S: *Psychiatry and the Dilemmas of Crime.* New York, Harper & Row. 1967.
5. Cormier BM: Depression and persistent criminality. *Canad Psychiat Ass J II (suppl):* 208-220, 1966.
6. West DJ: *Murder followed by Suicide.* Cambridge, Mass, Harvard University Press, 1966.
7. Dalman CJ: Criminal behavior as a pathologic ego defense. *Archives of Criminal Psychodynamics* 1:555-563, 1955.

couch and, laying a pistol down between them, stated: "I know you're big enough to protect me now."

6. Somatization, hypochondriasis, or a recurrent medical problem occurred in ten cases. Headaches of increasing severity, persistent physical aches, and in two cases somatic delusions that a certain organ was diseased were among the patterns. No adolescent had a florid delusion such as those seen in psychotic adults, although states of guilt, self-depreciation, and worthlessness abounded. Again, somatic concerns were present in many anxious adolescents. General practitioners, family service agencies, mental health centers, school counselors, and clergy had all been involved; proprietary medications were sometimes implicated. The complaints were more typically chronic than occurring for the first time, although during the prodromal period an intensification of concerns occurred.

7. An emotional crescendo appeared in the form of an increasing buildup of agitation and energy, accompanied by motor restlessness and distrubed sleeping and eating patterns. For some, restless pacing and talking to themselves in an incomprehensible and unintelligible manner appeared in the prodromal period. Acute anxiety, panic, or a presaging of catatonic excitement were in the clinical pictures. A manic solution when he emerged from a depressed state was present in one boy; lucid intervals during which those who observed the boy reported nothing unusual were interspersed. Even observers who had contact with one of these adolescents the day of the homicide were rarely aware of the degree of internal turmoil. The same people, an hour or two later, were stunned to witness the fragmentation. Witnesses who saw an individual in a wildly agitated state or even making a suicidal attempt by shooting himself were still unable to accept the behavior as "real"; some believed it was faked to escape responsibility. When reintegrated, the adolescents themselves sought to deny they could have done such a thing. This was blatantly incongruous in view of the fact that the acts were witnessed. Depersonalization or ego-splitting, rather than dissimulation, appear to be better explanations.

A breakdown of ego control over affective discharge was evidenced in crying and sobbing spells and moody preoccupation. An hour preceding a homicidal outburst one mother had observed her son huddled over a chair convulsively sobbing. She was not sure at the time if he was laughing or crying. He subsequently dashed outside and shot an unknown passerby. In another case, after a night of restless pacing a juvenile fired a bullet through the head of the family cat. He accompanied this with wild laughter, which gave him a temporary feeling of relief. Within an hour he brutally assaulted a repair man working in the building.

8. Homosexual threats—overt or covert—raised the homicidal index. A boy of 16, involved with his stepfather in an incestuous homosexual relationship, plunged a knife into him when he realized "there was no other way out." In another case, an overt homosexual relationship existed between two schoolmates in which one performed fellatio and received physical beatings. This schoolmate obtained a gun, which he kept hidden under a mattress for months. Following a denial of oral intercourse one morning, his roommate came toward him and "to save my life I got the gun and shot him." He went to an airport and, although he had had only four hours of flying lessons, he took a plane up alone. He was eventually forced into landing by means of patrol planes buzzing him from the rear of his plane; he complained of severe rectal pain during the course of the chase.

A group of adolescents, two 15 years old and one 16 years old, would visit a single, 40-year-old bachelor who gave them beer. On one occasion the man displayed an overt interest in one of the boys by putting his arm around him as they were drinking. The intent of the boys preceding that visit was to rob the man, using his own gun, which they knew was in a drawer. After the display of affection the boy felt nauseous and faint. He went to another room and sat with his head in his hands in an effort to avoid passing out. When the man appeared in the doorway, he began shooting with the man's gun, which he had taken. Most interesting was the committing of a homicide by one of the other boys exactly one year to the day later. The "anniversary" was celebrated by the boy's shooting his mother's common-law husband.

Discussion

What is the final "breaking point" in individuals predisposed to this type of decompensation? Halleck holds that an ultimate feeling of helplessness and hopelessness is the predisposing factor that culminates in an act of violence.[4] I have been impressed by an additional specific component. A deep state of mourning may have brought the adolescent to a point of no return because of the seeming hopelessness of relief. It is as though an irretrievable blow or insult had been delivered to his integrity from which repair seemed impossible. Relationships between depression and acts of violence have been detailed by Cormier.[5]

This theme overlaps several diagnostic categories. Mourning need not involve a literal loss but can reflect an affective state attendant upon a sense of disappointment. The disappointment may be an accumulation of aca-

demic or vocational failures, social disappointments, fail lationships, heterosexual or homosexual disillusionment, someone has betrayed one or has been dishonest. A brief intervene. In some cases episodes like this had occurre which grief work commenced, but repetitive self-defeatin later established.

The closeness of the homicide-suicide phenomenon the observations of West in England.[6] Fifteen of his patie preoccupations during the week of the homicidal episo seemed an option in the immediate hours before the homi preoccupation had been present in the past. The combinat ing of variables that pass the breaking point for an ego rup be unknown. The homicide can serve the illusory function self and ego from a disintegration by displacing onto someo for aggressive discharge. It may be a last desperate effo lesser evil is then "chosen" in preference to the grea dissolution.[7] Could one go so far as to hypothesize juveni miscarried triumph based on a continuing desire to live rath

References

1. Kent v United States, 383 US 541 (1966).
2. *A Staff Report to the National Commission on Causes and Preventiol and violence*, in *Crimes of Violence*, vol 12. Washington, D.C., US G Office, 1969, pp 603-637.
3. Ellinwood EH Jr: Assault and homicide associated with amphetan *psychiat* 127:1170-1175, 1971.
4. Halleck S: *Psychiatry and the Dilemmas of Crime.* New York, Harp
5. Cormier BM: Depression and persistent criminality. *Canad Psychi* 208-220, 1966.
6. West DJ: *Murder followed by Suicide.* Cambridge, Mass, Harvard Uni
7. Dalman CJ: Criminal behavior as a pathologic ego defense. *Ar Psychodynamics* 1:555-563, 1955.

Violent Persons: Treatment Issues

The management of persons who manifest violent behavior is a complex and often anxiety provoking experience. Dr. John Lion, a pioneer in the development of "violence clinics," describes his experiences with individual patients and as the director of a violence clinic. It is clear that the potentially violent patient can be managed effectively in outpatient settings and that eclectic treatment approaches must be employed. Dr. Sherwyn Woods focuses attention on a subgroup of violent patients—those for whom violence is an attempted escape from the anxiety of feelings of male inadequacy and impotency. Such persons often categorized as "pseudo-homosexual" may become violent as psychotherapy progresses. Dr. Woods makes sound psychodynamic suggestions for the conduct of psychotherapy. Another factor involved in work with violent patients are the often intense conscious and countertransference reactions to such patients among psychiatrists and mental health workers involved in their care. More than one therapist has overreacted to the fantasies of an aggressive patient with violent fantasies of his own, particularly "ambush fantasies." And in an age of assassinations, skyjackings, and bizarre kidnappings, psychiatrists sometimes seem overly sensitive to violent preoccupations on the part of their patients. Case examples and treatment suggestions are found in the article by Dr. Lion and Dr. Pasternack on countertransference reactions to violent patients. Keeping in mind that violent patients are confronted in inpatient and outpatient settings and that there is increasing utilization of mental health resources by forensic services there is a clear and present need for "cool hands" and masterful approaches to violent patients.

51

IV.

Countertransference Reactions to Violent Patients*

John R. Lion
and
Stefan A. Pasternack

Treating violent patients can evoke countertransference reactions of fear and anger in therapists that may interfere with effective management. The authors present six case reports in which countertransference reactions deleteriously affected the treatment outcome. They stress the importance of the physician's being aware of his fear and of how this fear may distort, by projection, his view of the patient as being dangerous.

In previous work we have described the clinical features of patients who appear in emergency room and clinic settings with complaints relating to assaultive and destructive urges.[1-4] In the course of treating and supervising the therapy of such patients, we have noted recurring countertransference reactions that interfere with their evaluation and management. We describe here the nature of these reactions, using the term "countertransference" to mean any emotional reaction that the clinician has toward the patient.[5] Probably no group of patients evoke as many anxieties in the clinician as those who relate such violent urges as the fear of running amok and of killing someone or those who describe patricidal or infanticidal impulses. While the suicidal patient's aggressive urges have

*Reprinted from the *American Journal of Psychiatry* 130:207-210, 1973. Copyright American Psychiatric Association 1973.

not yet transcended his personal boundaries, the violent patient—particularly if he has been violent in the past—is an individual who may hurt someone besides himself. In the back of the clinician's mind is the possibility that the patient may turn his aggressive urges on his therapist if the latter does not fulfill the patient's therapeutic expectations. The clinician may also fear that his patient will develop a pathological distortion of therapy; stories about the paranoid patient who kills his psychiatrist are commonly fantasized. It is therapeutic wisdom for the therapist to have some anxiety about treating a violent patient. In the case of a paranoid patient, for example, concern for the development of a dangerous psychotic transference should continuously propel the therapist to carefully monitor the relationship with the patient. However, while hazards exist in treating the violent patient, we have observed that anxiety concerning the patient's dangerousness often gets out of hand.

Case Reports

Case 1.

A prisoner convicted of assault was transferred to the psychiatric unit of a hospital because of suspicious behavior. He was evaluated by a staff psychiatrist, who found that he was not psychotic but that he did have definite paranoid traits. The patient blamed all of his difficulties on the police and prison authorities. He was negativistic and hostile and spoke of physical force as a solution to emotional problems. Interviews with him were difficult, and his psychiatrist emerged from a particularly frustrating session with marked anxiety and an irrational fear that the patient, who still had a one-year sentence to serve, would try to ambush him at home and kill him. In a discussion with a colleague he came to the realization that he was furious at the patient and actually had the desire to physically strike him. As he came to grips with these feelings, the fear of harm subsided, and eventually a more positive relationship prevailed during the remainder of treatment.

In this case the therapist did not have easy access to his angry feelings and became irritated because the patient continually projected all of his difficulties onto the environment and evaded introspection. This is particularly likely to be the case with paranoid patients. Patients who act out extensively, such as those with severe character disorders, also produce the same feelings in physicians. Although the acting out may be dynamically understood by the physician, he may still feel anger and helplessness in controlling an individual who translates affective issues into destructive behavior—behavior that the therapist may feel reflects badly on his therapeutic abilities. Anger and helplessness seem to us to be the basis for another not-uncommon fantasy expressed by therapists: that their patients will do something terrible (e.g., commit a mass murder) and that they, the therapists, will then be held liable. Such fantasies, of course, always require the most serious and urgent consideration as to their basis in fact. Yet we have observed that this particular fantasy often derives from a feeling of anger and helplessness which the physician has toward the patient. This helplessness is projected onto the patient, and he is perceived as an individual capable of doing immense harm. In case report 1, anger led to the physician's fearing personal harm even though no threat had been made.

Helplessness may also be evoked in the physician by the fact that the patient is apt to handled defensively, as the following case report illustrates.

Case 2.

A 36-year-old man was admitted to the hospital in a state of delirium tremens and was treated by a first-year resident psychiatrist. As he improved, he was allowed a special pass to leave the hospital. He returned from leave one night with a loaded revolver.

Apparently he had brought back a bulky package and had handed it in with his other personal belongings. When the package was submitted to routine inspection, the weapon was discovered. The patient readily admitted that it was his gun and that he had brought it to the hospital for "safe keeping." The resident hastened to the ward to discharge the patient because "those who bring guns to the hospital obviously do not belong here." He resisted understanding the meaning of the man's behavior. He ignored the fact that the patient could have kept the weapon concealed and that his turning it in to the hospital reflected an underlying conflict.

When instructed by staff supervisors to retain the patient in order to further investigate this conflict, the resident refused. He persisted in his wish "to be rid of the derelict." Only the threat of suspension made the resident alter his stance. It was subsequently learned that only six weeks before the man had been released from prison because of armed robbery. He had been approached by his friends to take part in a new holdup but had turned his weapon in to the hospital, hoping for protection. In discussion it became evident that the resident harbored a marked fear of the patient and of weapons. His insistence upon discharge was his means of dealing with his anxieties.

This case illustrates the physician's overreaction to the violent patient and the principle of denial. Denial is the most ubiquitous defense against anxiety generated by a violent patient. In its most common and most insidious form, it manifests itself in the clinician's failure to gather unflattering and anxiety-producing anamnestic data. Time and time again we have found it necessary to ask residents to inquire about patients' ownership of weapons and ammunition, their lethal skills, past criminal or violent acts, or driving habits. It has been our distinct impression that psychiatrists do not ask such questions, but defensively conceive of these queries as belonging more in the forensic realm than in the province of clinical psychiatry. The need to ask such questions has been stressed by Macdonald.[6] In certain other instances the predominant emotional reaction to the violent patient has been anger or rejection of the patient as a "prison case," an "untreatable psychopath," or a "harmless drunk"—this despite the knowledge that drinking is implicated in a very large proportion of violent crimes and automobile fatalities.

The following case report is an interesting, although extreme, case of denial.

Case 3.

A 19-year-old college student barged into the office of his therapist armed with a .22 rifle. He fired, but the gun failed to discharge, and the student attempted to strangle his would-be victim. The therapist fought back enough to discourage his patient, who then wept. The patient called out for help and protested that once aqain he was the victim of racist plots that might destroy him. He begged for mercy. The therapist took the gun and gave it to his secretary. He than escorted the tall, heavy-set patient to the emergency room—a long walk over the hospital grounds and through a complex series of dark tunnels. Once there, he notified the emergency room clerk to summon the psychiatrist on call, since he wished to admit the patient to the hospital. He gave the clerk no information regarding the urgency of the request. The doctor then left the patient sitting alone in a room. Two hours later the psychiatrist on duty, who had still not been notified about the case, found the patient. The referring psychiatrist explained his approach saying, "I did not want to influence your decision regarding the need to admit the patient."

This is a frightening case and an unusual one. The denial can well be understood in the face of the crisis but is nonetheless glaring. An additional interesting fact about this case was that in therapy the resident overlooked the dangerous potential of the patient and focused instead on his earlier life conflicts, his mistreatment at the hands of cold and controlling parents, and his difficulties facing the vicissitudes of life. He avoided dealing with the negative aspect of the patient's psychotic ambivalence and hostilities until, at length, this omission was pointed out to him in supervision. Both the resident and his supervising therapist had made extreme attempts to form a positive therapeutic alliance with a patient they sensed to be dangerous.

To face the issue of dangerousness is very threatening to the physician, much as it is to face the seductiveness of a female patient; the therapist's human vulnerability emerges, and he must deal with his own strong emotions. Aggression is a subject that revives conflicts which the psychiatrist is apt to have about his own urges. It has long been our opinion that the psychiatrist is in closer dynamic harmony with suicide and the introjection of hostile urges than he is with the externalization of such impulses. Violence directed outwardly is apt to be threatening. Events in the physician's life may be stirred up, as the next case report illustrates.

Case 4.

A hospital staff psychiatrist sought informal consultation because he was afraid of a patient. The patient, who had a severe character disorder, had difficulty with hostile urges and had verbalized a desire to shoot another person. The psychiatrist, although never threatened, expressed fears for his own safety. In the course of conversation the psychiatrist related that several weeks before, he had gone on a camping trip with his wife in the mountains. The couple stopped to look at the scenery. Another car drove up, and a man got out and engaged in conversation. He then abruptly drew a revolver, fired at the psychiatrist at point-blank range, but missed. The psychiatrist instinctively tackled the man, throwing him over a ledge. The couple then immediately raced off, encountering a state trooper who ordered an immediate search of the area. The man was eventually found; he had a broken limb and was discovered to be an escaped prisoner.

This case demonstrates the revival of an actual, past attempt on the physician's life; this memory led to a distortion of the patient's dangerousness and interfered with a working relationship. In other cases we felt that the patient's patricidal or infanticidal impulses reawakened conflicts that the clinician himself had about similar impulses. This seemed to be the case when the therapist had ruminative, obsessive preoccupations about the dangerousness of the patient. Our speculation was, of course, difficult to prove in the course of supervision, since personal exploration is inappropriate in such settings. Ventilation, however, proved to be immensely useful and led to a more realistic appraisal of the patient. Fromm-Reichman [7] has described a personal case in which she was irrationally afraid of a patient; consultation led to a therapeutic relationship unhampered by such emotions.

Patients on ward settings can generate negative countertransference reactions among nursing personnel.[8] This happens most typically when the patient is agitated and exhibits motor restlessness or belligerence, together with flouting of ward rules and regulations; as a result, nursing staff members become alarmed and angry.

Case 5.

A 19-year-old college student with a long history of drug abuse was readmitted to the hospital in a state of toxic psychosis. He was unkempt, incoherent, agitated, and menacing. A well-developed, muscular young man, he acted bizarrely and unpredictably reached out for those who passed by him. During patient group meetings, he would pace nervously and suddenly thrust his face close to the face of another. At times he shouted wildly and refused to obey instructions. He talked of wishing to kill his father for being "a bastard." The patients decided to exclude him from the group meeting. Staff members reacted to the fears of the patients and gave the patient increasing amounts of medication. The patient was also placed in seclusion where he became violent and banged on the walls. This behavior generated even more anxiety, and more repressive measures were taken.

In viewing the situation with ward personnel, it became apparent that the patient had responded to verbal intercession in the past, although persistent efforts were indeed required in this direction. Because of frustration and fear, necessary attempts to talk with the patient had been abruptly abandoned in favor of sedation and isolation. When attempts were again made to talk with the patient about his anger, he responded positively, and the other measures were not needed.

This case points out how a patient's dangerousness can become exaggerated by the very measures that are prematurely instituted to control him. The staff members withdrew from interacting with the patient and handled him punitively. This intensified a bad situation, since it removed the patient from therapeutic human contact and worsened his alienation. Since patients with aggressive urges fear losing control of such urges, they become even more agitated when they sense that everyone is afraid of them. In the situation described here, ventilation of the staff members' frustration with and fear of the patient led to a reduction in their perception of him as threatening.

Identification with an aggressive patient can occur in ward settings.

Case 6.

A 26-year-old soldier was hospitalized because of bizarre, violent behavior. It was learned that he was a former boxer and professional football player, with a long record of violent outbursts for which he had been hospitalized. He was a powerfully built man who projected an aura of dangerousness. His arrival on the ward caused great concern among the staff. All of them wished to know what to do in case he "went wild" since they feared that no one could restrain him.

Within several days an interesting reaction was noticed. Some nursing staff members began to supply him with cigars; several of the patients and staff members began to imitate his mannerisms, and his colloquialisms became widespread among certain male patients. Weight lifting became a fad on the ward, and a number of younger staff members and patients were soon participating in physical exercises with this patient, who regularly performed his own. Within several weeks the patient was elected to a leading ward government position. These events had a beneficial effect on the patient, who seemed transformed into a well-liked individual.

One night, however, when aroused from bed by a policeman who had come to investigate a recent act of violence, the patient became enraged and threatened to kill "the goddamn cop." He was on the verge of losing control when patients and staff approached him and assiduously encouraged him to contain himself. He ranted and raved and broke a chair but did not attack his accuser. This explosive incident exposed his deep-seated problems and his barely submerged potential for violence, issues that had not come to light until then.

More subtle variations of identification are occasionally noted on ward settings. Staff and patients, as well, may take a special interest in the patient, find him "charming" or "interesting," and listen avidly to his accounts of past antisocial acts without coming to grips with and challenging the patient's aggressive propensities.

Patients who experience violent impulses desperately want help in curbing such urges.[2][3] Violent patients are terrified of losing control and welcome therapeutic efforts that restore a sense of control and prevent them from acting on their urges. To this extent the therapist must explore all avenues of aggression with the patient and squarely face issues of destructiveness, pointing out to the patient that the goal of this exploration is to prevent the very aggression that disturbs him. The physician must be aware of his own fear of and anger at the patient and of the effect these feelings may have in distorting the dangerousness of the patient via projection. The therapist must be careful not to reject the patient or to forget to inquire about situations that could result in the patient's becoming violent. Finally, the clinican must be aware of the emotions evoked in nursing staff by violent patients and the role these emotions play in complicating management of an already problematic group of individuals.

References

1. Bach-Y-Rita, G, et al: Episodic dyscontrol: a study of 130 violent patients. *Am J Psychiatry* 127:1473-1478, 1971.
2. Lion JR: *Evaluation and Management of the Violent Patient.* Springfield, Ill, Charles C Thomas, 1972.
3. Lion JR, Bach-Y-Rita G, Ervin FR: Violent patients in the emergency room. *Am J Psychiatry* 125:1706-1711, 1969.
4. Pasternak SA: Evaluation of dangerous behavior of active duty servicemen. *Milit Med* 136:110-113, 1971.
5. Colby KM: *A Primer for Psychotherapists.* New York, Ronald Press, 1951.
6. Macdonald JM: The prompt diagnosis of psychopathic personality. *Am J Psychiatry:* 122 (June supple.): 45-50. 1966.
7. Fromm-Reichmann F: *Principles of Intensive Psychotherapy.* Chicago, University of Chicago Press, 1952.
8. Schwartz MS, Sockley EL: *The Nurse and the Mental Patient: A Study in Interpersonal Relations.* New York, Russell Sage Foundation, 1956.

V.

Violence: Psychotherapy of Pseudohomosexual Panic* †

Sherwyn M. Woods

Psychotherapy of patients with a genuine potential for violence is difficult and dangerous. This is particularly true of the frequently encountered heterosexual patient for whom violence represents an ego defense against intolerable psychic pain associated with a crisis of masculine self-esteem. This often results from dependency and power conflicts which are unconsciously symbolized as homosexual acts. Such pseudohomosexual panic states may follow any adaptive failure, be it social, sexual, or vocational. Violence is a restorative act, attempting to restore masculine self-esteem via aggressive demonstrations of power and strength while at the same time denying the passivity and dependency symbolically linked to femininity. Avoidance of violence requires the rapid identification of pseudohomosexual vs. true homosexual anxiety, and active interpretive involvement with the associated pseudohomosexual conflicts.

†Reprinted from the *Archives of General Psychiatry* 27:255-258, August 1972. Copyright 1972 American Medical Association.

Perhaps some of the most difficult moments in the professional life of a psychotherapist are those spent with patients who present a genuine threat of violence. Not uncommonly the ongoing process of psychotherapy bogs down or halts as anxiety in therapist and patient unite to make both fearful of upsetting the delicate balance of the patient's controls. The therapeutic task is obvious, though at times extraordinarily difficult. It is, namely, to defuse the situation so as to be able to engage the conflict with full affective force, avoiding acting out.

As pointed out in an earlier publication concerning adolescent violence and homicide,[1] a violent act is the product of complex psychological and social forces impinging upon the biological matrix of ego controls, with such factors weighted differently in each individual. It is not within the scope of this paper to explore all of the combinations of violence. In addition, my remarks concern only men because of difficulties in accumulating sufficient clinical experience with the less frequently encountered violent woman. My discussion is directed towards those heterosexual men for whom violence represents an ego defense against the intolerable psychic pain associated with a crisis of self-esteem brought on by conflicts of dependency and power, which have been symbolized as homosexual acts and taken by the patient as presumptive evidence of homosexuality. Such conflicts have been labeled by Ovesey[2] as pseudohomosexual in contrast to true homosexuality which has an erotic motivation. The crisis of masculine self-esteem may result in an incipient pseudohomosexual panic state which the patient desperately attempts to ward off through acts of violence. It is of critical importance to distinguish pseudohomosexual conflict from true homosexual conflict in such patients.

Classical Psychoanalytic Viewpoint

Freud's[3] biological orientation led him to a theory of constitutional bisexuality with the childhood precursors of sexual behavior being activity vs. passivity. Environmental influences acted, therefore, to facilitate or inhibit an inherently strong or weak predisposition to the active-masculine or passive-feminine role. Homosexuality, according to the libido theory, represented such dynamics as narcissistic fixation at an autoerotic level to a person with similar genitals; defensive regression under oedipally induced castration anxiety to narcissistic identification with the incorporated image of mother, loving his homosexual objects as he wished to be loved by mother; and fixation of libido, in association with narcissistic identification with mother, submitting to a father-substitute in a passive receptive manner; transformation of competitive hatred into homosexual love, etc. In the overt homosexual these conflicts are translated into the seeking of sexual objects of the same sex, and the style of the sexual activity often reflects the underlying dynamic. When such homosexual conflicts are under repression the individual is said to have "latent" homosexual problems, and as such latent impulses strive for conscious expression, the resultant anxiety, guilt, and shame cause the mobilization of ego defenses and, therefore, neurotic or perhaps psychotic symptomatology. When defenses fail, castration anxiety may reach the proportions referred to as homosexual panic. Classical interventions[4] consist of bringing the conflict into conscious awareness, with resolution consisting of both an acceptance of innate bisexuality and release from psychosexual fixations and regression so as to permit progression toward "genitality" with its associated heterosexual object choice and sublimation of homosexual strivings.

An Adaptational Viewpoint

Ovesey's[2] dissatisfaction with classical theory led to conceptualization from the adaptational theories pioneered by Rado.[5] The term "sexual" designates only that behavior having orgastic satisfaction as the motivational aim. Assertion is a generic term for all behavior, with or without hostile intent, which is designed to gratify a need. Aggression is a specific form of assertion which has hostile intent for the object with the goal of injury or destruction, and violence pertains to the use of physical force. The primary goal of all behavior is survival, and gratification of nonsurvival needs is allotted secondary priority. Culturally determined psychosocial needs are not innate but develop and conform with exposure to the demands of one's society.

The earliest technique for survival and need gratification is dependency, an adaptation rooted in the biological helplessness of infancy. Adaptive failure in the adult may revive infantile dependency strivings. Fear aroused in response to adult sexuality often represents a revival of associated childhood fears of physical punishment (extended in fantasy to bodily mutilation, castration) and/or withdrawal of love (often symbolized as death or separation) and, therefore, loss of dependency. This may be a take-off point for a homosexual adaptation in an attempt to ward off such fears through choice of a safer object which also has the reassuring presence of a penis. The penis symbolizes not merely sexual adequacy, but also the strength, dominance, and superiority assigned to masculinity by our culture. Any adaptive failure, be it social, sexual or vocational, may be perceived unconsciously as a failure in masculine role and give rise to fears of homosexuality. The sequence is: I am a failure - I am castrated - I am not a man - I am a woman - I am a homosexual.

The fear of homosexuality is further increased by the ego's regressive attempts at restoration and repair. Infantile security is associated with omnipotence and magical control via possession, and this may be symbolized "homosexuality." Via the breast-penis equation there may be attempts to recapture masculinity by oral or anal incorporation of another man's penis. Or, there may be an attempt at restoration via compensatory power striving represented in fantasy by aggressive sexual domination of a male partner.

These dynamics are discussed by Ovesey[2] in his superb monograph entitled *Homosexuality and Pseudohomosexuality.* He had observed, as had Freud and many others, that heterosexual male patients frequently expressed wishes to be loved by men, to be dependent upon them, to dominate or be dominated by them, and to establish genital contact with them. Inevitably, such patients became fearful that they were homosexual, and in accordance with freudian theory the analyst had no choice but to ultimately confirm the patient's fears. However, except for those few heterosexual patients who were overtly bisexual or suffered from true latent homosexuality, the fantasies were unaccompanied by erotic feeling and there was no evidence of homosexual arousal or behavior in adulthood. Ovesey[2] states: "I found in every such instance . . . the fantasies were motivated either by dependency needs or by power needs . . . through the symbolic use of genital organs for nonsexual purposes." The patient misinterprets these fantasies as truly homosexual, but in reality they are only symbolically so.

Anxiety about homosexuality can be broken down into three motivational components: sexual, dependency, power. The sexual component is the only one that seeks sexual gratification as its motivational goal, and anxiety generated in the search is, therefore, true homosexual anxiety and the associated conflict is true homosexual conflict. The dependency and power motivational components use the genital organs to seek nonsexual goals, and sexuality is incidental. Pseudohomosexual motivations are also found in the homosexual male, alongside the true homosexual motivation, and may determine the form of the homosexual act and the psychosocial structure of the relationship.[6]

Violence as a Defense against Pseudohomosexual Panic

I have been impressed in clinical practice with the frequency with which pseudohomosexual anxiety and panic is encountered in patients with problems of aggression and violence. It was a far more frequent and important issue than was true homosexual conflict and anxiety.

The pressure of the impulse to violence was often reduced as there was psychotherapeutic engagement with the shame, humiliation, and hurt masculine pride that was associated with homosexual ideation which had been generated by the pseudohomosexual conflicts. Failure to deal directly and decisively with the patient's shame and hurt masculine pride, particularly when the pseudohomosexual elaborations were out of conscious awareness, would often lead to dangerously high escalation in the titer of violence. In virtually all cases, however, it would dramatically decrease or even abruptly cease when it became possible to engage therapeutically with the feared homosexuality via clarification of the pseudohomosexual issues. This was in sharp contrast to several of my early cases, and a number seen in consultation for other therapists, in which failure to distinguish homosexual from pseudohomosexual conflict, and interpretation along classical lines of inherent bisexuality, resulted in an escalation of anxiety and acting out. Is this based upon "simple reassurance" that the patient is indeed not a homosexual but struggling with "more acceptable" problems? I find this an untenable explanation. Any salutory effect of fraudulent reassurance cannot endure in the face of the introspective explorations of dynamic psychotherapy or psychoanalysis. There is no significant change in the clinical picture, the conflict continues to emerge in dream and fantasy, and new and significant productions fail to appear. The reassurance which accompanies accurate classification is quite another matter, and leads toward profitable exploration of real, rather than apparent, conflictual issues.

Clinical Examples

For most, the incident arousing the violent impulses was merely a precipitant and the history revealed a long-standing precarious sense of masculine identity. Common precipitants related to failures in self-assertion, often in power struggles with other men; competitive defeat by other men, especially in love or professionally; failures in achieving a sense of activity and dominance in relationships with women with intensely shameful feelings about submission or passivity; or threatened or actual exposure of intense and shameful dependency needs. Indeed, the cases studied might be subsumed under two general categories: (1) Attempted triumph or destruction over the object inducing shame, competitive defeat, or submissiveness; and (2) attempted destruction or removal of the object arousing or threatening exposure of dependency

Examples of the first general category included patients who became obsessively preoccupied with revenge and punishment of the girlfriend who jilted them, the spouse who betrayed them, or the man who cuckolded them. The patient reacts with righteous indignation, but the reaction generalizes, becomes obsessional, and moves toward violence for which the punishment often far exceeds the magnitude of the crime.

Example 1

The subject was a businessman who entered treatment because of severe depression precipitated by competitive defeat at the hands of an old business rival. The patient's fantasy of wealth and status were shattered by his rival's completely legal though unethical manipulations which won a coveted contract. In treatment the patient alternated between fits of depression and fits of rage with plots of vengeance and violent destruction. He finally hired someone with instructions to beat and cripple the offender on the anniversary of the incident. The patient defiantly clung to his plan until one day he appeared panic-stricken following a dream. In the dream he encountered a cripple on the street whose attempts to walk appeared ludicrous and caused the patient to laugh loudly. However, he jumped into the cripple's immensely powerful arms and was promptly stripped naked and impaled upon a huge erection. A crowd gathered and hooted at his humiliation.

The subsequent dream analysis led to the exposure of long-standing inhibitions in masculine assertiveness dealt with by overcompensatory power strivings. His shame concerned unconscious relief that his rival had rescued him from certain humiliation. His conviction was of gross inability to handle a masculine role of wealth and power, and through violent revenge he hoped to restitute his sense of masculine pride and deny his feeling of castration. Even his attempt at assertion via revenge was doomed, however, and he was shown to the world as preferring to offer himself passively for anal rape rather than face the alienation and destruction associated with masculine potency. No erotic motivations were apparent in this or in subsequent material. With clarification and psychotherapeutic focus upon the true issues, the patient's need for violence decreased and his contract with the underworld was cancelled.

Recapture of the maternal breast is the most primitive wish of the dependent person, but an alternative route is based on the equation penis-breast. Penis size, integrity, and functional capacity symbolize total adaptive success or failure, and the dependent male may strive to incorporate orally or anally the stronger man's penis, thus magically capturing the donor's strength. Awareness of such wishes are quite understandably interpreted by the patient as evidence of incipient homosexualty. Analysis, however, frequently fails to reveal a true homosexual motive. These patients comprise the second general category, namely those who through violence hope to eliminate the object arousing or threatening exposure of their infantile dependent and passive wishes. Such patients included those who attempted to destroy the child in themselves by violence upon their own children, another whose impulses to rape and murder were a part of his psychotic attempt to extinguish chaotic infantile dependent wishes toward women, and another with impulses toward matricide. For some there would be pseudohomosexual panic via the passive dependency aroused in close relationships with male friends and business partners.

Example 2

This man was at times dangerously close to injuring seriously his newborn child who inexplicably irritated him to the point of rage. Simultaneous with the child's birth he had begun to have dreams in which he was nursing at a breast which would subsequently turn into a penis. He became fearful that he was becoming a homosexual, and this generalized to compulsively recurrent fellatio fantasies. He entered treatment terrified that he would seriously injure his child, and these impulses abated when he became aware of his envy of the infant who was arousing his own infantile wishes. These wishes had been elaborated via regressive fantasies of oral incorporation of the penis to reclaim magically masculine potency and strength.

It is obvious that the therapist may be viewed as a similar threat, and may become the object of the patient's violent impulses. Such a circumstance arises from the transference relationship in which the patient plays out earlier conflicts of power and dependency, as well as the assault upon masculine pride from dependency upon the therapist and the therapy. Patients may experience psychotherapy as having their nose rubbed in their passivity and dependency, and the therapist's interventions as the equivalent of rape. They view the unfolding of their inner life as a submissive humiliating surrender of masculinity. Such patients often have strong paranoid dynamics, and when there is significant or psychotic ego disorganization the therapist may indeed be in danger. Ovesey[2] in a reformulation of the paranoid dynamic believes that survival anxiety is universal in such patients, and pseudohomosexual conflict of much greater frequency than projected homosexual wishes. Schwartz[7] stressed the issues of narcissism and fragility of self-esteem rather than repressed homosexuality. My experience would support these views, and for such patients classical interpretations based on latent homosexuality may escalate anxiety, at times to dangerous panic.

It is not surprising that these patients are often subject to severe depression and may present a high risk of suicide. The dynamics are those described by Bibring[8] and Jacobson,[9] namely, depression which is highly related to failure in self-esteem. It is but a short step from murder of others to murder of self. The danger of suicide may be greater in those also struggling with true homosexual conflicts.

The act of violence wards off pseudohomosexual panic via aggression, and there is simultaneous denial of the passivity, submissiveness, defeat, or dependency associatively linked to femininity. The pseudohomosexual equation is thus reversed: I demonstrate dominance, control and power - therefore I am not castrated - I am a man - I am not a woman - I am not a homosexual.

Issues in Psychotherapy

The patients under discussion were involved in the treatment spectrum from brief psychotherapy to analytic psychotherapy and psychoanalysis. As with suicidal depressed patients, modifications in technique may be essential.

Little dynamic psychotherapy can occur unless the initial phase of psychotherapy results in the establishment of a therapist-patient relationship sufficiently good to weather the storms of the ensuing transference distortions and vicissitudes of treatment. Similarly, the sooner both therapist and patient are freed from the anxiety concerning the immediate danger of aggression, the sooner the dynamic conflicts can be brought into focus. For patients with serious ego disorganization or unmanageable anxiety, the major tranquilizers are useful, as is reassurance, injunctions on the side of ego controls, and environmental structuring. Such interventions should be kept to the minimum necessary to accommodate the danger, and maintained no longer than absolutely necessary. Such activity may be drawn into the pseudohomosexual conflicts, heightening anxiety or inhibiting the developing sense of autonomy and self-control.

It is of crucial importance that confrontation follow all active interventions or transference response which involved dependency or power. Anxiety and shame regarding dependency upon therapist, therapy, or medication must be made immediately conscious. Castration fantasies of submission to the therapist' and loss of masculine pride in having to rely upon another man (or upon a woman), must be dealt with similarly. The fragility of the sense of masculinity appears, along with the historical material, and sets the stage for later engagement with the pseudohomosexual conflict. The therapist need not be reluctant to confront openly distorted concepts of masculinity and femininity, along with a forthright statement that the patient's shame is highly overdetermined, unrealistic, and undoubtedly the product of distorted life experiences. Identification with the therapist's greater flexibility and tolerance reduces anxiety.

Should aggressive impulses toward the therapist appear directly or in dreams, if the material is at all in evidence there should be an immediate attempt to reach the motivational issues of dependency or power, or both, as well as exposure of the wish to overcome the conflict through force. The therapist's failure to respond with counter-aggression interdicts the patient's expectation of combat and supports the alternative of introspective exploration. Frequently these patients will "put one over" or create a circumstance rendering the therapist helpless. There may be conscious deception, withholding, or stubborn proclamations of intent of aggressive activity. When the therapist readily admits his helplessness, fails to be humiliated or castrated, and fails to counterattack, the patient is often defensively depreciating, then confused, then relieved, and perhaps more open to alternatives to violence. Particularly with reference to the issues of violence and suicide, it is clear that the therapist must be secure in the recognition of his limitations, openly accepting with defiant patients, indicating that he strongly wishes to help them avoid self-defeating aggression, but realizing his helplessness without assistance. Should such behavior occur he will indeed be sad for the disaster in the patient's life, but not destroyed, humiliated, or ruined as a psychotherapist. Several patients with a classical negative therapeutic reaction were clearly the result of the therapist's failure to recognize and deal with this pseudohomosexual power struggle.

As is always the case, the therapist's greatest assets are his tact and sense of timing. The threat of violence raises strong temptations to clarify, confront, or interpret prematurely before the patient's productions have clearly removed such interventions from the category of high-inference speculations. Such activity can only lead to an intellectualization of treatment and will accomplish little if anything.

The rigidity of the patient's demands upon himself regarding masculine self-esteem, the case with which he experiences shame and humiliation, his panic over feelings of helplessness and dependency, and his extreme shame over passivity or competitive failure are all usually very much in evidence. These issues provide fertile avenues of exploration which usually lead rapidly to the conflicts underlying the patient's panic. As anxiety and shame decrease, previously unconscious homosexual symbolization may appear in dream or fantasy and pre-existing symbolization may be more openly discussed. It is useful to call immediate attention to the dependency and power issues manifested often by the style of the fantasied "sexual act." When the evidence is clear that the issue is pseudo rather than true homosexuality, as Ovesey[2], [6] has stated, the patient should immediately, forthrightly, and unequivolcably be told he is not a homosexual but is using homosexual constructs to symbolize his dependency and power conflicts. When there is evidence of true homosexual motivation it must be analyzed separately.

When significant aggressive danger is past, treatment may proceed in typical fashion. Other dynamic issues and conflicts will, of course, emerge. There may be an attempt to return to the original problem of violence in order to recapture the more active early therapist-patient relationship or as resistance to further work. This is particularly true in the termination phase with its capacity to revive the original anxiety and conflict associated with the upswing of self-assertiveness and independence. Indeed, one hallmark of successful treatment is the patient's capacity to reach full potential for assertive self-definition without anxiety or resort to aggression in moments of failure. There are now viable alternatives to violence.

References

1. Woods SM: Adolescent violence and homicide: Ego disruption and the 6 and 14 dysrhythmia. *Arch Gen Psychiat* 5:528;234, 1961.
2. Ovesey L: *Homosexuality and Pseudohomosexuality.* New York, Science House, 1969.
3. Freud S: Psycho-analytic notes on an autobiographical account of a case of paranoia (1911) *in* Strachey J (ed): *Standard Edition of the Complete Psychological Works of Sigmund Freud.* London, Hogarth Press, 1958, vol. 12, pp. 3-84.
4. Fenichel O: *The Psychoanalytic Theory of Neurosis.* New York, WW Norton & Co. Inc. Publishers, 1945.
5. Rado S: *Adaptational Psychodynamics.* New York, Science House, 1969.
6. Ovesey L, Gaylin W, Hendlin H: Psyshotherapy of male homosexuality: Psychodynamic formulation. *Arch Gen Psychiat* 9:19-31, 1963.
7. Schwartz D: A re-view of the "paranoid" concept. *Arch Gen Psychiat* 8:349-361, 1963.
8. Bibring E: The mechanism of depression, in Greenacre P (ed.): *Affective Disorders.* New York, International Universities Press, 1953.
9. Jacobson E: Contribution to the metapsychology of cyclothymic depression, *in* Greenacre (P (ed.): *Affective Disorders.* New York, International Universities Press, 1953.

VI.

Developing a Violence Clinic*

John R. Lion

In this paper I will describe the functioning of a small specialized clinic for violent patients which I have been operating at the University of Maryland Hospital for the past two years. This "violence clinic" involves nothing conceptually new in the evaluation of violent individuals nor is it a large-scale operation with a sizeable administration and research budget; instead, the Violence Clinic is a small affair in which I and some colleagues see a regular number of aggressive patients for evaluation and treatment. More important, however, the clinic serves as a teaching function for mental health personnel and also serves as a place to conduct clinical research on a population of aggressive and destructive men and women. This clinic and my interest in work with violent patients has developed sequentially over recent years. It is important for me first to review this development.

My interest in violence stemmed from work I had done in Boston in the area of brain dysfunction—including epilepsy—and violence. Having seen a number of epileptic patients who manifested violent outbursts, I became interested in the general area of cerebral dysfunction as manifested by EEG parameters, psychological testing for organicity, and careful neu-

*This paper was presented at the Georgetown University Medical Center Symposium on Violence, October 26, 1973.

rological assessment. The role of brain dysfunction in violence is highly controversial at present. Much has been written and said about epilepsy as one extreme example of brain dysfunction and violence. In a recent book entitled "Violence and the Brain" Drs. Vernon Mark and Frank Ervin[1] advance the general thesis that there exists an etiological link between psychomotor epilepsy and violence. They purport that in certain circumstances, neurosurgical procedures are justified in cases refractory to anticonvulsant control. Further literature exists on the use of neurosurgical procedures to control non-epileptic behavior disorders[2] [5] and the entire area field of epilepsy and violence has become clouded by highly charged emotional issues. Both the National Institute of Neurological Diseases and Stroke[6] [8] and the American Psychiatric Association[8] are directing attention to the problem of violence, brain dysfunction, and the neurosurgical control of behavior. We will have to await further scientific data on all aspects of this problem. Suffice it to say the literature linking psychomotor epilepsy to violence is unclear and that there is no consensus in the literature showing that psychomotor epileptics are any more prone to violence than other epileptics.[9] [12] Furthermore it can be directly stated that the vast majority of epileptics are certainly not violent.[13] I emphasize these points immediately because the issues are very important. We must gain scientific understanding of the role brain dysfunction plays in violence if we are to treat violent patients.

Having seen a few epileptic patients, I became interested in non-epileptic violent patients. I was very interested in violent patients who entered the emergency room of the large general hospital where I worked.[14] It became evident first, that violent patients *do* come to acute psychiatric facilities asking for help, and second, that they present with specific chief complaints and common psychodynamic features. In previous work I have described a breakdown of violent patients into various classifications.[15] Patients can present with diffusely directed violent urges (I'm afraid of doing something terrible; I'm afraid I'm going to harm someone) where *no* target or vector is specified. Or they can present with *specifically directed violent* urges (I'm going to kill my wife). In the first class of patients, the *diffuseness* is usually defensive, and protects the patient from realizing the true source of his anger which is directed at an ambivalently held object. That is, the patient adopts an intense and brittle reaction formation against hatred at, for example, a parent. This reaction formation breaks down under appropriate stress and leads to anxiety and the expression of diffusely violent urges. Patients with *diffusely directed violent urges* demonstrate intense anxiety. The anxiety propels them into treatment. In patients with *specifically directed violent urges,* anxiety is more often absent. The sadomasochistic interaction of patient and victim are obvious and the pathological and provocative role of the victim is also apparent.[16]

There are two other classes of patients seen in emergency room settings. One very common type is the patient who complains of "blackouts" and violence, i.e., violence in association with drinking (small amounts of alcohol). There is an extensive forensic literature on the topic of pathological intoxication. Suffice it to say that a "blackout" may be nothing or it may be something. It may be a patient's manipulative story, or, it may be a true psychosis activated by alcohol or a seizure state activated by alcohol. Dr. George Bach-Y-Rita and I have intravenously administered alcohol to a group of patients complaining of "blackouts" in association with violence and found no EEG or behavioral changes.[17] However, other workers[18] have found behavioral arousal and EEG activation when alcohol was orally administered. Much confusion still surrounds this issue. In any event, patients with this problem deserve careful psychiatric and neurological assessment. Suffice it to say that aggressive alcoholics are not necessarily benign people when it comes to violence; a majority of violent crimes[19] and motor vehicle fatalities[20] involve the use of alcohol.

A final group of patients seen in the emergency room are those who describe spells of violence-paroxysmal and episodic outbursts of violence. Such patients relate explosive recurring rage attacks with histories of auralike and postictal-like events. They can sometimes relate histories of convulsions, head injury, family histories of epilepsy, and other data suggestive of central nervous system dysfunction, if not psychomotor or temporal lobe epilepsy itself. It is this group of patients which interest me the most. However, it is this group of patients about whom there is much clinical and scientific debate, and I shall discuss these patients further.

The main lesson I learned in emergency room work was that violent patients seek help.[21] I also learned that violence can be a *dystonic* event for a patient. I believe that for most patients violence is dystonic. It is perceived as unpleasant; it represents a defense against helplessness and passivity and depression; it is something which arouses great anxiety and is a cry for help. If you can ever recall being very angry or furious about something, you can appreciate just how unpleasant is the affective state of anger. If you multiply this by a hundred fold, you get an idea of what a violent or impendingly violent patient feels like when he is mad enough to kill. I learned also that it is possible to work with violent patients. They can be educated to respond to premonitory signs and symptoms which herald future violent actions. Violence is, after all, a response to something unpleasant. If we can acknowledge that unpleasantness, we can do business with violent and potentially violent patients.[14]

I hasten to qualify this generalization by pointing to a large group of severely recidivist offenders in our jails and prisons around the country. These people have been violent over and over again. They do not necessarily see their acts as dystonic. Perhaps we should label them as just good old-fashioned evil men. Yet this generalization, too, requires qualification. There are certainly bad criminals who are refractory to help. But many criminals have never had a chance at help. Of course many, if not most, have never really been evaluated, and many do, when you sit down with them, complain of their violence and perceive it to be dystonic. Some have exceedingly poor impulse control over violent urges. Some fit the classification of Explosive Personalities where one wonders whether brain dysfunction might not play some role in the genesis of their behavior. I am involved currently in collaborating on a large research project in a local prison in which we will systematically examine a group of violent offenders. in order to answer this type of question.

Having seen violent patients in an emergency room setting and having treated such patients in individual and group settings, I decided to begin a violence clinic in the Baltimore area. Actually, I did not use the term violence clinic because it appeared that the term led hospital administrators to fantasize a waiting room filled with people carrying machine guns. I called the clinic "Clinical Research Program for Violent Behavior." This title sounded scholarly and noble, and so we proceeded. I planted stories in the local newspapers[22] announcing our program and informing the public that a clinic for violent individuals was opening and that patients with assaultive or destructive urges would be seen on an appointment basis in the clinic. I stressed the nature of self-referrals, hoping that most patients who would call would be self-referred. This has since not turned out to be the case, and most of our referrals currently are from other physicians, social agencies, and members of the legal profession or correctional officers. Along with the newspaper story, I included three photographs of violent people.[22] One photo showed a man sitting slumped in a chair, surrounded by broken furniture and broken dishes. A caption read: "This man has temper outbursts. He becomes violent when angry. Do you get like this? Call — — — — 528-6475." Another showed a man bending over a dresser upon which lay a gun. A caption read: "This man is afraid of doing something violent. He goes out of control when he is angry. Do you have this problem?" A third poster showed a man speeding in a car with an analogous caption. I particularly included a speeding car, since so many of our patients have misused and still do describe the misuse of the car in association with violent urges. This, by the way, is a question that always needs to be asked of violent patients and a question we often forget to ask. Other questions which need to be asked of violent patients involve ownership and use of weapons (guns), past criminal acts, and past violent acts. These questions can be tactfully asked.

I stated that patients required an advance appointment. I did this, because I was tired of emergency room work and because I wanted time and a relaxed environment to see patients. Too often, violent patients are handled dispositionally, shunned and shunted off to state facilities because they evoke anxiety, fear, or disgust in examining personnel. This problem, by the way, of the countertransference is one that interests me greatly, and I have had the privilege of working with Dr. Pasternack on the production of a videotape on the subject of countertransference reactions to violent patients.[23] [24] This tape, available through the Network for Continuing Medical Education contains numerous interviews with frightening patients. It deals with the emotional reactions of clinicians and how such reactions distort and skew the diagnostic process. For example, paranoia and projection in an agitated patient often leads to anger in the clinician who may deal with his own emotions in a similar way. This may all result in the patient being perceived as very "dangerous." As dangerousness is a very ominous label from the legal standpoint, much attention must be paid to this process and we need to know what goes on inside of us when we deal with violent patients. Incidentally, I should say that I feel dynamic factors also account for the fact that we are much more prone to work with depressed patients than with violent patients. We are, as a profession, more prone to depression in ourselves than we are to become violent. Depressed patients are often seen as more treatable than violent patients, particularly patients with severe character pathology. This may be partly true, of course, but I have often wondered whether our reactions toward violent patients springs more from our being in dynamic harmony with the introjection of aggression, rather than its externalization. Unfortunately, this is sheer speculation and I have no data to support even the speculation.

The violence clinic, as it is known in the Baltimore community, now functions without much difficulty. A regular flow of about 3 to 5 new patients a week is handled by several psychiatrists, residents, or students choosing to spend elective time with us, and by members of the community who wish to learn something about violence. At the moment, for example, a psychologist spends time in the clinic, and a local psychiatric practitioner spends one morning a week with me. Various social workers and probation officers have frequently asked for consultations regarding management of a particular patient, as do students, interns, and residents. This teaching aspect of the clinic is important, and has, so to speak, given violence a decent name, or, more specifically, has reduced some diagnostic and therapeutic nihilism which is so prevalent in the area of the treatment of this group of patients.

Since the inception of the clinic, I have seen about 200 patients and formally reported on 150 patients.[25] The bulk of these patients fall into personality disorder classifications of a mixed type with antisocial, explosive, and passive-aggressive, paranoid features. A smaller number are schizoid or obsessive in character structure, and a yet smaller number are psychotic, usually chronic schizophrenic. The patients are usually in their twenties, though we have seen patients up to the age of 67. The backgrounds of the patients, as would be expected, reflects much emotional deprivation and a high incidence of intrafamilial violence. Nine patients have killed others, and 53 have related histories of convictions for assault or other crimes of violence. One interesting finding is a high incidence of suicide attempts of 30%. This business of suicide is an interesting finding and often attests to boderline ego functioning. Certain patients when under stress show impairment in reality testing and an inability to appreciate body boundaries. Thus such patients freely internalize and alternately externalize aggression. When the object of their anger is not available, they tend to internalize aggression leading them to suicide. I would draw your attention to the classic study of suicide in police written by Paul Friedman in Shneidman's Essays in Self Destruction[26] where this clinical point is made. Suffice it to say that a history of suicidal acts is of little consolation to me when I see a violent patient. That is, I cannot rely upon him to internalize his aggression because that internalization may be a manifestation of an impaired ego process, rather than a strong superego process. For example, I saw a patient who wanted to kill his wife; when she abruptly walked out of the house, he took an overdose. In the hospital, he vehemently denied any suicidal intent and professed puzzlement over his behavior. This is a common story with such patients.[27]

There are recurring dynamic themes. Violent patients often try to defend against negative thoughts about members of their families. Thus when a friend insulted a patient's mother, he tried to kill the friend. In another case when a patient's mother was called a prostitute, he erupted with homicidal rage. Violent patients seem provoked by threat of separation. Indeed loss of control over hostile urges commonly arose when patients were threatened with abandonment by a spouse. I would judge abandonment to be one of the most prevalent dynamic issues in violent patients of the type I have seen. Threats of separation or divorce and threats of leaving on the part of the spouse could trigger murderous rage in a patient. On closer examination, it frequently appeared that such abandonment revived affects related to earlier infantile abandonment the patient had experienced in childhood. Another important dynamic theme was that of homosexuality. Patients vigorously defended against passive yearnings and underlying homosexual strivings by adopting pseudomasculine stances that became easily challenged with physical attack.

Here[25] are some representative case examples of patients to give a flavor for the clinical material encountered.

Case 1.

A 27-year-old laborer was referred to the clinic because of severe anger outbursts and a homocidal ideation directed at his girlfriend, who had rejected him. There was a history of previous criminal convictions, and the patient was awaiting trial for assault. Mental status revealed a paranoid, agitated man who saw little reason for therapy and who projected all difficulties onto the environment, refusing introspection.

An organic evaluation showed some equivocal findings on neurological examination, organicity on psychological testing, and a borderline abnormal EEG.

The patient was placed on anticonvulsant and tranquilizer medications and was scheduled for group therapy. He attended a few times but eventually stopped coming and was lost to follow-up. Attempts to reach him by telephone and mail were unsuccessful.

These types of patients are common and pose difficulties in evaluation and treatment. Many seek only to involve the psychiatrist with the hope that this may favorably influence their legal status; others seek hospitalization to avoid court action. Seeing neither possibility materialize, they lack motivation and disappear. In some cases, they have learned enough about anger and the role of the clinic to contact us in acute panic states, as the next case illustrates.

Case 2.

An unemployed 21-year-old man was referred by a physician of another hospital because of temper outbursts and self-mutilative behavior. A past history revealed multiple state hospitalizations for depression, self-mutilative behavior, and aggressive outbursts. He had attacked his landlady and often harbored thoughts of killing people for no apparent reason. Judged schizophrenic, he had been unsuccessfully tried on a variety of medications including anticonvulsants, tranquilizers, and lithium, but he did not reliably take these.

He was hospitalized for evaluation. Mental status revealed a pleasant young man who demonstrated bland affect and often smiled inappropriately. No clear delusions or hallucinations were apparent. He had limited insight into his difficulties. He showed mood swings and tolerated group discussions poorly, often becoming upset by what another member said about him. Hostile urges continued, and on one occasion, he became violent on the ward, breaking some furniture. Eventually, he responded to chlorpromazine medication. He attended group therapy but remained a peripheral member. He frequently contacted the clinic when he felt himself decompensating. Such brief contacts with hospital staff were a positive experience for him, and apparently sufficed to keep him functioning without his becoming dangerously aggressive.

This case illustrated an important aspect of treatment which I have previously described. The violent patient can perceive violent urges as dystonic, and can seek help to avoid them. Such a patient, at the least, can be taught to *use a clinic or emergency room service in times of stress* thus avoiding potentially destructive action. An institutional transference can develop. I introduce such patients to members of my staff and my secretary with the expectation that future contacts, even telephone contacts, with such people can be of help to them.

Case 3.

A 27-year-old sanitation worker was referred by his probation officer after the latter read about the clinic in the paper. The patient anxiously related that he had shot a fellow employee after the employee had teased him about being a homosexual. The patient had intended to kill the employee, but only wounded him. After being convicted and serving a portion of his sentence, he was paroled and made to attend the clinic. No previous criminal history existed.

Mental status revealed a tall and powerfully built individual with little formal education but much native intelligence. He was mildly anxious and suspicious, but not psychotic. He had little initial insight into conflicts which might have led him to react so strongly to the insults.

patients with convulsive disorders.[30] But even if you make the diagnosis, you are still faced with the conceptual problem of accounting for the aggressive behavior and reconciling that behavior with any seizure state.

In our series of 150 patients, we found 4 temporal lobe epileptics on the basis of EEG. Eight other patients had EEG findings such as slowing or dysrythmias which seemed suspicious. Some of these patients also had equivocal neurological examinations which revealed "soft findings": difficulties with coordination, reflex asymmetries, and mild apraxias, and still others showed evidence of organicity on psychological testing. Some of these patients looked as though they had signs of minimal brain dysfunction; in fact, some gave histories of learning disabilities and hyperkinesis in childhood so that our suspicions were not so far fetched. The concept of minimal brain dysfunction in young adulthood and adulthood has recently received some attention in the literature.[31] [32] I have often wondered whether or not some of these patients calm down with amphetamines just as certain hyperkinetic children calm down with central nervous system stimulants. Indeed I saw one violent patient who told me that amphetamines did calm him down and made him less violent. Unfortunately he disappeared.

I have seen other interesting patients. This past month, I saw a 19-year-old paraplegic who was violent and throwing temper tantrums at home. He came from a household of violence and had been shot and made paraplegic by his stepfather, a policeman, with whom he started a violent argument over a woman. I also saw a very successful dentist who in the midst of a bad argument at home hit his wife in the face, and then riddled with remorse and shame, called me for a private appointment. He was quite depressed, and is in treatment now.

Please note that some of the case reports I have summarized are quite esoteric. This is not surprising, since any specialty clinic sees a fair number of complicated and esoteric cases.

We now turn our attention to the *treatment* of the violent patient. Please recall first, that violent patients need a place to come to or a number to call when they feel their impulses going out of control. These patients can be taught to use emergency room facilities or phone a physician when dangerous urges begin to break through. This simple statement needs to be made over and over again. Violent patients, like suicidal ones, utter a cry for help. The violent act is rarely random but is in response to dynamically significant stresses which evoke anxiety and to which the patient can be told to pay attention.

Treatment of violent patients is eclectic. For some patients, individual therapy is most useful, while for others group experience is better. There are many serious problems in the treatment of these patients and part of the problem is getting them into therapy and making them stay there—the same problems one has with the treatment of any severe personality disorder. In my work with groups of violent individuals[33], I have described their great sensitivity to issues of self-esteem and intimacy, their preoccupation with masculinity and power, and their fear of insight and discomfort with introspection. Attendance at group therapy is a major problem. The therapist must change his traditional role [34] from a passive observer to an active, more outgoing, and supportive person. The therapist must be the concerned medical doctor with whom the patient can identify. Identification is a prime factor in treatment, I feel, and there have been major deficits in the early identification processes with these types of "acting-out" (I use this word loosely as behaviorally oriented individual rather than as a transference phenomenon) patients. The term "acting-out," by the way, leads me to a prime strategy and agenda in therapy. Actually, there are two agendas. First, there is the need to teach the patient how to fantasize, and second, there is the need to teach the patient how to *recognize affect and describe it verbally.* Let me take up the issue of fantasy first.

Many of the impulsive violent patients I have seen seem to demonstrate an impoverished ability to fantasize. Any kind of an adverse stimulus leads to direct behavior without intermediate intervening, ruminations, fantasies, or thought. These patients act first, and think, if they do think, afterwards. It is as though there were an "eipleptiod" short circuit in the brain from sensory to motor areas. In any event, these patients do not sit around like you and I wonder about another person's sarcasm, for example, "what did he mean by that insult?" They strike out or they go out and get drunk and then punch. Now in therapy it becomes important to get the patient to elaborate on his thoughts regarding a particular incident. For example, if the patient says he wants to kill his wife, he must be asked how he would do this. Where would he buy the gun? What would the gun feel like in his hand? Where would the bullet hit? Press the fantasy to the logical conclusion of murder and incarceration (fantasies of that?) Do this over and over again. Repeat this often so the patient learns, in some primitive way (and the way they learn it is to report that they "think more now") to interpose thought and fantasy between stimulus and response. One presses for detail because *with detail comes affect.* I have described in one report the role of depression in the treatment of aggressive personality disorders and described in that report the need to deal with frustration, disappointment, and depression in aggressive patients.[3 5] This means that the therapy must uncover, gently, the weaknesses and fragilities against which the patient expends so much energy defending himself. A patient is aggressive and will remain so only as long as he is unable to come to grips with the depressive aspects of his position and unable to reflect on it. As long as he must avoid realization and toleration of emotional pain, he is a risk.

A second agenda and another area to focus on in therapy is the *realization of affective states.* Many violent patients do not know when they are mad or angry. Now you and I can sit around for hours talking about the nuances of our feelings, and we have a mental thesaurus in our heads. But these aggressive and impulsive patients do not. They perceive negative affective states in a globally unpleasant way. Anger is felt as something which you have to go out and get drunk about to escape from. Thus I try to train patients to experience affect and to describe it: the sensations, the bodily sensations, the muscle tone, and the subjective inner affective states. This is vital and important because once they can feel their anger and identify it and pay attention to it, they can then talk about it, and talking about it is always better than acting on it. Verbalization follows articulation; patients must be educated to respond to their emotions, in a verbal way. Then they will not be taken by surprise by violent impulses which quickly follow their angry feelings.

Another important aspect of treatment is the relationship the patient has with his therapist. In a previous report [36] I have stated that I talk of the relationship with aggressive patients in terms of trust and dependency. Most patients with an aggressive personality disorder have never sat down and seriously talked to another human being about their emotions. This transaction is bound to evoke anxieties and mistrust. The patient usually sees the therapist as being similar to some authority of the law. For that matter, he usually sees the world in general as hostile. I capitalize on this by pointing out to him how restricted his views of people are and how unsatisfactory and depressing this must be for him. This identifies, then, the area we must work hardest to correct.

Some words about medication are in order. There is very sparse literature on the pharmacology of aggression per se. Most of the literature deals with anecdotally or more systematically (controlled studies) with varying population of patients labeled delinquent, psychopathic, or manic. Some reports describe the effects of a byrophenone on aggressive psychotic patients and some of the work with the anticonvulsants was done with juvenile delinquents. It is not clear how aggressive these populations are, and the target symptom or sign of violence is difficult, perhaps impossible, to clearly identify. A violent manic patient is different from an antisocial individual who is in turn different from a paranoid schizophrenic with persecutory delusions and questions arise regarding the action of a drug. That is, does the drug work because it has an effect on the thought disorder? On the depressive core? On the epileptoid mechanism? These are complicated questions; what we can say now is that there is no one drug for aggression, for aggression is, after all, just a symptom.[37]

Nevertheless, a variety of medications have been touted as useful for patients with aggressive symptomatology. These include the major tranquilizers (phenothiazines and butyrophenones)[38] and minor tranquilizers (benzodiazepines)[39] lithium,[40] anticonvulsants[41][42] CNS stimulants[43] and experimental drugs such as the antiandrogen agents.[44][45] Drug choice is a problem. The anticonvulsants are often useful when the patient's violence is episodic, or explosive, particularly when there is, say, EEG evidence to support the notion of a dysfunction of an epileptoid nature. Lithium is useful in patients with aggression linked to cyclothmic disorders of mood. For some hyperaggressive patients who are paranoid, minor tranquilizers in high dosages may provide tranquilization without the disturbing side effects so frightening to such patients and the added anticonvulsant properties of drugs such as diazepam (Valium) may be useful. We are currently conducting research on the benzodiazepines in the clinic and I am also involved in a collaborative study with the Departments of Endocrinology and Psychiatry at Hopkins and McLean Hospital, in Boston studying the effects of Provera—a progestational agent on a small group of hyperaggressive men. This study follows the reporting of beneficial effects of female hormones on men who are not only just aggressive but hypersexual as well.[45] This study has just begun, and I do not have enough experience to report on the usefulness of hormonal agents in the control of aggression.

The amphetamine and methylphenidate compounds have, of course, been used to treat hyperkinetic children and may in that process reduce the impulsivity and aggression such children may show.[43]

I might mention that we are just beginning research on the use of Reserpine to enhance fantasy and affect in severe character disorders with aggressive tendencies. One of my interests is in getting patients who avoid introspection into a depressed posture so that they have to talk about their feelings and I want to administer an old psychotropic drug which may have this capacity, and which may facilitate psychotherapy. This research obviously has many conceptual problems.

Psychopharmacological treatment of violent patients is best carried out empirically, and the clinician should be ready to use a variety of medications in some systematic fashion and with some rationale in order to help the patient control hostile urges. Medications are rarely enough; some form of psychotherapy is always necessary.

Now I should like to turn to some *sociological considerations*. Violence rarely happens in a vacuum but, as I have said, occurs in response to psychological stress, and that stress can be in the *family* or in *society* itself. Ralph Nader has recently [46] coined a phrase "new styles of violence." By this he means the following: "violence exerted on a huge scale but somehow kept, by the workings of the prevailing system of power in our society, from reaching a popularly perceived threshold that triggers irresistible public pressure for reform . . . .. What we must get across to people is that endemic forms of violence are going on daily in this country on a scale that completely dwarfs the common concept of violence as meaning primarily crimes in the street . . . .. In New York City, there are far more people angry about cab-drivers than people disturbed by the combined depredations of all the banks and finance companies in the city . . . .. Oh those cheating cab-drivers! they keep saying. But the cab-driver knows a thing or two about corporate life. He listens to those corporate executives in the back of his cab. He gets some idea of how the big boys are stealing millions. He might as well get his share".[46]

Let me switch the scene now. I am sitting in a small interview room at Patuxent Prison, Patuxent, Maryland, talking to a prisoner who has been committed to Patuxent because of repeated armed robbery and assault. He is a violent man, and I asked him a naive question: Will he get involved in violent crime again when he is free? He smiles at me and says "Doc, I'm just doing what they do in Washington—the only difference between them and me is that I get caught." This statement is not surprising to hear and I have heard it many times. I have wondered what we are covertly saying to our violent prisoners. Psychotherapy and drugs may help the individual patient; that is important, but we must also wonder about the world which surrounds the patient. We can develop our clinical skills to the utmost and we can devise new behavior therapies and new pharmacological aids in reducing violence. We should advance the state of the art of helping those patients who are troubled by violence, but we must not be overzealous. And I want to make it clear that I do *not* support the notion of establishing a chain of violence clinics around the country and I do *not* believe that the suppression of violence is a viable desirable therapeutic concept or social concept. Our jobs as clinicians are not to supress violence, but to teach the patient to effectively modulate it himself. We must realize that social good can come from violence and that not all violent people are candidates for a violence clinic. If we invited all violent people to come in off the streets to our clinics, the streets might be quite empty; that might not be so bad. But what would be bad *is* if we then never had the time to look outside and see if the streets needed repair.

References

1. Mark VH, Ervin FR: *Violence and the Brain.* New York, Harper and Row, 1970.
2. Vaernet K, Madsen A: Stereotaxic amygdalotomy and basofrontal tractotomy in psychotics with aggressive behavior. *J Neurol Neurosurg Psychiat* 33:858-863, 1970.
3. Narabayashi H, et al: Stereotaxic amygdalotomy for behavior disorders. *Arch Neurol* 9:1-16, 1963.
4 Sano K, et al: Results of stimulation and destruction of the posterior hypothalamus in man. *J Neurosurg* 33:689-707, 1970.
5. Heimburger RF, Whitlock CC, Kalsbeck JE: Stereotaxic amygdalotomy for epilepsy with aggressive behavior. *J Amer Med Ass* 198:741-745, 1966.
6. Brown BS, Wienckowski LA, Bivens LW: Psychosurgery: Perspective on a current problem. *National Institute of Mental Health DHEW (HSM)* 73-9119; Washington DC; US Government Printing Office, 1973.
7. *Violence and Brain Dysfunction: Report of the National Institute of Neurological Diseases and Stroke Council on the Neurological Bases of Abnormal (Violent) Behavior.* (In press.)
8. *Report of the Task Force on Clinical Aspects of the Violent Individual, American Psychiatric Association,* Washington, DC (In preparation.)
9. Small JG, Small IF, Hayden MP: Further psychiatric investigations of patients with temporal and nontemporal lobe epilepsy. *Amer J. Psychiat* 123:303-310, 1966.
10. Small JG, Milstein V, Stevens J: Are psychomotor epileptics different? *Arch Neurol* 7:187-194, 1962.
11. Rodin EA: Psychomotor epilepsy and aggressive behavior. *Arch Gen Psychiat,* 28:210-213, 1973.
12. Sweet WH, Ervin FR, Mark VH: The relationship of violent behavior to focal cerebral disease, in *Aggressive Behavior.* Garattini S, Sigg EB (eds) New York, Wiley, 1969, pp 336-352.
13. Livingston S: Epilepsy and murder. *J Amer Med Ass* 188:172, 1964.
14. Bach-Y-Rita G, Lion JR, Climent C, and Ervin FR: Episodic dyscontrol: A study of 130 violent patients. *Amer J Psychiat* 127:1473-1478, 1971.
15. Lion JR, Bach-Y-Rita G, and Ervin FR: Violent patients in the emergency room *Amer J Psychiat* 125:1706-1711, 1969.
16. Macdonald JM: *The Murderer and His Victim.* Springfield, Illinois, Charles C Thomas, 1961.
17. Bach-Y-Rita G, Lion JR, Ervin FR: Pathological intoxication: Clinical and electroencephalographic studies. *Amer J Psychiat* 127:698-703, 1970.
18. Narinacci AA: Special type of temporal lobe (psychomotor) seizures following ingestion of alcohol. *Bull Los Angeles Neurol Soc* 28:241-250, 1963.
19. *Crime in the United States, 1972.* Uniform Crime Reports for the United

States,Washington, DC, Superintendent of Documents, US Government Printing Office, 1973.

20. Voas RB: Alcohol is an underlying factor in behavior leading to fatal highway crashes. *First Annual Alcoholism Conference of the National Institute on Alcohol Abuse and Alcoholism,* Washington, DC June 25, 26, 1971.

21. Lion JR, Bach-Y-Rita G, and Ervin FR: The self-referred violent patient. *JAMA* 203:503-505, 1968.

22. Baltimore Sun, p C-12, Nov 4, 1971; News American, p B-4, Nov 14, 1971.

23. Lion JR, Pasternak SA: Countertransference reactions to violent patients. *Amer J Psychiat* 130:207-210, 1973.

24. *Countertransference Reactions to Violent Patients.* Continuing Medical Education Series, Visual Information Systems, Inc. 15 Columbus Circle, New York, NY.

25. Lion JR, Azcarate C, Christopher R, and Arana P: A violence clinic. *Maryland State J Med.* (In press.)

26. Friedman P: Suicide among police: A study of 93 suicides among New York City policemen, 1934-1940, in: *Essays in Self Destruction.* Shneidman ES (ed) New York, Science House, 1967.

27. Cain AC: The presuperego "turning-inward" of aggression. *Psychoanalyt Quart* 30:171-243, 1961.

28. Blumer D: The temporal lobes and paroxysmal behavior disorders: A study of patients with temporal lobectomy for epilepsy. *Szondiana* VII 273-285, 1967.

29. Ervin FR: Brain disorders. IV: Associated with convulsions (epilepsy), in *Comprehensive Textbook of Psychiatry.* Freedman A, Kaplan M (eds): Baltimore, Williams and Wilkins, 1967.

30. Monroe RR: *Episodic Behavior Disorders: A Psychodynamic and Neurophysiologic Analysis.* Cambridge, Harvard University Press, 1970.

31. Quitkin F, Klein DF: Two behavioral syndromes in young adults related to possible minimal brain dysfunction. *J Psychiat Res* 7:121-142, 1969.

32. Hartocollis P: The syndrome of minimal brain dysfunction in young adult patients. *Bull Menninger Clinic* 32:102-114, 1968.

33. Lion JR, Bach-Y-Rita G: Group psychotherapy with violent outpatients. *Int J Group Psychother* 20:185-191, 1970.

34. Schmideberg M: The Borderline Patient, in *American Handbook of Psychiatry.* Arieti S (ed.): Basic Books, New York, 1959, vol. 1.

35. Lion JR: *Evaluation and Management of the Violent Patient.* Springfield, Illinois, Charles C Thomas, 1972. 36. Lion JR: The role of depression in the treatment of aggressive personality disorders. *Amer J Psychiat* 129:347-349, 1972.

37. Drugs in the treatment of human aggression. Audio-Digest Foundation. *Psychiatry.* vol. 2, No. 14, July 30, 1973. 1250 S. Glendale Ave., Glendale, California 91205.

38. Darling HF: Haloperidol in 60 criminal psychotics. *Dis Nervous Sys* 32:31-34, 1971.

39. DeMascio A: The effects of benzediazepines on aggression: Reduced or increased? in *The Benzodiazepines.* Garattini S, Mussini E, Randall LO (eds): New York, Raven Press, 1973, pp 433-440.

40. Sheard MH: Effect of lithium on human aggression. *Nature (London)* 230:113-114, 1971.

41. Looker A, Conners CK: Diphenylhydantoin in children with severe temper tantrums. *Arch Gen Psychiat* 23:80-89, 1970.

42. Lefkowitz MM: Effects of diphenylhydantoin on disruptive behavior: Study of male delinquents. *Arch Gen Psychiat* 20:643-651, 1969.

43. Arnold LE, Wender PH, McCloskey K, Snyder SH: Levoamphetamine and dextroamphetamine: Comparative efficacy in the hyperkinetic syndrome. *Arch Gen Psychiat* 27:816-822, 1972.

44. Money J: Use of an androgen-depleting hormone in the treatment of male sex offenders. The *J Sex Res* 6:165-172, 1970.

45. Cooper AJ, et al: Antiandrogen (cyproterone acetate) therapy in deviant hypersexuality. *Brit J Psychiat* 120:59-63, 1972.

46. New Yorker Magazine, October 18.

47. Carney FL: Three important factors in psychotherapy with criminal patients. *Amer J Psychother* 27:220-231, 1973.

THE RAPIST, THE RAPE VICTIM
AND VICTIMS OF ASSAULT

This summer a young college student was raped by three men who accosted her outside her summer school dormitory. She was so traumatized by the "gang assault" that she dropped out of her study program, became profoundly depressed, and lives in terror of another attack. Meanwhile across the town a young congressional aide was raped when she entered a private locked women's lavatory by a man who had concealed himself there. At gun point he forced her to perform sexual acts which she found particularly repugnant. In a nearby suburban area a housewife was beaten and raped by an armed intruder. When she pressed charges against the man, whom she easily identified as a man who once had made deliveries to her home, she found herself caught in a conflictual malestrom. Her husband withdrew into an angry shell, unable to offer emotional support, and somehow feeling that his wife "should have resisted." Her children, aware of the tension and unfortunate notoriety, suffered humiliation and guilt. The woman's belief in justice was shattered when she could not prove the charges against her assailant. The man was subsequently arrested when caught in the act of rape under nearly identical circumstances. These cases point up the tragic consequences and disastrous effects of rape which simple clinical statistics do not amplify. Yet in spite of the dramatic increase in rape, now over 30,000 reported cases each year, few medical and scientific investigation into rape victims and rapists

89

have been made. Recently in the District of Columbia a special commission has been attempting to revise police investigation techniques and civil procedures with a special emphasis on aiding the rape victim. But there have been too few scientific studies. What is it like to be raped? What are the sequellae of victimization? Dr. Martin Symonds has made a study of a number of victims in different types of assault, including rape and offers clear empathic insights into the tragic occurrence. In the forefront of the effort to aid rape victims is a group of dedicated women, themselves rape victims who have organized under the banner of W. A. R.—women against rape. Included herein is information from their booklet for rape victims. This is an extremely valuable collection of *do's* and *dont's* with which all emergency room police investigators and mental health professionals should be familiar. While there are many predictable responses on the part of the rape victim, each person handles such a trauma in a personal way. It is crucial to realize that many victims are further traumatized by a society which does not understand them and by families which too often fail to provide warmth and needed emotional support. Rape is much more than just a physical assault: it is an attack against the integrity of a woman's personality. Rape victims should have available to them every type of aid. Certainly the energetic efforts of the urban rape crisis centers deserve further attention and these fledging groups should receive appropriate community assistance.

But what about the rapist? There are few scientific studies of such men and before many predictions dare be made there is a great need for hard data. Cohen, Garofalo, et al. some insights provide just that in their report on the psychology of rapists.

VII.

The Accidental Victim of Violent Crime*

Martin Symonds

Literature on violent crime generally focuses on the criminal or the criminal act. It has only been in recent years that the third element in violent crime, viz., the victim, that has attracted professional interest. However, even these studies of victims have dealt solely with the participant aspects of the victim. The newly developed field of study of victim behavior called victimology examines victim-stimulated or victim-precipitated crimes. Unfortunately, this tendency of investigators to assign responsibility for criminal acts due to victim behavior reinforces similar beliefs and rationalizations held by most criminals themselves. The purpose of this paper is to share my understanding of the innocent or accidental victim of violent crimes.

Early in my explorations of the subject of victims of violent crimes, I became aware that society has strange attitudes toward victims. There seems to be a marked reluctance and resistance to accept the innocence or accidental nature of victim behavior. This reluctance is shown by community responses, police behavior, the family reactions to victims and, surprisingly, by the victims themselves. This reluctance or resistance to accept or believe in the total innocence of the victims of violent crimes is

*This paper was presented at the Symposium on Violence, Georgetown University Medical Center, October 26th, 1973 and is reprinted with the express permission of the author.

shown by the early responses to victims after the initial shock response of the nonvictim listener wears off. "Didn't you know this neighborhood is dangerous to walk in after dark? Did you have your door locked? Weren't you suspicious of that man in the elevator? Why didn't you scream? Did you look before you opened the door?" In general, the theme is aggressive questioning of the victim and these questions generally take the form of "Didn't you know?" or "Couldn't you tell?" and "why, why, why did it happen?" implying the victim's injuries could have been prevented or avoided by them. If we could talk to the tragic victims who died as a result of violent street crimes, we would ask: "Why did you walk alone in that neighborhood? Didn't you know that was dangerous?"

This general early response to victims stems from a basic need for all individuals to find a rational explanation of violent crimes, particularly brutal crimes. Exposure to senseless, irrational, brutal behavior makes everyone feel vulnerable and helpless. It then can happen at any time, any place, and to anyone. It is relieving to find that the victim has done something or neglected something that plausibly contributed to the crime. It makes the other individual feel less helpless and less vulnerable and so feel safer. These questions to determine the rationality of the crime are directed toward the victim since the criminal is not available for examination.

As part of this study to fully understand victims of violent crimes, I decided to interview men who were convicted of violent street crimes commonly known as "mugging" as well as individuals who admitted to such behavior. One of the questions I tried to seek an answer for was "Why the mugger beat the victim after he took their money." In one series of these interviews I spoke to four sentenced men, each one of whom implied that he had committed more than a hundred muggings. Instead of finding that these individuals were irrational, violent, impulsive, sadistic men, I experienced them (remember I saw them in a prison setting) as quiet, rational, and not psychotic. However, they were singularly lacking in insight and frightening in their degree of unrelatedness to anyone else's needs but theirs. One individual expressed his thought as follows: "I am not a sadist. I don't beat people—only if they are slow in giving me my money." I have interviewed other individuals outside a prison setting who admitted to mugging. They, too, showed this common pattern of marked social unrelatedness, living only in egocentric time with no hope for the future. Their crimes are not particularly thought out nor are they particularly impulsive. Their criminal behavior isn't essentially sadistic; it is commonplace and gross. Their crimes are primarily money-oriented and they have no sophisticated patterns of victim selection. Most of them are surprised at victim cooperation and yet would beat them senseless if they didn't cooperate. Some of these muggers have themselves been mugged and I asked them what they did. Each said: "I got angry and fought back." I asked "Why?" and they responded by saying, "I worked hard for the money, I wasn't going to give it up." They failed to appreciate that their victims felt the same way.

The community has other attitudes that blocks sympathetic responses to the victim's plight. One is the primitive fear of contamination by the unlucky victim. The result of this primitive response of fear is to isolate or exclude the victim.

Teachers of primary grades are upset when they witness their pupils' response to a classmate's misfortune such as the death of a parent or divorce of his parents. These classmates frequently will ignore the unfortunate child; often they will tease him and some even will hit him. It is as if the other children feared contamination of this tragic event and tried to isolate or exclude the victim. Similar behavior is also seen by community response, particularly working class community attitudes toward the individual who has been raped. The victim experiences isolation and exclusion through notoriety. There are whispering campaigns, questioning the innocence of the victim. If she is young and single, she can be subjected to annoying behavior by men in the community without the usual protective interference of other individuals. Some rape victims who had experienced this exclusion through notoriety had to move from the neighborhood.

Finally, there is a third response of seeming indifference to the victim's plight, and this is the most common complaint of victims of violent crimes when they discuss community responses to what happened to them. A frequent recipient of this complaint is the police. This attitude of seeming indifference of the community, as well as the police, is due to the fact that by the time the victim is seen, the criminal act is in the past with the criminal gone. There is nothing active that the listener can do and the victim's expression of her distress is experienced by the listener as an implied demand that something be done, as well as an implied criticism that the listener failed to protect her from this tragic experience.

This reaction of seeming indifference of the police, that the victim experiences, is due to a common misinterpretation by the police of the concept of professionalism. In their zeal to be neutral, and since it is a crime in the past with the criminal gone, they aggressively question the victim as to the details of the crime. This behavior rejects implied expectations of comfort to the victim, as well as rejects the victim's implied criticism that the police have failed to do their job of protecting him from crime. One woman who was the victim of a mugging told me that when the radio car responded the patrolmen sat in the car and she had to lean on the ledge of the open window of the car and talk to them. In addition, these men said: "You aren't the only one who has been mugged. We get plenty of other calls." Such behavior or comments are hardly comforting to the victim and make her feel worse.

Up to now I have described society's responses to victims of violence. Let us now explore the psychological reactions of victims themselves. Whenever one is the subject of a sudden, unexpected attack of violence there is the initial response of shock, numbness, and unbelief. When this initial response subsides, depending on the individual, there will follow either fright or anger. In street crime where the victim is knocked to the ground, their purse or wallet taken, with the criminal running away, this response of fright or anger ensues without the criminal being present. In many street crimes the psychological response of fright or anger arises in the victim with the criminal still present with his threat of bodily harm if the victim doesn't comply. These are the crimes of rape, some other sexual crimes, kidnapping, hostage taking, as well as robbery. It is this second type of violent crime where the time element of the crime permits responses of victim other than shock and unbelief with the criminal still being present that is more likely to result in psychological repercussions long after the criminal act. In these crimes the fright response of victims is usually a frozen, frightened reaction. The reaction of fear is so profound and overwhelming that the victim feels hopeless about getting away. All hope of survival is dependent on appeasing the criminal. Years ago, I examined a young girl of 8½ who was thought to be a victim of incest. I found a young, extremely bright, very friendly, vivacious, and cooperative youngster. When I ended the interview and told her she could go, she took a deep breath, sighed deeply and said, "I thought I'd never get out of here alive." At that time, and even in retrospect, I see no direct evidence of fright. Since then I have collected many clinical examples of frozen fright where the individual has confused the listener with their surface pleasantries, ingratiating, extremely cooperative, and seemingly friendly behavior. Though this behavior is deeply rooted in profound fright, it is confusing both to the victim and the criminal. Later on when the victim reviews his behavior under peacetime conditions, he plays down the ingratiating aspects of his behavior under stress because he is ashamed of it and thus lays down the seeds of guilt. The appeasing, ingratiating, compliant behavior of a victim of violence during the phase of frozen fright often leads to the false conclusion that the victim produced or participated in the criminal act.

There are individuals whose response to sudden, unexpected violence is not frozen fright but anger. Even though their behavior is rooted in profound fright, the victim recalls only being angry. They screamed, hit, or yelled. They have said to the criminal: "Get the hell away." "What are you doing?" "Leave me alone, I'll call the police." Some have attacked the criminal with their purse or their hands or thrown things at the criminal. What happens to the victim depends on circumstances and mental health of the criminal. While some back down and even run away, more often the criminal feels frustrated and angry, which results in a violent attack on the victim to beat them into submission and compliancy. A woman said to a criminal who was robbing her store: "I'll never forget your face." He shot her in the head and blinded her.

As I reviewed the early, acute responses to violence, it seemed to me that these responses were rooted in early life experiences. The frozen, frightened response to sudden, unexpected, and violent aggression is more commonly seen in women. It is my impression that men and women who grow up from middle class backgrounds generally tend to freeze and propitiate the aggressor while those who have working class backgrounds tend to be action-oriented and fight back. In the postacute phase, the dramatic events of the crime are continually replayed by the victim. Those who fought back and weren't hurt seem to have a minimum amount of psychological trauma. They feel exhilarated and potent. Those who fought back and were hurt still feel supported by society. They easily find sympathetic responses, though some have felt annoyed by police reactions. They felt the police were defensive. It took the tone: "You didn't let me do my job. Next time you'll let the police protect you." In general, victims who fight back seem to have greater social acceptance than the victims who have followed society's rules and have complied with the criminal. This double bind attitude of society is strikingly evident toward victims of rape.

From a widely accepted book on Criminal Investigation Technique (1970) [1] by Charles O'Hara, I have selected the following passages that deal with behavior of a police investigator with a victim of rape.

p. 281. "The victim should be interviewed as soon as possible after the occurrence. The victim should be questioned thoroughly concerning the occurrence, the circumstances surrounding it and her movements before and after the commission of the offense . . . ..

p. 282. "The victim of an alleged rape should be requested to submit to a medical examination as soon as possible after the occurrence. No delay should be permitted."

p. 283. "Where a vigorous woman alleges ravishment it is to be expected that signs of violence such as wounds, bruises, and scratches will be present and their absence should induce a moderate degree of scepticism unless the girl avers that she fainted from fear, became panic stricken or was otherwise rendered incapable of physical resistance. The acts and demeanor of the female immediately after the alleged commission should be subjected to very critical investigation in these cases."

This attitude of treating the victim of rape with scepticism and cynicism, especially if she complies with the criminal due to profound shock and fright, is at wide variance with the generally accepted advice given by society.

In a book "How To Keep Crime From Happening To You"[2] the repeated advice is: "The best single thing you can do to protect yourself from bodily harm is "Tell me what you want and I'll give it to you."

A young adolescent girl was the victim of rape. The police who investigated this crime continually questioned the parents about their daughter's behavior. These questions followed the textbook dicta: "critical investigation of the acts and demeanor of the female." However, the parents became confused, angry, and frightened by the detective's attitude. In their desire to protect their daughter, they developed a collusive attitude of silence with their daughter. Though there was a grandmother in the house, this conspiracy of silence kept her unaware of what had happened to her granddaughter.

As I continued to talk to victims of violence, I became aware that the general reactions of these victims were similar to the psychological response of an individual who experiences sudden and unexpected loss. Loss of any kind, particularly if sudden and unexpected, produces the following sequence of response in all individuals. The first phase is shock and denial. When the person's attempts at denial fail he becomes frightened. This fright is usually accompanied by clinging behavior. Very frequently the individual finds himself compulsively talking and obsessively ruminating. This phase is followed by apathy with periods of recrimination and inner-directed rage. There are occasional outbursts of outer-directed resentment and anger to individuals until resolution occurs with either replacement or restoration of the lost object.

The foregoing description of the psychological response to sudden and unexpected loss is easily recognizable as the same phases seen in depression. This concept is of clinical value in the psychological treatment of victims. What has the victim of violence lost? It is more than just the loss of money and the loss of physical functioning. They have lost the feeling of individual invulnerability. They have lost their trust in society, which they have depended on to protect them from harm. Many have lost their self-respect when gained the unenviable status of being a victim.

For some individuals, particularly conforming and dependent ones, there is prolongation of one or more phases of the victim reaction just described. Some victims remain for months in the phase of fright with clinging behavior. Extra locks, extra precautions, and excessive suspicious substitutes for judgment. They cling to their family and obsessively ruminate about what happened to them. Their family begins to feel that this compulsive talking of the victim is bad for them and encourage the victim to be silent. I have had difficulty to get to talk to some of these victims because of this protective attitude to their families. Yet, when I have managed to talk to the victims, I have found them anxious and eager to talk and some have mobilized their resources to become less frightened. It seems to me the mistaken concept of protective silence prolongs the depressive reaction of victims.

In this phase of fright of the victim reaction some report persistent recurrent fantasies or dreams which have a similar theme. The most frequent theme is the criminal will come back and either kill them or injure them more seriously. Sometimes the victim has a fleeting but recurrent thought of killing the criminal, but this thought is completely submerged by a counter thought—what if they fail or if they succeed his family or his friends will get revenge and kill them. Some individuals in their fright try to deny what happened to them. One man was robbed. A few days later he thought he recognized the robber. The suspected robber was working in a store where the victim rarely shopped. The victim walked away and later couldn't remember what store the man worked in, nor could he remember what street the store was located. When I asked him what he was shopping for he angrily refused to talk about the incident anymore.

Other individuals have a prolonged period of apathy with inner- and outer-directed rage. The loss of feelings of invulnerability, the disillusionment in society's ability to protect the individual from harm quite often intensifies his feelings of resentment and anger. Commonly heard expressions in this phase are: "The hell with people, who needs them. You got to look out for yourself. People are animals. The world is a jungle. No one gives a damn." The woman victim expressed her thoughts as follows:

"What hurt me the most was the complete indifference and lack of consideration for my feelings in my hour of need by people I know and work with." There are also frequent comments attacking police behavior. Police make an ideal scapegoat because of a traditional policy of silence even if attacked.

The experience of being a victim of a violent crime is tragic enough when we add to this the paradoxical attitude of society. Then the victim feels isolated, helpless, and alone in a world experienced as hostile. This response has been defined by Dr. Karen Horney [3] as basic anxiety. It produces profound adaptive and defensive patterns which form the core of the psychological responses of victims. Any measure the community employs that reduces the victim's feelings of isolation, aloneness, and helplessness will also reduce his secondary psychological trauma.

The growing awareness that anyone can be vulnerable to crimes of violence has caused the community to be more genuinely sympathetic to the victim. However, there is one segment of society that the victim must come in contact with as a result of his misfortune that seems to lag behind in this growing sympathy and empathy for the victim. This is the criminal justice system. Judges, prosecutors, the legal profession, and the police still are somewhat removed from the personal plight of victims. I recently spoke to a judge about victims and he said: "You know, I never really thought about it. My concern was always the application of the law. I thought of the criminal act and what to do about the criminal, but not the victim." This diffident attitude toward victims is derived from the legal model which is based on the adversary principle. It is not the truth but the better argument pro or con that wins the case. The victim's plight is exploited or attacked when the adversary principle of law is applied. It would require another paper, and a long one at that, to discuss fully the psychological trauma that victims receive from all aspects of the administration of criminal justice. While the public cannot change the entire legal system, there is one aspect that they can substantially influence. That is the police. The police are usually the first individuals the victim meets and most of the time they meet the victim after the crime has been committed with the criminal gone. Police attitudes can be quite crucial in reducing the acute psychological trauma of victims and also help prevent the debilitating secondary trauma that most victims undergo. Though from personal experience, I know the police are sensitive to criticism and resent anyone telling them how to do police work, police officials have a high regard for professionals in their particular specialities. They are receptive to ideas that will improve their ability to be of help to the public. If we in the helping professions support the concept of victims needing psychological help, the police, who are in a unique position to administer psychological first aid, will turn to us for help in how to do it.

In conclusion, victims want something from society for the injuries they recieved. They have suffered loss of money, sometimes severe and permanent physical injuries, their self-respect has been damaged, and their illusions of trust that the community will protect them from harm has been shattered. They cannot get back anything from the criminal. Revenge and retribution will not heal their psychological wounds. What is needed is a wholehearted, sympathetic, and empathetic response from the community toward the victim. A woman who was mugged sent me a letter in which she described what happened to her and what she would like done. I could do no better to end this paper than by quoting her. "It is not that the victim wishes to wallow in self-pity; it is that at such a crucial time—a very frightening experience at least and one that could have resulted in the victim's being actually killed or seriously hurt—that such a person should immediately be given the same moral support, and words of comfort and caring, that you would give one who has just lost a loved one."

References

1. O'Hara E: *Fundamentals of Criminal Investigation.* Springfield, Illinois, Charles Thomas Publisher, 1970.
2. deCelle J: *The Safety Strategy, How to Keep Crime from Happening to You.* Joseph Rank Publ Co, 1971.
3. Horney K: *Our Inner Conflicts.* New York, W W Norton, 1945.

VIII.

Rape:
Medical and Legal Information*

RAPE CRISIS CENTER,
BOSTON, MASSACHUSETTS

Introduction

W.A.R.—Women Against Rape! We are a group of women who have been raped or who know someone who has been a rape victim. We got together to figure out what we could do to change things. We want to prevent rapes and other violence against women. We want to challenge and attack the male myths that claim women ask for and secretly want rape. We found that many women have felt that the police and hospitals often are brutally insensitive to women when they turn to them for help. We also want to see a woman's feelings of fear, isolation, and vulnerability changed into feelings of strength and unity in order to confront and attack the rapist and his male supporters.

We, W.A.R., along with other groups of women have been getting media coverage around the issue of rape. As our first project we are opening a Rape Crisis Center with a 24-hour emergency phone service that can be easily reached by dialing 492-RAPE. We have several goals for this center. First, to provide support and services for our sisters who have been raped. Women need to know what their medical needs are in the case of rape. Women also need to be familiar with the legal process, police, and

*This material is reprinted with the permission of the staff members of the Rape Crisis Center, Boston Mass.

courts. This pamphlet is our first step toward educating women in the medical and legal areas. We will accompany and support any woman who has been raped (and contacts us) through the hospital, police, and court systems. We also will provide counselling for rape victims to help them overcome the emotional consequences of the rape. We want to see the guilt and fear turned outward into constructive anger. We hope that other women will contact us to talk about their experiences and set up other kinds of projects like neighborhood patrols. The Rape Crisis Center hopefully will be a place to figure out and put into effect more actions and projects that not only will support other women but threaten and confront the sexism within the rapist and the institutions that support him.

The obvious immediate needs for the rape victim are medical and legal. This pamphlet was written to dispense information to women so that they get adequate medical care and have enough information to make their decision about legal matters (reporting the rape and/or filing a complaint and prosecuting). All the women answering the phone at the Rape Crisis Center will be familiar with this material and will use it to help rape victims get good medical care and know enough to make decisions about what legal actions to take.

We advise women to call us (492-RAPE) or a friend to accompany them for support and strength. We recommend that if raped, you first go to a hospital emergency room. There are several reasons for this. First, your medical needs are most important (having bruises and possible pregnancy and VD attended to). Generally the hospital staff will be more considerate of you and your feelings than the leering, interrogating police stations. Going to the hospital first will give you time to collect your thoughts, calm down, and seek psychological help if you feel you need it. Then you will be in a better position to make decisions about reporting the rape and/or filing a complaint with the police.

Emergency Medical Needs of the Rape Victim

There are several basic medical needs that every woman should have attended to immediately after she is raped. They include the prevention of pregnancy, prevention of VD, and care of general body trauma. The following is a description of these needs and their treatment in more detail.

1. General Bodily Injuries and Trauma

These injuries may be in the form of lacerations, stab wounds, bruises, etc. Surgical care, X-rays, dressings, and medication may be necessary. If so, you can expect to be seen by a number of hospital personnel, and you can expect to spend time waiting.

2. The Police

Most hospitals will routinely report a possible rape to the police if the victim hasn't already. The police should be informed as soon as possible if you want the rapist arrested or to collect evidence in case you later decide to prosecute in court.

3. The Possibility of Pregnency

If there is a chance that you are pregnant as a result of the rape, there are only two possible alternatives to avoid pregnancy—the "morning after" pill or an abortion.

A. Diethylstilbestrol ("morning after" pill)

Many facts must be taken into consideration before a woman decides to take this notorious drug. This estrogen is given in large doses to prevent the implantation of a fertilized egg in the lining of your uterus. The treatment is commonly 50 milligrams a day by mouth for five days and must be initiated within 24 hours of the rape. It is necessary to take the full course of medication for it to work correctly.

The important hazard of diethylstilbestrol is that it is a *known potent carcinogen* (cancer-inducing ingredient). It has been barred from beef in this country and it has been banned from use as an anti-miscarriage drug in already pregnant women.

Its effects take years to determine; only recently has it been discovered that some daughters of women who took DES in the 1940's and 50's have vaginal cancer. There is as yet no proof that the woman who takes the "morning after" pill will get cancer.

The choice is yours to make, but be certain of the following facts before you consider further:

1) Ask your mother if she took an anti-miscarriage drug when pregnant with you. If the answer is yes, we strongly recommend not taking DES yourself. You should follow-up this knowledge by having an iodine stain test done of your vaginal walls and a pap smear taken every six months, to screen out the possibility of cancer.
2) Ask yourself whether you may be already pregnant at the time of the rape. If so, have a pregnancy test done to be sure you don't take DES after pregnancy has begun. It *won't* stop the pregnancy.
3) Be certain that your medical history is taken to screen out any contraindications to DES, such as:
—any family history of cancer or diabetes.
—diseases of the liver, kidneys, lungs, or heart.
4) Be aware that the side effects of DES are severe nausea and vomiting. Therefore you should take some anti-nausea pills. Other effects may be vaginal spotting, diarrhea, breast tenderness, insomnia, and skin rash.

5) It is possible that after the "morning after" pill treatment you will have greater increased fertility. Therefore be careful to consider contraception.

B. Abortion

In six weeks after your last period a pregnancy test will show for certain if you are pregnant. Legal abortions can be obtained in Boston for $150.00 or for a sliding scale fee in New York.

If you don't wish to wait as long as six weeks; menstrual extraction can be done four weeks after the last period. This actually is an abortion procedure, but is done without positive knowledge of pregnancy. Menstrual extractions are obtainable in New York for $30.00-$50.00 and some private physicians do them in Boston often for a higher fee.

Be aware that any pregnancy test done in the emergency room will only determine if you are already pregnant when assaulted.

4. Venereal Disease

A. Testing

Emergency rooms generally do VD testing of rape victims. As with the pregnancy testing this VD testing determines only if you already had VD at the time of the rape. Therefore it is up to you if you wish to be tested at this time. (Take the extra cost into consideration.) A vaginal culture for gonorrhea and a blood test for syphilis would be involved.

It is essential for your own welfare that you do get diagnostic tests for VD at some point after the rape. We recommend six weeks after the rape because:

1) the gonorrhea culture can be taken one week to three months after contact.
2) the syphilis blood test can be taken as soon as three weeks after contact.

A negative VD result six weeks after exposure does not mean it won't read positive at a later date. In other words, regular VD testing at six month intervals is essential. VD clinics are state-run and do free testing. Most large hospitals have a VD clinic. A good resource material for further information on VD is the Montreal Collective's free *VD Handbook*.

Note: Women on birth control pills are said to have an increased susceptibility to gonorrhea.

B. Treatment

Preventive penicillin treatment can be given to the rape victim in the emergency room to prevent possible VD infection from the attacker. This treatment is effective if administered correctly, but keep in mind that you will never know for sure whether or not you would have had VD. Later testing should of course prove negative.

1. The type of penicillin used should be (procaine) Penicillin G and no other kind. (i.e. not Benzathine penicillin, or PAM-Penicillin with Aluminum Monostearate.) This is because gonorrhea must be treated only with fast-absorbed penicillin and only Procaine Penicillin G is fast-absorbed. You can expect one shot in each buttock.

2. In a large coastal city such as Boston, very often there will be penicillin-resistant strains of gonococcus. Probenecid is then given along with the penicillin. Probenecid is an oral medication which increases the absorption of penicillin from the injection site.

3. You can receive an oral form of penicillin for gonorrhea called Ampicillin. It is usually given with Probenecid and should be taken on an empty stomach. Avoid eating for an hour after. These precautions are because food in the stomach and especially milk products greatly decrease the absorption of the medication.

4. Allergic reactions to penicillin are rare, but do happen. They occur five to fourteen days after treatment and may be a red skin rash or a fever. They will disappear, but you should notify the doctor who prescribed it.

5. People with a known allergy to penicillin receive instead Tetracycline in oral form every six hours for about four days. Take it with the same precautions as for Ampicillin. Side effects most commonly experienced are heartburn, nausea, vomiting, and diarrhea. The only antacid you should take for heartburn here is sodium bicarbonate. Report the symptom of diarrhea to a doctor.

6. One fact women should be aware of with any antibiotic therapy is that it may disrupt normal existing vaginal bacterial organisms by allowing an organism foreign to the area to grow. The result can be a new vaginal (nonvenereal) infection with accompanying symptoms of unusual and/or increased discharge, etc.

5. Pelvic Examination

There are two reasons for having a gynecologist examine you soon after the rape: 1) To determine if you have been injured internally; 2) To obtain possible evidence of sperm in the vagina for the police if you should decide to prosecute.

The American College of Obstetricians and Gynecologists advises physicians to obtain written and witnessed consent for:

1. the examination
2. collection of specimens
3. photographs
4. release of information of the authorities.

The examining doctor is at all times urged to be as objective and nonjudgmental as possible since both the doctor and medical record can very well be subpoenaed in court. In any case you can tell by your treatment whether any judgments have been made.

The following is what the doctor should note:

1. general body appearance—presence of scratches, lacerations, bruises, etc. (Photographs taken for evidence should be of non-genital injuries.)

2. condition of "patient"—whether she appears to be "hysterical" or "drunk," etc.

3. clothing—whether it is torn or bloody. The doctor may request to keep an item of clothing as evidence. (or you can request it.)

4. any evidence of trauma to the external genitalia.

The vaginal examination will involve insertion of a speculum as in a routine exam. But after you've been raped this part of the exam will be particularly distasteful and it would help to have a sympathetic nurse present. A nurse must be there, but we all know it's no help to have the nurse reiterate "just relax, dear" as the doctor himself will often say. Most doctors will be uptight about allowing a friend to be present during the internal exam, but if you do want someone with you, ask. She could stand by your head.

Once the speculum is inserted the doctor will take a swab from the vaginal pool and put it in a test tube for the lab to detect evidence of semen. One slide will be made for immediate examination for sperm, and another swab may be taken from the vulva.

Most hospitals are required to label slides and specimens as "? rape" and this or the medical record is released to no one, not even police, without the victim's consent.

6. Emotional Needs

That a rape victim is very upset is one important aspect of rape which is often unrecognized or even denied by hospital personnel, both male and female. It's ironic—how can a woman gain sympathy when her claims of rape are not even believed? So in this crisis a woman will need support from someone she knows will be sympathetic. The most desirable person to have would be a close friend. Another alternative is a woman who will come just because you talked to her on the phone after the rape (from the Crisis Center). The point is to get support. Support means strength and with strength you can insist on the humane medical treatment you deserve.

Support means also that you can better recognize your rage. It means you may better deal with the guilt that society and you may impose on yourself.

Concerning medical treatment, a sympathetic physician may prescribe a sedative for short-term use. Don't be afraid to ask for it.

7. Follow-up

The rape is not always over a few hours after the actual experience. You may experience more mental and emotional distress for a period of time. We feel that a large part of this distress is valid anger which, if recognized, can motivate you to take positive actions in your life.

We'd like for you to keep in contact with us to let us know how you're doing. We want to bring women together to discuss in groups their feelings about their rape experiences and possible things that could be done about rape. We don't recommend it, but if you feel psychotherapy is necessary, we'll try to refer you to a sympathetic therapist. Most of all we want to see the feelings of isolation, guilt, and helplessness dispelled from the mind of the woman who has been raped.

For further peace of mind, please follow-up on later medical needs caused by the rape, that is, VD testing and pregnancy testing.

8. Cost

What you pay the hospital is a very real concern. A woman who's with you in the emergency room could find out, and we also have information on the major hospitals. If you have no money, a couple of alternatives are Medicaid and the Massachusetts Victims of Violent Crimes Act which legally makes the state responsible for your medical bills (if the rape is reported).

The Rape Victim and the Legal System

The most immediate reaction of many women who have been raped is to call the police. Whether the incident occurred in the woman's apartment or on a desolate street, the police call box or the police emergency telephone number may be the most accessible means for the victim, who has been injured or shocked, to find a quick response to her call and consequently some form of relief from the fear of another attack.

For some women, a call to the police station has provided quick and needed protection. For many others, however, the police questioning and subsequent legal proceedings have made them feel like they have been raped twice, first by a violent assailant, and second, by a system of justice that is supposed to offer support and protection but offers instead unsympathetic policemen and attorneys who make implicit or explicit accusations that she invited the rape and got what she deserved.

There may be many situations in which a woman's only recourse is to contact the police as soon as possible. If you do have the time to make a choice and feel that despite the incident, you want to think things through, you might consider going to the hospital for treatment before you go to the police station. Even if you have no serious injury, your medical and psychological needs demand primary attention. While you are being treated, you can decide whether or not to report the incident to the police and whether or not to bring charges against the rapist.

1. Filing a Complaint

Generalizations may be erroneous, if not dangerous in some cases, but we do suggest that you at least report the crime to the police to ensure the greatest accuracy possible in documenting the violence against women. Reporting the rape does not mean that you must prosecute. We strongly urge that despite the difficulty of making a choice in such a moment of crisis, you understand as well as possible the legal system, consider the pro's and con's involved in bringing charges against the rapist, and lastly, but most importantly, apply them to your own situation. A real consideration for many women is the threat or fear of retaliation by the rapist. Some law enforcement officials interviewed in the Boston area believe that the actual incidence of retaliation against women who have filed complaints is very small, and they encourage women to press charges. A woman may be able to obtain a police watch to ensure her safety, but as a practical matter, there may be little effective protection, and in the last analysis it is the victim herself who must decide how real the threat of retaliation seems to be. Weighed against the fear of retaliation may be equally strong considerations of preventing the rapist from attacking other women, getting psychological help for him, or even protecting yourself against a greater threat of repeated attacks if you don't take action.

Once you have made the decision to press charges against your assailant, which you can do whether you know who he is or not, you should do so immediately. The slower you are in reporting the crime, the less likely it is that the assailant will ever be convicted. Any delay in filing the complaint should be a matter of hours, not days, because any delay may make it less likely to find the assailant, and any delay gives the defense a strong argument against your credibility at the time of the trial.

Going to the police is your prerogative, but that does not mean that your charges are automatically accepted. The police may not believe the story. Such questions as "Why were you there?" need not be answered, but you must remember that as a practical matter, the police have discretionary power to accept or not accept the charges. You may find it more useful to be as cooperative as you possibly can with the police to ensure that they take and investigate your complaint. You may refuse to answer a personal question by indicating that you will speak to a physician about it; the physician's statement can be used as evidence.

The statement given to the police can and most likely will be used as evidence at the trial. You may feel some confusion immediately after the incident about details of time, place, or identity. You should try to be as absolutely accurate in your description as you can be. For your own use and the later use of the prosecution, it is then advisable for you to keep a record of details as you remember them.

2. The Trial Procedure

You can expect to have to recount your story two times before the court and once before a grand jury. First, there is a preliminary hearing before a single judge of the district court, or lowest court, level to determine if there is sufficient evidence about the charge to possible support a finding of guilty. The rape victim must tell her story and then be cross-examined by the defense attorney. The cross examination at this stage is usually used to find out the details of your story and any potential discrepancies rather than to try to prove his client not guilty. If the judge finds that there is "probable cause," the case is sent to the next level, the Superior Court. You will have to tell your story again to a closed grand jury hearing, which is a jury that sits only to hear evidence favorable to the victim's case, includes no cross examination, and indicts the rapist if the jurors believe that there is sufficient evidence to do so. Lastly, you must tell your story before a Superior Court judge, usually with a jury, and you will be cross-examined again. At this final and major hearing, the defendant rapist also presents all of the evidence he has to prove his innocence.

3. Punishment

If a man is convicted of rape, what sentence is he likely to get? The maximum sentence for rape is life; however, to receive this extreme sentence, the rapist would usually have had to have a previous record of rape or have killed his victim. Lesser penalties vary according to the circumstances. Generally, the chances of conviction and the likelihood of a long sentence are unlikely.

If the rapist knew his victim and has no previous record, the sentence could be as little as three to four years; if the rapist was a stranger to the victim and forced the rape at gun- or knife-point, the sentence will probably range between ten and twenty years. The convicted rapist will usually spend some time in the Bridgewater state prison for the criminally insane. Another consideration in sentencing is the general climate of public opinion. For example, with the latest rash of rapes and murders thought to be related to hitchhiking, the sentences for hitchhiking-related rapes have been higher.

4. Preparing for the Trial

A woman who has been raped and wishes to press charges against her assailant should realize from the time that she goes to the hospital that a conviction of the rapist rests upon her testimony. Therefore, you will want to obtain as much accurate evidence as possible.

First, the hospital report is crucial. The examining doctor's report will state penetration, if any, and the presence of semen, if any, in the woman's body. If injuries were obtained during the rape, they too should be reported and treated.

Also, the police have equipment to photograph all injuries. You may have to ask to have pictures taken, since the police may hesitate to do so for fear of upsetting you. Photographing that might upset you, e.g., photographing upper leg areas, etc., is usually inadvisable anyway because a jury might think that anyone who would consent to have such an area photographed must have invited the rape. But most pictures of bruises or scratch marks can be used at a trial to counter any defense argument that you consented.

Pre-trial preparation of testimony and familiarization with lines of questioning and the types of evidence the court is looking for will be invaluable to you. The responsibility of proof is on the victim, and you should talk as long as possible with the district attorney who will handle your case. Often the D.A. has very little time to prepare for the trial, while the defense prepares extensively. You can, and if confused, should seek additional counsel, a role that a private attorney can fill. You should be careful not to discuss the case with every person who calls you, because defense attorneys have been known in this way to have obtained a complete statement from the victim.

5. The Trial

The final hearing and the most important one is before the judge of the Superior Court and a jury, unless the defendant waives his right to a jury.

At the end of the trial, the judge directs the jury to determine the guilt of the defendant beyond a reasonable doubt. Therefore, the role of the jury is crucial. The men and the women of the jury tend to be older and conservative; it is wise to be cautious about the terms you use in testimony. Try to decide for yourself what terminology they would fully understand as well as language that is unoffensive. For example, many jurors would prefer to hear "private parts" as opposed to penis or vagina, and also, by not understanding expressions like "make out," they might infer "make love."

Since identification in a rape case tends to be less difficult than some other violent crimes, the defense usually centers on whether the victim "invited" the rape. Questions along this line usually involve "What was she wearing? Was she hitchhiking? Was it dark? Was she drinking with the defendant?"

Another line of questioning may seek to discredit you by proving that you had a bad or promiscuous reputation in the community. The defense will attempt to find out whether you are "loose," whether you live a rather "free" lifestyle, for example, live in a communal situation, etc., or have a "suspect" occupation like that of a stewardess.

Also, you have to be careful to differentiate in your testimony and in later questioning that you did not consent to intercourse, but that you were forced to submit, by threats or fear of physical injury. "Submit" is a crucial word. If the defense asks you, "Did you in fact consent?," the response should be something like, "No, I was forced to submit." In New York state, the laws concerning rape are so strict that many women feel they have to be beaten to death before they can prove that rape occurred. In Massachusetts this is not the case, and submission under force or fear is acceptable. Consent, of course, is not.

Photographs from the scene of the incident are helpful, particularly if they show cut phone cords, broken windows, etc. Initial and follow-up medical reports are very important. Also, if the rapist contacts you to talk, apologize, or make a threat, this may be used as evidence.

IX.

The Psychology of Rapists*

Murray L. Cohen, Ralph Garofalo, Richard Boucher, and Theoharis Seghorn

In a series of papers by Sarafian,[1] Kozol et al.,[2] and Cohen and Kozol,[3] a Massachusetts law for "sexually dangerous persons" and a treatment center established by the law has been described. Although the specific purpose of this paper is to present some observations on the psychological factors involved in rape, the clinical data are based on experiences with this law and the treatment center, and therefore a discussion of both will be profitable.

Special legislation concerning sexual offenders is frequently enacted as the result of a social outcry to a particularly brutal or heinous crime[4]. This was the case in Massachusetts in 1957. Six weeks following his release from prison a child molester kidnapped two boys and sexually assaulted and murdered them. In immediate response to this crime, Chapter 123A of the General Laws of Massachusetts[5] was written into law as a method for preventing the premature release of a potentially dangerous person.

Even prior to 1957, Massachusetts had special laws governing sexual offenses. The first was enacted in 1947 and was entitled The Psychopathic

Reprinted from "Seminars in Psychiatry" Vol. 3, No. 3, August 1971. Copyright Grune Stratton.

Personality Law. This statute was applied in only one instance and was repealed 1 year later when an alternative law was passed that removed the term "sexual psychopath" and substituted the term "sex offender." There was no provision for retaining the offender after the expiration of his sentence, whether or not he had shown any change in his proclivity for sexual aggression. In 1957, the legislature revised the 1954 statute and provided for a commitment for an indefinite period if necessary for the protection of the public. Sections of this statute were found unconstitutional, and the entire law was replaced by the present statute, Chapter 646 of the Acts of 1958. This law ordered the creation of a treatment center to achieve its purposes and fashioned a new term "sexually dangerous person."

Under this law a person found guilty of a sexual offense may be committed for one day to life under a civil commitment in lieu of a criminal sentence. Section 2 of the statute ordered the Commissioner of Mental Health to establish a treatment center for such commitments, and in 1959 a psychiatric facility was created within the Massachusetts Correctional Institution at Bridgewater. The center is staffed by psychiatrists, psychologists, social workers, and educational, occupational, and recreational therapists, who are responsible for the care, treatment, and rehabilitation of persons who come under the purview of the law.

The law provides for a truly indeterminate commitment—one day to life. Indeterminate sentence laws usually have relatively narrow limits within a fixed minimum and maximum term. The basic legal consideration here is that the commitment is civil and not criminal. The offender is not given a fixed penalty for his crime, but rather the period of commitment is determined by his mental condition. His release occurs when the psychiatric staff judges that he will offer a minimal risk to the safety of the community.

Since enactment of this statute a number of articles have appeared containing critical comments of the law and the treatment center[6-10] These criticisms discuss the legal, ethical, and scientific aspects of the legislation, but only those criticisms of interest to the mental health professional will be presented here in brief. These include problems of treatment and diagnosis and limitations of the statute to "sexually dangerous" (thus not including those who may be aggressively dangerous in nonsexual ways).

Many papers critical of the law recognize the paradox that although the indeterminate civil commitment is for the purpose of treatment, many of those offenders most subject to the application of the statute do not appear treatable by current techniques. This is a valid and worrisome observation. In a recent study of psychotherapy completed at the center, only 36% of the patients were found to be responsive to psychotherapy. This is supported by the finding that 35 % of the patients committed during the first 6 years (the first half of the total period of the existence of the center) are still committed patients. However, society has clearly taken the position that it has the right to protect its members from harm. The objections to a life commitment on the grounds of treatability are valid only when it can be demonstrated that the intent and application by society of civil commitment is not treatment and rehabilitation, but simply preventive detention.

Section 1 of the statute defines a "sexually dangerous person" as "any person whose misconduct in sexual matters indicates a general lack of power to control his sexual impulses, as evidenced by repetitive or compulsive behavior and either violence or aggression by an adult against a victim under the age of sixteen years, and who as a result is likely to attack or otherwise inflict injury on the objects of his uncontrolled or uncontrollable desires"[5]. This section has been criticized for its vagueness and for its limitation to the sexually aggressive. It is pointed out that "sexually dangerous" is a social-legal concept and not a psychiatric entity. It is a term that refers not to etiology, current process, or immediate symptom, but to future behavior. Thus, the very wording of the definition lacks the clarity required for consistent reliable application. The law imposes on the psychiatrist a relatively unfamiliar demand and a responsibility that it is not certain should be given to him, and one he is frequently loathe to accept.

The problems are clearly difficult ones. If sexually dangerous is going to be determined by the part of the section that refers to past behavior ". . . as evidenced by repetitive or compulsive behavior . . ." then it is not necessary to have the psychiatrist make the determination and there will be no way for the evaluation of change and release. If the emphasis is to be on ". . . is likely to attack . . ." there is then a behavioral predication problem, and social scientists, other than the psychiatrist, should clearly be involved by statutory action and not only in clinical actuality.

McGarry and Cotton[9] criticize still another aspect of Section 1, that aspect resulting from the exclusive features of the law" . . . if such programs for the sexually dangerous are justified, it makes no sense to exclude the repetitively aggressive dangerous offender without sexual overtones" (p. 298). Holden[8] questions this feature not only from logical, but also from legal considerations.

(The sex offender law represents) a special way of dealing with a particular class of criminal offender and such class is exposed to greater deprivation of liberty with less procedural due process that is the case for other criminal offenders. If society's particular concern is for its own safety, it is difficult to see why sex offenders alone should be singled out for indeterminate detention . . . (p. 29).

It is certainly a meaningful question as to why there is this peculiar separation of sexually dangerous from other forms of socially dangerous persons. It is clear that the answer resides within sociocultural and not psychiatric data. It is a matter of social attitudes to specific criminal acts and the social response to these acts.

Despite these and other criticisms of the law, it has operated (with three amendments) since 1958. In that year the Treatment Center at the Massachusetts Correctional Institution, Bridgewater, began to function, and over 2000 sexual offenders have been given preliminary examinations since that time. There was sufficient question regarding 800 of these men that they were sent to the Treatment Center for intensive study for a 60-day observation period. Of this latter group 240 men were found to be sexually dangerous as described in the law and were committed to the center.

It is quite apparent from the data gathered that the men seen under this statute are seriously sexually disturbed and represent a significant threat to society. Two of many findings demonstrate this. Unlike the general findings reported in the literature of 12-17% sexual offense recidivism, 62% of the total group screened had one or more prior convictions for a sexual offense. Of the group committed to the center, 73% had a prior record for a sexual crime. In 47% of the committed sexual offenders, force or violence was associated with the offense. This is quite different from the overall data on sexual crimes that indicates aggression is comparatively rare[11].

Thus the center sees a selective sample. It is precisely this selectivity that has given us the opportunity to observe characterological sexual pathology and features of character related to such pathology without the distortions created by clinical cases showing sexual deviancy as the result of transient neurotic regressions, traumatic environmental stress, the so-called accidental sexual offense (not a deviancy), or the deviances that are better ascribed to cultural disapproval than to psychopathology. This is not the man in alcoholic stupor urinating in an alley and arrested for exhibiting himself; not the disappointed lover misunderstanding the glances of a young girl as a seductive invitation and arrested for accosting; it is not the man on a date sexually provoked and then denied whose anger triggers off a sudden uncharacteristic, explosive rape; nor is the sexual assault an expression of a subcultural double standard or masculine culture "machismo."

The patient that is seen at the center shows serious defects in social relationships and social skills, lacunae in moral and ethical attitudes, impulse-control functions that are tenuous and break down under relatively normal life stresses, ego functions (judgment, reality testing, reasoning, etc.) that seem entirely intact until he is sexually or aggressively provoked and only then do the ego distortions appear, and major disturbances in his sexual development that leave him fixated at an infantile, primitive level or make him susceptible to sudden and precipitous regressions.

The following sections of this paper will be devoted to one group of such sexual offenders, the rapist. The data were obtained from extensive clinical study involving diagnostic and psychotherapeutic interviews and psychological tests. The elaboration, correction, and refinement of these clinical observations are the result of four research studies.[12] [15]

The Rapist

It is readily apparent that there is no congruence between rape and any specific diagnostic category. It is true that classic neurotic symptoms are a rarity, but all types of character neuroses, character disorders, and more severe borderline and psychotic states are represented. It is equally clear that there are some specific characteristics present in rapists that differentiate them from other criminals and from other sexual offenders. In addition, there is evidence that clear, differentiated classes of rapists can be observed, and such differentiation has significant clinical and research utility.

Guttmacher and Weihofen[16] have found discriminate classes among rapists and regard motivation as the basis for a classification.

Forced rape . . . has several basic motivational patterns. There is the rapist whose assault is the explosive expression of a pent-up sexual impulse. Or it may occur in individuals with strong latent homosexual components . . . These are the true sex offenders. Another type that is also sexual in origin, although not so manifestly so, is the sadistic rapist . . . Many of these individuals have their deep-seated hatred focused particularly on women. Then there is the third type of rapist who, paradoxically is not primarily a sex offender. He is the aggressive, anti-social criminal who, like the soldier of a conquering army, is out to pillage and rob (p. 116).

The authors refer to three types. However, it appears that four groups are described, and although they do not present them in such terms, the following more dynamic statements seem to reflect their findings: (a) rape motivated by sexual impulses whose intensity has become so great that whatever defensive or controlling factors were present were overwhelmed and the sexual desire is expressed; (b) rape that is not a breakdown of defense, but is itself a defense against strong homosexual wishes; (c) rape that is the expression not only of sexuality but this impulse combined with deep-seated hatred or aggressive feelings toward women; and (d) rape that does not so much express sexual or aggressive wishes but rather a more general predatory disposition.

In a prodigious statistical study based on interviews and data retrieved from case folders, Gebhard *et al.* [17] describe two major categories of rapists. In their taxonomy this group is referred to as "heterosexual offenders vs. adults." The two varieties of aggressive offenses include

(1) those in which the aggression is a means to an end, and no more force is used than is necessary to achieve the end (coitus usually); (2) those in which violence is an end in itself or at least a secondary goal; in these cases the female is either subjected to more force than is necessary or she is mistreated after coitus or other direct sexual activity has ended (p. 196).

The nature of the differentiation is the motive, dealt with this time in behavioral terms. The authors do go on to discuss seven additional varieties that have little or no relationship to the two major categories quoted above, but in some instances, at least, awareness of factors other than goal behavior is indicated.

Anyone who has worked with such sexual offenders will immediately recognize the "types" referred to in the two classifications. He will also recognize the superficiality of the descriptions that results from a lack of attention to other psychological characteristics. The act of rape clearly cannot be understood unidimensionally simply in terms of motivation or, in fact, in terms of any single factor.

Williams[18] eschews classification but does show an appreciation for the complexity of rape by considering both instinctual forces and controlling forces. The latter forces involve both the developmental level of ties to the external object and the quality of the internal, incorporated, restraining figures. The instinctual forces are those of sex and aggression. The act expressed is a result of these forces and the control forces developed from object relationships. The particularities of the act represent a point on a continuum.

> Sexual crimes directed against females are thought to form part of a graduated series of actions with minor assaults at one end of the scale and lust-murder at the other (p. 563).

No effort will be made here to resolve the issue of whether rape can best be understood in terms of discrete categories or a point on a linear continuum. The multidimensional nature of the factors involved and the clinical phenomena themselves make it extremely difficult to consider the differences simply in quantitative terms. On the other hand, when considered from a multifactor point of view, the clinical data do not fit securely into categories. The compromise adopted here is to present a set of clinical classes based on descriptive and dynamic characteristics with an appropriate caveat to the reader that a typology is not intended.

Descriptively, the act of rape involves both an aggressive and a sexual component. As noted above, and in accord with the observations at the treatment center, in any particular sexual assault the part played by these impulses can be quite different. The primary aim may be hostile and destructive so that the sexual behavior is in the service of an aggressive impulse. In other instances the sexual impulse is the dominating motive, and the aggressive aspects of the assault are primarily in the service of the sexual aim. In a third pattern, the two impulses are less differentiated, and the relationship between them can best be described as sexual sadism.

We have also observed a number of rapists within whom neither sexual nor aggressive impulses played a dominant role in the act itself. This is the group that Guttmacher[4] refers to as the aggressive antisocial criminal and Gebhard *et al.*[17] refer to as the amoral delinquent. We agree that this group should not be considered primarily as sexually deviant persons.

The remainder of this paper will be concerned with only the first three patterns of rape, since there are no new findings to contribute to the understanding of the antisocial character disorder.

The discussion of the classification will be concerned with those factors that appear to differentiate the three classes of rapists. These include the descriptive features of the act itself, the interrelationship of the sexual and aggressive impulses and the developmental level of these impulses, ego interests and attitudes, defensive structure, unconscious fantasies that appear to be the level of object ties. These factors can be conceptually considered as separate and distinct, but they do not exist as independent forces, states, or structures, and will not be treated separately.

CLINICAL CLASSIFICATION OF RAPE

Rape—Agressive Aim

In this pattern the sexual assault is primarily an aggressive, destructive act. The sexual behavior is not the expression of a sexual wish but is in the service of the aggression, serving to humiliate, dirty, and defile the victim. The degree of violence varies from simple assault to brutal, vicious attacks resulting on occasion in the victim's death. The savagery of the act clearly denoted the aggressive intent. When aspects of sexuality are present, they, too, enter the service of aggression as seen in biting, cutting, or tearing of the genitals or breasts, rupture of the anus through violent insertion of some object, or in other sexually mutilating acts.

The women certainly appear to be the victims of the offender's destructive wishes, and he, in fact, describes his emotional state as anger. These women are always complete strangers. This anger that is experienced is clearly a displacement of intense rage on a substitute object. The source of this rage is most frequently the mother or her representatives in the present, the wife or girlfriend.

The rape occasionally occurs in the offender's automobile where the victim is brought either by physical force or by threat with a weapon. However, the rape occurs most frequently in the victim's home with entrance gained by some ruse, the offender representinq himself as a delivery man, repairman, or someone looking for a false address.

The rape often occurs in a series, and they appear as isolated instances in an otherwise relatively normal social and psychiatric history. There is, however, a long history of difficulty in heterosexual object relations in conjunction with an active sexual life. Many of these men are married and those who are not are engaged or dating with regularity. There are, however, considerable difficulties in these relationships that are marked by episodic mutual irritation, and, at times, violence. They tend to experience women negatively as hostile, demanding, ungiving, and unfaithful, and frequently for good reason. The women they select are in fact assertive, active, and independent who, by their manner and attitude, ask them to accept passive components of relationships that they find intolerable.

Features of the oedipal situation are reenacted time and again in involvements with divorced or separated women who are themselves mothers or with girlfriends or wives who are sexually promiscuous and not infrequently pregnant through affairs with other men.

Most of these patients have an adequate occupational history showing not only stability of work, but high level skills and achievement with qualities of inventiveness and creativity. They are competitive but are able to enter into cooperative, sharing relationships with men, although here, too, the more active features are dominant, with the passive demands of such relationships leading to conflict and anxiety. The work they do is clearly masculine as defined by this culture—machinist, truck driver, plumber. etc.

They appear generally to have mastered the various developmental tasks of childhood and latency with no gross signs of disturbance appearing until adolescence. In this period there is an impairment in intellectual attainment and excessive, exaggerated masculine activity. With regard to the latter they become involved in street brawls, become preoccupied with high speed driving, enter aggressive sports, usually outside of formal organized high school activity, and are overzealous in physical contact. In a dramatic way there is an increase in partially controlled, socially acceptable (if not always socially approved and legally sanctioned) aggressive behavior.

In a striking number of such offenders, there is a history of prepubertal or postpubertal sexual traumata with older women, frequently the mother. These experiences appear to be directly associated not only with the generalized aggressive display, but also with the development of rape fantasies and with the rape itself. Two brief clinical cases will demonstrate this.

Bill was seen at age 14½. He was a large, well-built young boy, physically much bigger than his peers. In the summer following his tenth birthday, an attractive, married, 20-year-old aunt took him into a picnic area, parked the car, and disrobed. He recalled being in a state of panic as she took his hands and placed them on her breasts and her genitals. He remembers that the feeling of fear was accompanied by excitement and sexual curiosity. That evening he lay awake until midnight at which time he arose, dressed, and walked to her house feeling once again both apprehensive and sexually excited. Although he knew she was home, she did not answer his knocking at the door, and, disappointed and angry, he went home. Following this, he found himself preoccupied with memories of the sexual experience. He became intensely aware of older women, mentally comparing their covered bodies with the memory of the nude body of his aunt. At this time he began to have sexually sadistic fantasies involving a female teacher and his mother. In the fantasy, he would steal into a house and find the teacher or his mother fully clothed. He would assault and undress them, make love to them, and then stab or shoot them. This fantasy, with little change in content, became a nightly masturbatory ritual at puberty, and at the age of 14½ he acted out the fantasy with a neighbor. She had offered him money to help her move furniture and as he followed her up the stairs to her home which was relatively isolated, he had the thought that she was sexually provoking him. He became angry and when they entered the home he put his arm about her throat and throttled her until she lost consciousness. He undressed her and had intercourse with her during which he recalls giving vent to a steady stream of obscenities and feelings of increased anger. He wanted to stab and cut her but instead reached for a metal lamp and beat her until he thought he had killed her. Bill did not recapture the memory of the early sexual experience with his aunt until the third year of his therapy at which point there was a dream in which this aunt appears.

In the second case, the sexual traumata occurred with the patient's mother.

Following the death of his father when he was 13, his mother began to drink excessively and became increasingly promiscuous. At different times in her drunkeness she would behave in a seductive way toward him that both angered and frightened him. At the age of 19 he was making a telephone call and as he looked into the hall mirror he saw his mother, nude, walking into her bedroom, throw herself onto the bed with her legs spread in his direction. He was overwhelmed by a desire to run into the room and have intercourse with her. With this feeling there appeared the thought that at that moment any man could walk into the house and have her sexually. He became angry and wanted now to sexually assault her, specifically to kick her repeatedly in the genitals. This flooding of sexual and aggressive feelings so frightened him that he fled from the house and began a 2-week drinking spree. This period was marked by sporadic aggressive vandalism that involved smashing store windows and breaking antennae of automobiles and ended with a rape. One evening while waiting on a corner for his girlfriend, he became upset with the idea that she was out with another man. He then noticed a woman walking toward him and the thought entered his mind, "if she turns right, she wants me to follow her, but if she turns left, she does not." Unfortunately she turned right. He ran after her, threw her down, carried her to a deserted lot, and sexually assaulted her.

In these two cases, although different in many respects, the clinical material leaves little question that intense rage was present, that this rage was related to sexual anxiety, and that the victim was clearly a substitute object.

In nearly all of these patients there is body concern and a body narcissism. They are physically attractive and tend to be attentive to body health and hygiene. There are moderate obsessive features and clearly the explosive outbursts represent an anal-sadistic regression as a response to certain types of stress. They are capable, however, of finding socially acceptable outlets for this aggression under normal circumstances and similarly capable of aim-inhibited feelings of warmth, kindness, and love. The characteristic mode of relating, however, is in a cool, detached, overcontrolled manner. They are active, assertive, excessively counterdependent, and intolerant of the passive aspects required of true mutuality in relationships. True friendships are rare because of their hyperalertness to narcissistic injury and, more important, because of the absence of depth and intensity in the formation of object ties. The ease with which feelings and concern for others can be withdrawn facilitates the release and expression of unneutralized aggression. What is noteworthy is the frequent reappearance of the concern with feelings of compassion and efforts to undo or make some kind of restitution to the victim. The full dynamic meaning of the compassion and remorse is not clear but it is evidently not understandable by a simple formula of guilt.

One observation may contribute to understanding this phenomenon and also helps to clarify the intensity of the rage and its displacement. In this type of offender there is frequently a splitting of the ambivalent feelings toward mother. Their own mothers, and women in abstract, are overidealized as the sources of fulfillment of all infantile and narcissistic needs. Real women are unfaithful, untrustworthy, and depriving. In usual circumstances these two images are fused in their relationships with women, with the splitting occurring in situations of stress.

This splitting of the mother ambivalence is only one feature of the defensive structure that includes displacement and isolation as primary mechanisms. Counterphobic attitudes prevail to assist in the defense against castration fears, but it is the ineffectiveness of this defense that gives rise to the primitive aggression when a woman is the source of the castration anxiety. Their inability to develop real devotion and loyalty makes them incapable of experiencing such traits in others, and this presents an appearance of paranoid mistrust. However, it does not have the quality of basic distrust, and the paranoid mechanisms are not seen as primary adaptive features, although they do come into play during the regressive episodes.

There is nothing noteworthy about perceptual or cognitive functioning or generally with the autonomous ego functions while such patients are in confinement. No gross impairments are present nor is any specific pattern discernible. The average IQ of this group is somewhat higher than the other groups of rapists and is in fact higher than all other groups found to be sexually dangerous (pedophiles, incestors, etc.).

In additional comparisons with the other groups of rapists to be discussed, this group has the highest level of social and occupational adjustment, the most mature relationships with both men and women (although relations with the latter are less adequate), they are most responsive to treatment, can be released following the shortest commitment period, and the postparole adjustment is made with fewer difficulties and is most successful.

Within the center, disciplinary action occasionally must be taken because of surly or unruly behavior toward security personnel or for fighting with another patient. Even when these offenders are not so involved, they frequently appear to be actively suppressing such behaviors and for the most part they are successful. They do not have an excessive disciplinary rate and among their peers they are the most socially desirable patients.

Thus, what is seen during the confinement is quite different from the behavior immediately preceding their confinement and is quite at odds with the primitive, brutal acts of sexual violence that brought about the commitment. The data seem to be best understood in terms of decompensation approaching psychotic proportions in men who have been able to deal with their intense rage toward women in relatively successful ways. The aggression itself appears to be both the result of a splitting of the mother ambivalence and also a defense against the experience of helplessness they feel in all object relationships, but with particular intensity with women.

Phillip was born 25 years ago in an urban, industrial community in the Northeast. He is tall and well built and although his walk, carriage, voice, and manner is active and assertive he carries a boyish smile enhanced by a cowlick and deep blue guileless eyes. His crime belies this impression of innocence.

He was committed to the center 4 years ago following a sexual assault on a young girl. He was driving along a city road when he saw a girl, whom he did not know. He stopped his car beside her, stepped out, and asked her where she was going. He didn't hear her answer and asked again in an angry manner. She turned to walk away and Phillip felt that she was trying to make a fool of him. He believed that she had first shown an interest in him and when he exposed his own interest to her, she was rejecting it. He punched her in the stomach, grabbed her under her chin, pulled her into his car, and drove to a secluded area. After he had parked the car he told the girl to get into the back seat. When she refused, he climbed into the back and dragged her over the seat beside him. He undressed her and violently penetrated her. He states that he then withdrew, without having an orgasm and let her out of the car, threatening to kill her if she made mention of the attack. When he was arrested shortly thereafter, he immediately admitted his guilt.

During the diagnostic interviews subsequent to his trial, he discussed the incident, describing himself as enraged at the time, not sexually excited. He had gone to visit his girlfriend, a "good" girl whom he had been seeing off and on since early adolescence with no sexual activity throughout the courtship. He found her necking on the porch with a black man and he drove from her house in a blind rage. He was partially aware as he drove away that he was going to look for someone to attack sexually.

Phillip had an active sexual life, but only with girls whom he considered to be "bad." These relationships were short-lived, ending when he was directly confronted with their promiscuity. Terminating the relationship always occurred with violence either in assaults on the girls or on the boyfriends that had replaced him.

His late adolescence was marked by the repetitiveness of these experiences. Over and over again he became involved with promiscuous girls who would then prove unfaithful. Although this behavior has meaning in the compulsion to repeat the oedipal situation, it must also be understood in terms of an ego split and an underlying masochism. On the one hand he could only permit himself to have intercourse with girls known by him to be sexually indiscriminate. On the other hand, he maintained the fantasy that they would be faithful to him. This latter belief he would test, not consciously, by setting up occasions for the girl to meet and enter relationships with other men. He would then feel ashamed, foolish, and hurt and would react aggressively.

Aggression characterized Phillip's behavior throughout the latter years of the latency period and through adolescence, although at no time did this behavior bring him before the authorities. Outside of the sexual offense described above, he has a negative criminal history.

Phillip began masturbating at age 13, and there appears to be nothing remarkable about the frequency or method of masturbating or the accompanying fantasies. Although there is no history of homosexual experiences, his behavior toward homosexuals indicates the presence of homosexual desires and the tenuousness of their repression. Within the center, he reacted with exaggerated, explosive anger toward homosexual invitations. Sexual intercourse began at 15 with the girls described above. His memory of his first heterosexual experience was that it was somewhat traumatic. When he was 9 or 10 year old, he was approached by a girl who said she wanted to play ball with him and then engaged him in sexual play telling him that girls liked this kind of play. Shortly thereafter a neighborhood girl asked him to play with her and he began to fondle her believing that this was what she desired. She ran home, told her parents who in turn called the patient's father. According to the patient, the father felt so disgraced by this that they moved to a different part of the town.

This father was a strict man, the disciplinarian of the family. The mother was a somewhat passive, quiet, religious woman, who rarely differed overtly with her strong though emotionally uninvolved husband. Family life was quite stable with the father working for the same company, as a machinist, for 25 years. There were two other children in the family, an older sister and a younger brother, both of whom appear to be living normal lives.

Phillip is a very likeable young man, well thought of by the officers and his fellow patients. His anger appears to be very specific to threats to his sense of independence or challenges to his sense of his masculinity, and with projective identification, to protection of the younger or weaker patients. Under these threats, his anger explodes impulsively but not brutally. Although there is a regressive or infantile quality to what he experiences as a threat and a similar infantile quality in his inability to control the release of the aggression, the qualitative features of the aggression itself are less primitive with a relative absence of sadistic features.

Phillip was released from the center after 2½ years, continuing in outpatient psychotherapy. Despite the fact that his life style has remained unchanged so that he must be considered a risk to repeat his sexual assault, sufficient changes have occurred to make the risk worth taking. A brief review of his postparole life will be instructive.

His first year on parole was a traumatic one, not only for the patient but for his therapist as well. Shortly after his release, he began seeing a girl, Ann, whom he had dated prior to his committment. She had been married, had a child, and was currently separated from her husband, although she continued to see him occasionally. Phillip became very involved with her and her son, purchasing furniture for her apartment and taking the boy on outings. He was fully aware that she was still seeing her husband and that she was having affairs with other men. In therapy he was able to discuss his sense of helpless rage and began to look more deeply into his pattern of getting involved with such women.

One evening Ann announced that she was going to invite her husband to return to live with her. A stormy scene ensued during which Phillip beat her rather severely. He then left the apartment and while driving away he saw a girl walking along the street. He stopped the car, asked her if she would join him and when she refused he jumped from the car and grabbed her about the waist. She screamed and Phillip released her, terrified at what he had done. He then returned to his car and began to drive at speeds exceeding 90 mph directly at telephone poles in an effort to kill himself. He sheered off two poles, totally wrecked the car but received only a head laceration.

He dealt at some length in therapy with this self-destructive behavior, showing some awareness of the masochistic aspects of his relationship with Ann. The pattern, however, continued. He began dating bar girls or other pick-ups and soon became intimate with a divorcee. He was seeing her for about 8 months in a stormy relationship marked by his jealousy of her continuing contact with the parents of her former husband and with what he felt to be too close a relationship with her own brother. A serious fight erupted between Phillip and the brother, followed by an argument with his girlfriend and he lost control and struck her.

He had been living in and out of his own parental home, but shortly after this incident his father died suddenly and Phillip decided that he would move in with his mother to care for her. This takes Phillip up to the present. Whether his father's death will have the meaning of an oedipal victory and effect a change in his aggression toward self and others remains an open question.

Rape—Sexual Aim

A second pattern of characteristics that has been observed is quite different from the above. Here the act of rape is clearly motivated by sexual wishes, and the aggression is primarily in the service of this aim. The degree of aggressive behavior varies, but there is a relative absence of violence and the act lacks any of the characteristics of brutality.

The offense almost always takes place out of doors in isolated places such as darkened streets, a park, or wooded area. Most frequently the offender embraces the woman from behind touching her breasts or genitals, holding on to her with some force but not to any excessive degree. If the victim should struggle and thus require more physical effort in order to be held, the offender will release her and flee. Thus, most of the offenders are charged with assault with intent to commit rape. At other times the victim is so frightened that she passively submits, and the rape takes place without any additional force. When apprehended it is discovered that he has carried out such acts many times.

He is always very sexually aroused and fully aware of what he is doing, although at times he feels as if he were performing under a compulsion.

The victim is always a stranger but not one that he comes upon by accident. She is usually someone he has seen while on a streetcar or bus and follows her off when she leaves.

It is not an impulsive act, however. This is a scene he has lived through many times in fantasy. It is a fantasy that is not only used in masturbation but one that preoccupies him throughout his waking day and is composed in a relatively fixed pattern. In the fantasy, the woman he attacks first protests and then submits, more resignedly than willingly. During the sexual act, he performs with great skill, and she receives such intense pleasure that she falls in love with him and pleads with him to return. This differs from the not unusual adolescent fantasy in that he spends a large part of the evening hours traveling about the city searching for its fulfillment and in fact acts out the fantasy over and over again.

Rape is not always a feature of his sexual fantasies. When it is, the aggressive component of the fantasied assault, although somewhat erotic, never approaches a sadistic quality and is always secondary to the sexual aim. There is no evidence from the behavior, the conscious fantasy, or what we have learned of the unconscious dynamics of the act, that the aggression is eroticized to the degree seen in the third pattern of rape to be described below.

These sexual fantasies and the frequently impotent efforts at rape are not the only indicants of a disturbed sexual life. From early in adolescence he was acting out in perverted ways. Perversions involved partial aims, part objects, and substitute objects. Although he developed erotic feelings toward both boys and girls, there was a marked inhibition to any form of interpersonal sexuality. He was voyeuristic, fetishistic, and exhibitionistic, but a real heterosexuality existed only in fantasy, and homosexuality was intensely repressed. The repressive defenses against the latter were not entirely successful, and although no direct acting out of the homosexual feelings occurred, this was accomplished only by withdrawing and isolating himself from his male peers.

As he developed through adolescence, the guilt and shame that he felt regarding his perversions together with the need to defend by avoiding the homosexual wishes affected all peer relationships. The sense of lonliness increased, he became shy and increasingly inept and defective in social skills. The passive-feminine features of his personality became more dominant and were accompanied by intense feelings of impotency and inadequacy. Active masculinity was temporarily suspended for the passive gratifications offered by fantasy.

As such offenders approach the end of adolescence or enter young adult life the passive solution gives added strength to the underlying homosexual feelings and a break through of such feelings becomes a real threat. The acts of rape occur at this time but not only as a defense against the homosexual wish. They are also efforts at renewal, an adaptive effort to escape the implications of the passive-feminine resolution. The acts also serve to protest and deny the feelings of being an impotent castrate. They are also attempts to relieve the shame related to the pregenital perversions. (These offenders are able to describe the acts of rape in great detail including their thoughts and feelings and they do this in diagnostic interviews and early in the psychotherapy. In contrast, it is frequently many years of psychotherapy before the patient brings the material on the perversions into treatment.)

This type of rapist shows little or no antisocial behavior apart from the repetitive sexual offenses. He is, in fact, socially submissive and compliant. His friends and neighbors see him as a quiet, shy, "good boy," more lonely than most, but nonetheless quite normal. There is generally an absence of even a moderate amount of aggressive and assertive behavior. His approach to the tasks of life are tentative and have a phobic quality. This lack of assertiveness combines with a very negative self-esteem and a low level of aspiration, preventing him from making significant attainments in either educational or occupational areas. There is a stable employment history, but the level of work is far below his aptitude or potential abilities. Although intelligence varies across a wide range from dull normal to bright average and above among the rapists in this group, in no instance is the potential realized. Scholastic records show poor performance and frequently withdrawal from school prior to graduation. A brief description of one young man will illustrate some to these latter observations.

Donald was first seen at age 17 following his commitment for a sexual assault. He had been walking home when he saw a young girl walking through a park. He came up from behind, placed his arms about her and threatened that he would hurt her if she resisted. She was 16 years old. He pushed her to the ground, undressed her, and attempted intercourse, but as he penetrated her, she cried that it hurt. He withdrew and ran away. He recalls feeling sexually excited and frightened that he might be caught and that he might not have an erection or might have a premature ejaculation.

He was apprehended soon afterward and immediately confessed to an additional assault that had taken place a few weeks earlier. On this occasion, the victim had screamed despite the threats and Donald had run away.

He has always felt that he was the unwanted member of his family and described himself as "lower than a snake under a rock." He had no friends, male or female. From ages 10 to 15, he was placed in special classes as the result of being classified as retarded. The Weschler Adult Intelligence Scale administered at the Center 5 years following his committment showed a verbal IQ of 93, performance IQ of 107, and full scale IQ of 99, which is clearly not retarded. He describes the 5 years in special classes as "one long, unhappy nightmare."

Less than 2 years before he committed the rape, he was convicted of being a voyeur, and since this was his first offense, the case was filed. Four months later he was again convicted of peeping and was sentenced to a training school for 1 year. One month following his release he began his sexual assaults on girls.

The defensive structures, apart from the avoidance, repression, and inhibition described above, include introjection mechanisms, reflecting the diffusiveness in identity formation, projection of the severeness of the superego, so that he feels despised and anticipates rejection, and a type of denial leading to a naivete that permits him to be victimized and used by others.

A very particular family pattern was noted. This pattern included a weak father, not a passive submissive man but one who found the demands of family responsibility too much and reneged in his role as father and husband. The mother tended to very cold and ungiving, and an inconsistent, but harsh disciplinarian who infantilized her son by overwhelming control and suppression. This mother appeared to be preoccupied with sexual morality, and the most excessive repression occurred in response to any expression of erotic interest or pleasure.

· Despite her coldness, the young boy was completely dependent upon her. By virtue of her restrictive and repressive behavior he felt quite safe and protected not only from external dangers but from the threats of his own sexual wishes.

For the most part, these patients respond very well to group and individual psychotherapy and to planned programs of vocational, educational, and skill training, but the psychotherapeutic work requires a rather extended duration of from 4 to 6 years.

Ted was committed to the treatment center after having been found guilty of a series of sexual offenses, legally described as "assault with intent to rape" and "assault and battery." There was a fixed and stereotyped quality to these offenses. He would approach a woman from behind and place one hand on her breast and the other between her legs. If the neighborhood was sufficiently secluded he would try to force her to the ground. If the surroundings were more public he would simply caress and fondle her until she screamed or vigorously resisted whereupon he would release her and flee. The patient admits to over 100 such assaults. There were two exceptions to the behavior described above. In one instance he threw the woman to the ground in a deserted park and choked her until she lost consciousness. When he became aware of what he had done, he fled, leaving her lying on the ground. On another occasion, in the same park, he held a knife to a woman and in her continued struggle a superficial wound was made. He became frightened and again fled.

Despite his freely admitted sexual desires, and the numerous assaults that occurred, he did not have intercourse with any of his victims. In his treatment, a great deal of time was spent in attempting to reconstruct the thoughts and feelings that preceded the assaults. For the most part, despite active effort, he was not able to recall much before the acts, although his memory was intact and surprisingly complete for the acts themselves. It was as if a veil of amnesia covered this period somewhat similar to a dissociative experience. He was able to describe a feeling that his "whole body seems to expand, and my ears would get very warm." Frequently before accosting in the evening he would be preoccupied throughout the work day with his anticipation of going out to search for a possible encounter. On other occasions, he claimed there were no such preparatory thoughts. In these instances, he would be on a bus or walking when suddenly a girl or woman would demand his attention at which point he would be overwhelmed by erotic feelings and thoughts.

These acts of rape took place over a 5-year period, beginning when he was 17 and ending with his commitment at age 22. At the time of his arrest he was living at home with his mother, an alcoholic stepfather, and a half brother 9 years younger than he in an industrial community, a part of a large metropolis. His mother was working to assist in the support of this lower middle-class family. His natural father had died a few months before he was born, and his mother had remarried four years later. This marriage was never a stable one and shortly after the patient was committed, his mother separated from the second husband. Also in the family, but away from home, were an older sister and two older brothers.

He describes his mother as very cold and unloving person whose primary relationship to him was built around moral prescriptions and proscriptions. He speaks of her as one who gave him no feeling of warmth and affection but who always seemed present to confront him with his badness. He was always very dependent upon her in a manner that the mother reinforced and perpetuated. She prevented him from developing any initiative or sense of independence so that he was unable to make important occupational or other life decisions without her direct advice and suggestions. Although he loved her very much he was very afraid of her and was not able to share with her the enormous psychological discomfort he experienced throughout his life. In his earliest years there was no father present and he recalls no contact with his older siblings. His stepfather was a moody, alcoholic man, given to moments of brutality who apparently took no interest in him whatsoever.

Ted is 5' 5" tall, of slight build, and fair complexion, looking much younger than his 22 years. His voice is somewhat high-pitched and nasal and there is a slight speech impediment. These physical characteristics contributed to rather severe problems beginning in early adolescence. Although he is of average intelligence, he left high school after his freshman year as a result of an inability to form any peer relationships and of being subjected to ridicule with which he could not cope. He was accused of being a "fairy" and on a number of occasions he was attacked by groups of boys who removed his trousers and threatened sodomy, although he always managed to ward off actual sexual contact. The following years produced no change in his social status. He had no boyfriends, he dated only rarely and tentatively, and he became increasingly shy and retiring.

He saw himself as a very lonely boy, unattractive, unlikable, socially and sexually inadequate with no self-expression outlets. He was employed on a factory assembly line in a monotonous task. Each time he would try to leave to seek out more meaningful and gratifying work, his mother would ridicule his plans and defeat his efforts before they could begin. He ultimately resigned himself to the work and established an excellent and stable work record.

As indicated, the patient never had a mature heterosexual relationship. His sexual outlet had been through fantasy and pregnital sexual behavior. He recalls that at age 8 while playing with a little girl he inserted his penis between her thighs. This type of sex play continued for some years, terminating when the girl had her first menses. When she told him of this he experienced such feelings of fear and revulsion that he avoided all heterosexual contact until his sixteenth year. At age 13 he began to develop intense voyeuristic and exhibitionistic desires so that he spent a great deal of time and effort peeping at women and exposing himself. Also at this time he found himself aroused by his mother's underclothing. The peeping, exposing, and the feel of the undergarments would excite him, and it is at this time and in these situations that he began to masturbate. The masturbation soon became compulsive and later would follow the sexual assaults that brought him to the center.

The entire pattern of his sexuality reflects the immaturity of his sexual aims and the social impotency of effecting real heterosexual relationships. The latter were reserved for his fantasies. At the age of 16 he began to go with a girl who, he stated, was quite willing to have intercourse with him but this never occurred. They did, however, engage in extensive petting, although even this was a source of great discomfort to him for he would very quickly have an orgasm and lose his erection. On numerous occasions he would masturbate or drink alcohol before going to see her in an effort to maintain his potency, but even these efforts were unsuccessful.

Rape—Sex-Aggression Defusion

The third pattern of characteristics we have observed reveals the presence of a strong sadistic component. There appears to be no ability to experience sexual excitation without some degree of violence being present. The degree of sadism is quite variable with the extreme position seen in lust murders where excessive brutality and mutilation occur before, during, and even after the murder. This is relatively rare. The most usual behavioral pattern is forcible rape where violence is used to excite the offender, and after intercourse there is no further aggression. Such an offender is frequently impotent with women until there is resistance. To become sexually excited he will provoke in a teasing, playfully aggressive sexual manner, eliciting resistant or angry behavior from his partner. Her resistance arouses in him aggressive feelings that become, as his sexual play continues, more intense and autonomous. The arousal and maintenance of the sexual desire appear to be a direct function of this initially mild arousal of aggression. It should be noted that the affect of anger is not present.

In most patients in this group the sadistic quality of their sexuality is projected onto the victim. He sees her struggle and protestation not as a refusal but as a part of her own sexual excitation. "Women like to get roughed up, they enjoy a good fight." This belief is maintained even when the victim is literally fighting for her life and the offender has to brutally injure her to force her to submit to intercourse.

Although there is some neutralization or toning down of the aggression in relationships unrelated to sexual partners or to sexual situations, even here there are qualities of untamed aggression. He is assertive, overpowering, and somewhat hostile in all situations. Warmth and affection are completely absent. The most friendly meeting is punctuated by a touching and pushing so that any encounter wich such persons is a "bruising" one. In less pathological cases this is the extroverted football player type who crushes you in his narcissistic exuberance.

Such patients are usually married and in fact many have been married and divorced a number of times with, of course, never a sense of commitment to the marriage. The patient, and often his wife, are quite active in extramarital affairs. For the offender this constant search and seduction is essential for his sexual excitement, not as a defense against feelings of inadequacy but to satisfy the aggressive component of his sexual wishes.

Intercourse with his wife is described as physically relieving but unsatisfactory; not infrequently, he has difficulty in obtaining or maintaining
an erection. Quite often feelings of revulsion follow connubial coitus. In
some instances the patient is successful in having his wife play a masochistic
role and he can obtain satisfaction with the aggression modulated within
the fantasy. The wife permits herself to be tied up and verbally abused as
she acts out a scene of being physically assaulted and raped by a stranger.

In many ways such men are similar to the psychopathic character.
There is an extensive history of nonsexual, antisocial behavior, an absence
of stable object ties, a lack of concern for others, difficulty in tolerating
frustration, poorly structured control functions, and a relative absence of
endopsychic discomfort. Most different and most perplexing in view of the
more primitive organization of their instinctual life is the presence of
industry and initiative in skill development, although this cannot be used
for a socially successful occupational career. The psychopath obtains gratification in getting away with things, with getting by with active manipulation of others rather than with his own active efforts. This aspect of
manipulation of others is present to a great degree in our patients, but
gratification is also obtained through active mastery and personal accom-
plishment. These patients will manipulate, demand, and exploit in order to
gratify felt needs, but there is little or no gratification simply from the act of
manipulation.

Developmentally there is an absence of the latency period. Sexual and
aggressive behavior toward younger children, peers, and animals is prominent throughout the prepubertal years. Other indications of impulsive
behavior and general lack of control, expressed in truancy, stealing, running away, ·and lying, are also present.

This is a history also seen in the psychopathic character. In adolescence significant differences appear in the organization of aggression
that distinguish the antisocial character from the sex-aggression rapist. In
the psychopath, the aggression comes under the control of the ego and
serves it in its adaptive efforts. Although there certainly is a basic hostile,
angry attitude that requires little to release it in uninhibited ways, the
aggression is relatively organized, controlled, and directed. In this type of
rapist the aggression continues to be diffuse and unorganized; it maintains
its primitive quality and cannot be pressed into the service of the ego's
adaptive needs. The sexualization of the aggression (or the aggressivization
of the sexuality) so overwhelms the ego when the aggression is aroused that
the control and discharge mechanisms fail to function. The psychopath may
commit an assault or a murder through the absence of concern for objects or

to prevent detection of his pillaging. Here the behavior is organized in the service of survival, and the ego is in direct control of the aggressive discharge. In the assault or murder of the rapist the ego is completely submerged.

In comparison with the other types of rapists discussed above, patients in this group show the greatest degree of paranoid features, and under certain conditions these are of psychotic proportion. The world is perceived as a hostile place where one's survival is constantly under threat. Every human contact is made tentatively with mistrust and suspicion, experienced as a battle in which someone wins and someone loses. They cannot experience any sense of interpersonal mutuality.

Their entire life is tempestuous. Family life is marked by cruel and abusive behavior of the family members toward each other, except for the mother. Oddly enough she appears as the only member of the family with warm and compassionate feelings. Her major fault lies in her need to give that is so intense it takes on bizarre qualities. Her pathological need to give distorts her judgment of her children's behavior. She denies, rationalizes, and excuses the defective development of internal controls and actively supports a primitive oral demandingness.

The fathers of these patients were physically and psychologically cruel and sadistic not only in their own behavior, but would incite, support, and often demand physically aggressive behavior among the children.

Frank is a 42-year-old, white, divorced man who, since age 13, has spent a total of only 5 years out of prison. He was committed to the treatment center with a history of brutal sexual assaults on women; assaults that began shortly after his marriage at age 18, and that would occur while he was on parole from the previous offenses. In all, he has been found guilty of six separate sexual crimes.

Only one of these offenses will be described, but it is quite typical. When he was 22 years old, 5 months after having been released from prison where he had spent 18 months for a sexual assault, he met a girl in a dance hall. He was married at the time, but almost from the time of the ceremony he had been involved in one illicit affair after another.

He spent the evening dancing with the girl and then offered to drive her and her two girlfriends home. He drove one girl to her house, but when he reached the home of the second girl he learned that both she and the girl he had spent the evening with planned to leave together. He sped away, drove outside of town to a small cemetery, parked the car and told the girls he wanted to have intercourse with them. The two girls jumped from the car but Frank was able to catch each of them and knock them to the ground. One girl fell on her stomach whereupon he leaped astride her pressing her face into the earth until she lost consciousness. Leaving her lying there for a moment, he turned to the other girl, throttled her until she too was in a semiconscious state. He then carried them back to the car, forced them to undress lighting up the interior of the car so that he might watch. He then forced each girl to fellate him under both physical and verbal threats that they would be killed. Following this he had intercourse with one of the girls. He sat for a while with the two girls, took some money from one, and then drove them home. The girls were in an hysterical condition when they arrived and a physician was immediately called. He treated each of them for multiple contusions and sedated them. The police were notified, given a description of Frank and his car and he was apprehended about 1 week later.

When Frank was interviewed, he expressed disbelief that the police were called immediately. He stated that he may have been rough with the girls but he felt that they were quite agreeable to his advances. He had concluded that they only reported him when they saw him some nights later in a tavern. He was with his wife and therefore could not respond to their invitations to join him at their table. It was his conviction that the girls were angry out of jealousy and not because of his sexual assault.

Frank was the fourth of five children born into a very unstable and chaotic family. Only the patient's younger sister appears to be without physical or psychological stigmata. His two older brothers have criminal records that go back to early adolescence and a history of antisocial behavior in their prepubertal years. His older sister was born with a deformed hand. After some years of marriage her husband committed suicide. His father has a criminal history, and three half brothers, children of his father's from a previous marriage, all have extensive antisocial history with the oldest currently serving a life sentence for murder.

His father was an alcoholic and physically abusive to his family, especially to the patient. On one occasion, he hung the patient by his tied hands in order to beat him. On still another occasion, he sat on the porch firing a rifle into the ground about Frank forcing him to ridicule himself in front of other family members. The father's criminal record included assault and rape of a young girl.

His mother was a very passive, compliant woman, who although completely unconcerned about the social or educational development of her children, was very nurturing and giving; in fact in excessive and unrealistic ways. She appeared oblivious to the social and psychological pathology in her family. Although, she herself was not actively antisocial, her intense needs to mother resulted in either a denial or passive support of the psychopathy. For example during one of Frank's imprisonments she kept him supplied with contraband drugs.

The cruel and abusive treatment he received from father was only a part of the violence that surrounded Frank through his early and late childhood. His mother states that as a baby he would frequently beat his head against a wall or hit himself on the head with objects. At the age of 7 he was in an automobile accident and suffered fractures of the right leg, right clavicle, right forearm, and pelvis. At age 16, he was caught in the blades of a manure spreader and received a fracture of his left leg and extensive damage to his penis and testicles.

His memory of his first sexual arousal has the same violent quality. He recalls being in a hayloft with one of his brothers and two or three of his cousins, one, a girl 2 years older. They were jumping up and down thrashing the hay, when he noted that as she jumped her dress rose above her waist. He became sexually aroused and jumped closer and closer to her until they bounced against each other and tumbled together into the hay. This vivid memory in many ways represents the quality of

Frank is of medium height, extremely stocky and muscular with a short thick neck. During his commitment at the center he was on disciplinary report repeatedly having difficulties with both security personnel and fellow patients. These patients were seriously injured in separate altercations with him and each one under similar circumstances. They had gotten him angry in some face-to-face disagreement, but he waited until he could assault them from behind or take them by surprise. In a sociometric study, Frank scored as one of the least desirable men among the patients.

His voice was loud, raucous, and demanding. His needs were preemptory and his requests were orders. Certainly a prison is a paranoid community, and Frank has spent most of his adult life in correctional institutions. Nevertheless, his suspiciousness, lack of trust, unprovoked hostility, and the projection of this hostility reflects a characterological paranoid quality that is not simply institutional.

Summary and Discussion

This paper organizes some clinical observations of sexual assaultive behavior and of the men who commit such acts. Although for purposes of exposition the data were organized into classes of rape, the heterogeneity among the patients who seem to represent types leaves no room for conviction regarding classification. However, it is obvious that character patterns exist. Paranoid features are predominant in the group rape—sex-aggression, less so but still present in rape—aggressive aim, and relatively absent in rape—sexual aim. The primitive quality of the aggressive impulse shows the same pattern. Sexual perversions are far more common in rape—sexual aim, with excessive defenses against homosexuality through exaggerated masculinity, predominant in rape—aggressive aim. The level of object ties, the capacity to experience love, tenderness, and warmth, the ability to be kind and generous are clearly different among the three groups.

Their response to therapy, psychotherapy, and other rehabilitative procedures is different as is the progress of such therapy. We have had little success with the group of patients classified as rape—sex-aggression. With the group rape—sexual aim an alliance is established readily, but the passive, oral demanding quality of these patients makes movement slow and arduous. The primary difficulty with the rape—aggressive aim group is the tendency to fall back to paranoid mechanisms wherein a negative therapeutic alliance develops and treatment is then broken. The relative absence of the capacity for warm and intimate object relationship does not permit the relationship to be sustained in the face of the regression.

We are planning a study that will evaluate the extramural adjustment of patients who have been released. On the basis of some data from an earlier study and from clinical impressions, the rape—sex-aggression group represents the greatest risk of maladaptive behavior. Although the numbers are small they are still informative. Only six patients from this group have been released from the center. Two patients were released by court action with no parole or probation supervision prescribed and therefore there has been no follow-up with regard to social adjustment, but there is no evidence of any criminal acts. Of the remaining four, three have had their release revoked and the fourth is having serious difficulties in his second marriage of 6 months.

The data for approximately 30 other rapists who have been released, although not broken down into subgroups and with no information on social adjustment, show that only one patient has committed another sexual assault. A diagnosis in terms of contemporary nosology cannot be made for the rapists we have seen; when such is attempted it is not helpful. However, there are some similarities in the three groups of rapists discussed to three diagnostic categories of personality disorders appearing in DSM II, which perhaps the reader has already noted.

Explosive personality disorder as a diagnosis is most descriptive of the group described as rape—aggressive aim, but it is not adequate for it fails to reflect the pervasive hostility toward women and the feature of repetition compulsion. In our group the explosive outburst is not simply over-responsiveness to environmental pressures.

The second group, rape—sexual aim, has many descriptive features in common with the category Inadequate Personality Disorder, but this diagnosis does not communicate the extensiveness of the sexual perversions against which the rape was expressed as a defensive act.

There is most clearly a similarity between the group rape—sex-aggression and the diagnostic category Antisocial Personality Disorder. The clinical features of the correspondence and the dissimilarities were discussed above.

The clinical classification presented here is based almost entirely on descriptive features, and the problems attendant on such a procedure are fully recognized. It has been our experience, however, in clinical and research activity that the classification has a utility not afforded by any other currently available. It is, to state the obvious, that its usefulness or validity will be determined only by further empirical studies.

The men who have been described in this paper are clearly dangerous. Even in those instances where the aggression is minimal, each of these men has placed himself in situations with women where there is a possible threat to the life of the victim. It is also clear that we are not able to determine without extensive clinical work when, if ever, this danger is at a minimum.

We are fully aware of the objections to special sex offender statutes. These objections are not only legal and moral, but also include the diagnostic, therapeutic, and predictive inadequacies of our clinical science. Nevertheless, society has a right to be protected from such narcissistic violence. The lifelong pathological relationships with women seen in these three groups of rapists give no reason to believe that a prison sentence will make them less dangerous.

References

1. Sarafian R: Treatment of the criminally dangerous sex offender. *Fed Probat* 27:52, 1963.
2. Kozol H, Cohen M, and Garofalo R: The criminally dangerous sex offender. *New Eng J Med* 275:79, 1966.
3. Cohen M, and Kozol H: Evaluation for parole at a sex offender treatment center. *Fed Probat* 30:50, 1966.
4. Guttmacher, M: *Sex Offenses.* New York, Norton, 1951.
5. Mass. Gen. Laws. Ann. Chapter 646, Acts 1958, Chapter 123A. Ammendments: Chapter 615, Acts 1959, Section 2, chapter 123A. Chapter 347, Acts 1960, Section 9 Chapter 123A. Chapter 608, Acts 1966, Section 9, Chapter 123A.
6. Cotton R: Civil commitments from prison: Abuse of process or protection of society? *Mass Law Quart* 54 (No. 3):249, 1969.
7. Gould D, and Hurwitz I: Out of tune with the times; the Massachusetts SDP statute. *Boston Univ Law Rev* 45 (No. 10):391, 1965.

8. Holden L: Sex psychopath laws generally: Commitment of sex offenders in Massachusetts specifically. Unpublished, 1969.
9. McGarry AL, and Cotton R: A study in civil commitment: The Massachusetts sexually dangerous persons act. *Harvard J Leg* 6:263, 1969.
10. Tenney C: Sex, sanity and stupidity in Massachusetts. *Boston Univ Law Rev* 42 (No. 1):1, 1962.
11. Ellis A, and Brancale R: *The Psychology of Sex Offenders.* Springfield, Illinois, C Thomas, 1956.
12. Calmas W: Fantasies of the mother-son relationship of the rapist and the pedophile. Doctoral dissertation, Boston University, 1965.
13. Cohen M, Seghorn R, and Calmas W: Sociometric study of sex offenders. *J Abnorm Psychol* 74:249, 1969.
14. Lopez T: Emotional expression in the adult sex offender. Doctoral dissertation, Boston University, 1969.
15. Seghorn T: Adequacy in ego functioning in rapists and pedophiles. Doctoral dissertation, Boston University, 1970.
16. Guttmacher M, and Weihofen H: *Psychiatry and the Law.* New York, Norton, 1952.
17. Gebhard P, Gagnon J, Pomeroy W, and Christenson C: *Sex Offenders.* New York, Harper and Row, 1965.
18. Williams, AH: Rape-murder, in *Sexual Behavior and the Law.* Slovenko R, (ed), Springfield, Illinois, C. Thomas, 1965.
19. Allen C: *A Textbook of Psycho-sexual Disorders.* London, Oxford University Press, 1962.

SOME ASPECTS OF VIOLENT BEHAVIOR
OF MILITARY PERSONNEL.

A 19 year old enlisted man won combat ribbons while in Vietnam. Following an honorable discharge he resumed work at his former place of employment; he wished to resume his life as if he had never been away. Then he was disturbed by anti-war protesters. He developed nightmares, had anxiety attacks, withdrew from his family, and drank excessively. He was finally persuaded to enter therapy at a nearby Veterans Administration Clinic. He was, however, defensive and evasive during interviews with clinic staff. He became depressed and attempted suicide. He was hospitalized. He finally confided what he had previously concealed: he had committed and observed the commission of atrocities while in Vietnam. He had tried to put it all behind him but the protesters made him feel like a war criminal. Could he ever overcome his guilt?

A 22 year old marine private was disgruntled by orders to take "the point" of his patrol winding through enemy infested terrain. He had long distrusted his junior officer and had plotted to "frag the bastard." During an altercation when they returned to base he stabbed the lieutenant in the arm and was barely prevented from killing him. Psychiatric evaluation revealed the private to be psychotic and he was evacuated for further evaluation.

These two cases illustrate what we have finally realized: Vietnam was unlike any other war in which we were involved. The focus was on "body counts" and it was a dirty guerilla war. The men who fought the war were under incredible stress and extraordinary inner conflict. At home campus discord, race riot, and political protest reached violent levels and undermined the morale of the boys "overseas" who were in constant contact with the homefront news. The homefires were really burning! As the war dragged on year after year and as the civilian and military casualties mounted, the citizenry increasingly doubted the morality and legality of the war as well as its necessity. The troops in the field were increasingly caught in a double bind. They had to fight a war in which they did not believe. They had to follow leaders they often did not trust. They had to protect themselves, to "come back home," and therefore had to be extraordinarily vigilant in guarding against sudden attack. Their orders were sometimes unclear and their firepower awesome. In some cases they simply killed officers they distrusted (those REMF's — the rear echelon mother fuckers trying to win braid). At other times they were exceedingly cruel to an enemy they had dehumanized with profane terms, reduced to "gooks and slants." Veterans told of throwing prisoners to their deaths from helicopters to frighten other prisoners to give intelligence information. Sometimes there was needless slaughter when the troops lost control of themselves. We now know most of the story; it is almost history. But for the men who lived through it; the past is not so easily forgotten. Exactly how each atrocity was committed is a matter for individual investigation. Dr. Gault has written convincingly about the general dynamics of slaughter. Sarah Haley gives insight into the anguish of veterans who committed atrocities. These men are pursued by the shadows of their deeds. They deserve the most wise and humane treatment we can devise. Or else there will be more casualties . . .

X.

When the Patient Reports Atrocities Specific Treatment Considerations of the Vietnam Veteran*

Sarah A. Haley

All wars are "hell." Certain aspects of the Vietnam War, however, differentiated it from World War II and the Korean Conflict: guerrilla tactics predominated; this was was undeclared and became increasingly unpopular; and for the first time the exposure of war atrocities committed by Americans became a national issue. Many Vietnam veterans reflect the impact of these differences in their conflictual attitudes toward their combat experiences and in their psychopathology.

The Vietnam combat veteran who reports atrocities presents a special therapeutic challenge. The therapist's countertransference and real, natural response to the realities of the patient's experience must be continually monitored and confronted. If the therapist is honest with him/herself, a therapeutic relationship becomes possible for men whom many therapists are, or would be, repulsed and frightened by and would never treat.

> Sacrificing a portion of your
> consciousness so you won't have
> to deal with
> Being there
> and
> building mental blocks
> so you won't have to deal with
> having been there.
>
> Al Hubbard from *The New Soldier*

*Reprinted from the *Archives of General Psychiatry*, 30:191-200, 1974. Copyright, American Medical Association. 1974.

In 1969, before any publicized reports of My Lai or other atrocities, I began to evaluate Vietnam veterans for psychotherapy at the Veterans Administration clinic. A small percentage of these men revealed the fact that they had participated in, or witnessed war atrocities. Since that time I have evaluated and/or treated 130 Vietnam-duty veterans; 40 of these men have reported responsibility for atrocious acts. (These figures do not imply a generalizable percentage of Vietnam duty veterans seen by the Veterans Administration. Many came or were referred as a result of an informal communication system among veterans and from the veterans' self-help groups.) These atrocious acts range from those provoked during the intensity and threat of combat to the kind of sadistic brutality unrelated to any immediate external threat or stimulus.

This study explores the subjective states of these 40 men in relation to a treatment process in which the therapist must confront his/her own sadistic and retaliatory feelings to an unusual degree. Psychotherapy with these men is not of use until the therapist is perceived as someone who can hear horrifying realities, and can tolerate natural feelings of revulsion, yet resist an equally natural tendency to punish.

Psychotherapy with veterans who have committed atrocious acts does not follow the traditional treatment model of the "traumatic war neurosis." It is never easy for a therapist to hear the painful details of combat reality. The degree of sadism actually associated with reports of "overkill" in battle and unprovoked massacre, however, prevents the therapist from focusing merely on reactivated guilt, depression, and the "survivor's syndrome." The therapist must "be with" and tolerate the existential reality of the patient's overt or covert view of himself as a murderer.

Psychiatric observations from the Civil War to the Korean Conflict delineate the impact of combat on the soldier and describe a variety of sequelae, especially the "classic traumatic war neurosis." Much of the early psychiatric literature on Vietnam presents the factual, though often misleading finding of a lower incidence of psychiatric casualties from Vietnam than from World War II and Korea. The 12-months' duty assignment in Vietnam exposed men to a time-limited stress and many veterans did not react immediately to this stress and only became "psychiatric casualties" months and even years after their return to the United States. In addition, the early literature (primarily stress studies) also reflected the war as it was fought prior to 1969; prior to the onset of disengagement, lowered morale, decreased combat, the exposure of the killings at My Lai, and the increased use and abuse of drugs.

The combat stress studies of Grinker and Spiegel, as well as case studies of the "classic war neurosis" do not examine acknowledge combat atrocities. The Vietnam combat veterans are now being studied and the results vary. Gault, speaking with recently returned combat soldiers, was impressed with the high incidence of reports of combat "slaughter" and with the varying degrees of/or lack of expressed guilt. Borus, however, interviewed 64 combat soldiers also recently returned from Vietnam, and found only 10% who reported feeling guilty or being upset about their experiences in Vietnam.

Lifton and Shatan have worked with antiwar veterans, discharged a year or more, and feel that these men represent the struggles of many apolitical Vietnam veterans. Lifton has developed the hypothesis that Vietnam was an "atrocity-producing" situation that created a "psychology of survival." Shatan has suggested a "post-Vietnam syndrome" to describe his observations of veterans who make use of self-help groups, and who appear to him to be "in mourning."

Polner, who interviewed veterans in a college setting, stressed the impact of an unheralded return from combat, "no victory parades." He described veterans polarized as either "hawk" or "dove," but called early attention to a group he felt were "haunted" by their combat experiences. Levy studied intensely a group of 60 Marine combat veterans, distinguished not by whether they were "hawk" or "dove," and found them more prone to violence after their Vietnam experience, and he suggested the instituting of a "boot camp in reverse."

Within the Veterans Administration, attempts to correlate Vietnam duty experience to readjustment or traumatic sequelae, again, yield varying results. Strange and Brown found that although Vietnam combat returnees "manifested more aggressive and suicidal threats" their reactions are generally internalized and that potential for violent aggression is no greater than those without Vietnam experience. Bourne, however, feels that "the psychological and social problems of the Vietnam veteran probably exceed those of any previous conflict . . ." and cites their difficulty in communicating their experience, sense of isolation, and drug abuse.

SETTING

The setting of this report is a large Veterans Administration Outpatient clinic that provides a wide range of clinical services—medical, surgical, dental, prosthetics. The psychiatry service includes an outpatient clinic, drug abuse clinic, problem drinking center, and a day-treatment center. Because many veterans shun the VA or other "establishment" health care facilities, we have attempted, where possible, to contact veterans' groups on campuses or other "antiestablishment" veterans' groups.

TREATMENT CONSIDERATIONS

The traumatic war neurosis, as described in the literature following World War II and the Korean Conflict, involved feelings of guilt, depression, anxiety, and/or suppressive symptoms that appeared related to combat experiences but were thought to be essentially "neurotic." That is, the combat experiences, traumatic as they may have been, were in the line of duty and persistent symptoms of guilt or depression were thought to be related to the stirring up of unacceptable, unconscious wishes and fantasies. The standard way to treat combat-related guilt and the depression of the traumatic war neurosis, therefore, was to alleviate the guilt and thereby aid repression by taking the responsibility from the individual and placing it on a higher authority (one was following orders). In addition, treatment consisted of exploring the unconscious wishes and fantasies if necessary, and to treat the consecutive depressions of the surviving soldier—the depression of leaving his family, friends, and the life he would have had if not for military service; and finally the depression caused by separating from his fellow soldiers either by their deaths or his discharge. The inappropriateness of this model for the veteran whose chief complaint involves responsibility for war atrocities is best illustrated by my first encounter with such a veteran.

John (Case 1), in his first interview, blurted out a story of atrocities that left me numbed and frightened. "I am a killer, no one can forgive me. I-we should be shot. There should be a Nuremberg trial for us." What should I say in response to his sobbing self-accusation? Trying to relieve this guilt by placing the responsibility on a higher authority was, as the veteran himself volunteered, a "copout." Treating the consecutive depressions of the surviving soldier was a luxurious clinical exercise to await the day (if he did not act on his intense suicidal impulses) when the initial life and death issues had been resolved. As my experience with these veterans grew, I learned that some had confessed to clergy but they continued to feel guilty; others spoke of "turning themselves in" but none had done so.

How can the therapist respond to the issue of actual participation in atrocities and the varying subjective states associated with those acts? As therapists we most often work with patients who have neurotic guilt over unconscious wishes or impulses, experience psychic distress at the breakthrough of such wishes or with patients who "act out," usually symbolically, their internal distress. The "crimes" of these patients are usually in the form of fantasies or non life-threatening behavior. Therapists do work with patients who have murdered or who have committed violent acts, but usually these patients have been or are in correctional institutions or, as in the situation of the "battered child," some outside authority is exerting superego control.

The "patient who reports atrocities" has been, until that moment in the treatment situation when the actions are revealed, his only judge and jury. These reports may be accompanied by varying degrees of guilt, casualness, or even pride and bravado. The therapist's ability to acknowledge and tolerate both the veteran's objective responsibility and his varying views of himself is of crucial importance in the therapist's sense of "being with" the veteran as they work toward understanding and resolution of conflict. In the cases that follow two veterans describe their responsibility for atrocious acts; only one veteran "feels" guilty. A third case is an example of neurotic guilt for purposes of comparison. (Names and identifying information are fictitious and have been altered to protect the confidentiality of the veterans.)

A CASE OF OBJECTIVE RESPONSIBILITY

Case 1. John was a 22-year-old veteran who came to see me at the urging of a close friend who had been in treatment with me for a year. I had heard that John was depressed, disillusioned, abusing drugs, unable to enjoy anything, and failing in college despite an excellent high school record. Upon entering my office, he said, "I don't know what I'm doing here—I'll be all right." He then began to sob uncontrollably, holding his hands over his face and rocking back and forth in his seat. John had been raised in a middle-class suburb, the second of five children in a family characterized by close family ties and service to the community. John had been accepted into college but when an older brother was killed in Vietnam he enlisted in the Marines and volunteered for Vietnam "to see where it happened."

Once in Vietnam he volunteered as point man—often the most dangerous assignment—and he "shot first and asked questions later." From the beginning he "refused to think of the Vietnamese as people," killed prisoners after entreating them to surrender, and killed civilians on little or no provocation. As his tour in Vietnam neared completion, he came to view his actions with disbelief and horror.

One of his last assignments was to guard a number of high-ranking

Vietcong and during that week he came to know them as people; they shared cigarettes, food, and family snapshots. After a week's interrogation he refused an order from his commanding officer to "blow them away" and stood frozen as the commanding officer and other soldiers killed the prisoners. He felt overwhelmed with guilt and the urge to return to the United States and confess to his father, who was "the only person who could forgive me." However, upon returning to the base camp, he learned that his father had died in an auto accident and he was returned home within 72 hours to attend the funeral.

Following his discharge, he entered but then left college and spent one summer spaced out on mescaline because "I can't stand how I feel straight."

John stated that he was a murderer, guilty of war crimes, that there were many who had done worse, and that there should be a Nuremberg trial for him, his officers, and all government leaders. "No one can forgive me—I don't deserve to live." He also despaired that people cared about what had happened in Vietnam. "It's just something on the news before the sports and weather."

He came to treatment sporadically and then attempted to kill himself while on LSD. He accepted hospitalization, panicked that he would try again to kill himself. However, he remained only a few days and kept only a few follow-up appointments, stating that talking couldn't help.

My next contact with John was a year later when he brought a friend, Mike, who was "cracking up" and whom John had correctly judged needed hospitalization. At that time, John appeared remarkable less depressed and less guilt-ridden. He had spent the year working against the war and had returned to college and had a part-time job.

John was intense, intelligent, and handsome. He seemed like a young man one might encounter in a college debate on the morality of the war but for whom the issue was literally one of life and death. When asked about the change, he said he had needed to believe that just one person cared, that one person could be trusted to know what he had done, and not reject him.

My experience with other veterans who reported guilt over atrocities had been that they were able to do so only after a trusting relationship had been established. My guess is that John had established a measure of trust in me before I ever saw him through his friend who had been in therapy with me. The friend, Mike, whom John brought to the clinic one year later, though paranoid and secretive, also accepted that we could be trusted. John feels that he must "pay his dues" and that telling people about the war and helping other veterans is his way. He also observed that he feels he loves people in general but doubts his ability to ever love in a close relationship. He had had the same girlfriend throughout this time. He expressed concern that he could not return her love but also stated, "she's nice, but plastic; she'll never try to get inside my head about Vietnam."

A CASE OF AN ABSENCE OF GUILT

Case 2. Bob was a 23-year-old ex-Marine referred by local Veterans Administration hospital following an episode in which he had threatened to kill his wife, who had requested an abortion. He had left the hospital against medical advice stating "talking doesn't help" but later agreed to outpatient follow-up.

Bob was the oldest of a large, poor family from a working class neighborhood. His father worked steadily, but his mother had become psychotic when Bob was a teenager. He had become involved in a number of gangs to ensure the protection a "tough guy" reputation would afford him, and when drafted chose to join the Marines because "the Army was too sloppy." He impulsively married his girlfriend "to have someone to write home to." He did well in basic training and was made a squad leader in Vietnam. He described quite mater-of-factly that the only chance for survival was to keep the squad tight and morale high. As the leader he remained "cool", was brutal to POW's and civilians alike, and refused to follow "shit orders" from inexperienced officers. Bob was 13 months "in the bush," refusing R & R because "I was too into killing."

When ordered by a new inexperienced officer to assault a hill strongly defended by the Vietcong, where there had been numerous American casualties in the preceding weeks, Bob reported, "It was me and my men or him." He left ambiguous who killed the officer but stated cooly, "We didn't go up no shit hill and next week we had a new lieutenant." Another time the squad passed through a supposedly pacified village and camped outside. The next morning one man was killed as he walked away from the campsite, and Bob found that during the night the squad had been encirculed by booby traps. Once safely out of the encampment, they returned to the village and "blew them motherfuckers away."

Return to the United States brought Bob face to face with all the problems he had left behind: continued family deterioration, an unfaithful wife, no job training, and tenuous control over his rage. He stated he felt angry and sad all the time. Although he denied any guilt over his actions, he spoke of a kind of resentment "that all that killing has done a job on my head—I'm not the same." He was unable to hold a steady job until he found one as a guard. At that time his symptoms subsided although he continued to speak of murderous rage toward his mother, wife, and "peace nuts." He broke off regular treatment except for "dropin" appointments and medication.

The incidents reported by John and Bob encompass many of the "six principles contributing to slaughter" delineated by Gault: (1) the enemy is everywhere; (2) the enemy is not human; (3) dilution of responsibility; (4) the pressure to act; (5) the natural dominance of the psychopath; and (6) fire power.

For Bob, accustomed to defining his enemy (the other gang) and confronting them face to face in the streets, Vietnam was a constant sneak attack. In fact, the invisible enemy who attacked in the night and "from behind" and the troops of the Army of the Republic of Vietnam (South) who were seen as not taking the war seriously were collectively referred to as "gooks" and "faggots." Bob said he had gone to Vietnam to help "stop Communism" but stated, "You learn pretty fast that that's a bunch of crap." Staying alive became his overriding concern, and anyone, even Americans or South Vietnamese who jeopardized that aim would have been killed, usually by the use of a fragmentation bomb—"fragging"—or "by Charley" in combat.

Certainly some murders between soldiers, committed in Vietnam, do not differ from the Saturday-night brawl, vendettas, or the person gone "berserk" in the United States. However, when Vietnam combat veterans refer to a "fragging," they are speaking of the killing of someone who (as they saw it) threatened their survival. Bob made a distinction between officers who were "OK" and those whom he felt were put in combat command for a brief time to gain promotion.

A CASE OF NEUROTIC GUILT

Case 3. Bill is a 21-year-old high school graduate, from a middle-class family, who described a close family relationship and a desire to "serve his country" before going to college. He joined the Marines and was a radioman in Vietnam.

Bill described great loyalty to his lieutenant and squad, stating that the lieutenant "looked out for us, he wasn't out for medals." He described soldiers who killed prisoners or took "trophies"—for example, cutting off the ears of dead Vietcong and then having their pictures taken—as "animals." He refused R&R not wanting to be separated from his lieutenant and feeling that his safety and survival in Vietnam were linked with the high morale and "morality" of his unit. However, he came close to atrocity himself. His unit was called in to assist an Army unit and when they later found that 23 men of his unit and only two men from the Army unit had been killed, he ran through the camp vowing to kill the Army commanding officer. Instead, he sprayed the bush with machine-gun fire but fears that if there had been Vietnamese "handy" they would have been scapegoated/killed.

He had been in the bush for 11 months when he was sent to a field hospital for evaluation of a 40-lb. weight loss. He was told he had tuberculosis but was returned to combat with a month's supply of medication, "if I lived that long." Despite efforts by his lieutenant, he was not relieved of duty and with one week left to serve, his unit was overrun in the night. The lieutenant was killed but Bill survived multiple gunshot wounds to his chest. He was shot while attempting to pick up the already dead lieutenant, who "fell apart in may hands." He remembers waiting helplessly as the enemy soldier (later to be identified as a 12-year-old boy) prepared to "finish me off." However, the enemy soldier was shot by another Marine and fell dead across Bill. Bill was pinned under the dead Vietnamese for more than an hour and then waited on a launch pad more than six hours for air evacuation. Bleeding profusely and having multiple sucking chest wounds, he credits the medic with saving his life but turns tremulous with rage remembering what he observed of the evacuation priorities—"officers before non-coms, whites before blacks." (It should be noted that most combat veterans and air-rescue personnel report more "democratic" priorities; the critically injured were treated first, even though the relative scarcity of officers with combat training and experience was a factor in evacuation.)

Upon return to the United States and long months of surgery and convalescence, no explanation could be given him regarding his having been sent back into combat with tuberculosis. His recovery was further aggravated by being "isolated" because of his tuberculosis.

He was referred from the medical clinic to the psychiatry service the day before Christmas, stating, "I can't go through with it (the holidays, family gatherings). I can't enjoy anything. I feel guilty and depressed all the time. Why did I live, why did I survive? Lieutenant K. should have lived; he had a wife and children." And then with an anger and a despair that could not be comforted away but only experienced with him, he said, "The war was a farce—we got carved up for nothing—I'm no peace nut but we were used."

COMMENT

My purpose in presenting these three cases is to distinguish "the patient who reports atrocities" from the patient suffering classical traumatic war neurosis and to suggest, on the basis·of my clinical experience, how patient and therapist can best work toward a therapeutic alliance. My purpose is not to explore the individual psychodynamics of each case—for example, why John rather than Bill became involved in atrocity—but to suggest ways by which these patients are best approached and "engaged" in a trusting relationship so that treatment of their individual problems can proceed.

These three young men, from differing backgrounds and with differing personality structures and strengths were changed by their experiences in Vietnam. They had each served in Vietnam during 1967-1968 and came to the Mental Hygiene Service between one and three years after their return to the United States. They, like the majority of veterans I have seen who have reported atrocities, did not speak of them immediately upon return to the United States, as did Gault's subjects, nor would they have been seen as having a difficult or traumatic readjustment had they been evaluated immediately upon reentry to either stateside duty or civilian life. As one veteran described it: "I was playing my cards pretty close to the chest." Each of these three men had held positions of strategic importance to their combat units; each was in receipt of one or more Purple Hearts, and each had been decorated for bravery. They each sought help at a point of crisis after a period of time spent trying to "forget." This pattern of "delayed reaction" is typical of the Vietnam combat veterans I have seen who have been involved in atrocities.

When the patient reports atrocities, where does the therapist begin? Perhaps we start by reminding ourselves that atrocities are as old as man and as close at hand as our own well-defended but nontheless very real sadistic potential. Atrocities have occurred in all wars, but perhaps what made Vietnam different was the concentration of atrocities. (due in part to the guerrilla nature of the war, superior firepower, and the phenomenon of the "body count") and the exposure of these atrocities. The isolated reported episodes of the killing of POWs, civilians, or fellow soldiers known in previous American war efforts have now been documented by the hundreds in Vietnam.

When the patient reports atrocities, my experience has been that the first task of treatment is for the therapist to confront his/her own sadistic feelings, not only in response to the patient, but in terms of his/her own potential as well. The therapist must be able to envision the possibility that under extreme physical and psychic stress, or in an atmosphere of overt license and encouragement, he/she, too, might very well murder. Without this effort by the therapist, treatment is between the "good" therapist and the "bad" out-of-control patient, and the patient leaves or stays only because he has found the censure he consciously or unconsciously feels he deserves. The therapist should not deny the reality of the patient's perception of his Vietnam experience because if he does the patient may correctly assume he is being "cleaned up" or "white-washed" in order for the therapist to tolerate and treat him. For patients who express guilt about their actual participation in atrocious acts, the therapist must align himself with that part of the patient's ego that now views his actions as ego-alien, and explore with the patient those factors that occurred when his usual sense of right and wrong gave way. The establishment of such an alliance is difficult but critical.

Hopefully, by seeking out a therapist the veteran is seeking under-standing and resolution of his conflict and confusion, rather than pun-ishment or rationalizations. The veteran needs the strength of the ther-apeutic alliance in order to tolerate "remembering," working through, and eventual repression. His ego-ideal has been drastically compromised and many veterans complain of feeling "dead" or "wasted." Reports of feeling dead have been observed by a number of clinicians including Lifton and Shatan. For many veterans there seems to have been an identification or introjection of the people they killed or saw killed. To "cease living," therefore, is a form of atonement. John described the dilemma: "Before Vietnam, I only cared about sports and having a good time; now, I want to scream at friends and relatives that people are still dying while the NFL is playing—but how can I? If it weren't for Vietnam, I'd be watching the game, too; so I just walk away."

Patients most easily discuss the external precipitating stresses of an atrocity and tend to deny or avoid internal factors. The loosening of the usual constraints on sadism may involve some soldiers in atrocity for very personal reasons, such as the opportunity to release repressed anger at a primary object or defense against castration anxiety. For others, however, the very loosening of these constraints mobilizes a signal anxiety that may propel them out of the combat situation. An indication of who was really being killed or what was being defended against may be found in serial combat dreams. Many Vietnam combat veterans complain of night terrors, nightmares, insomnia, and they relate these concerns to the fact that night was the most dangerous time in Vietnam. "I guess I'm OK during the day, but it all piles up on me at night." During the first year away from Vietnam

John had a progression of dreams that at first repeated actual combat experiences but then began to incorporate buddies and later friends and relatives as the enemy. During the treatment he had a recurring dream that he and his dead brother were fighting and "he was beating the shit out of me." John's worst fear was that he had gone to Vietnam to avenge his brother's death and that in the dream his brother was punishing him. It also seemed that he was furious at his brother for dying, thereby "forcing" him to give up college and go to war.

There are clear difficulties and dangers to this type of exploration. During treatment the patient may bolt from the painful feelings and either cope maladaptively or become suicidal. My experience, however, is that this type of veteran comes to treatment because repression is not working and, although he is coping, he feels unworthy to live. Patients like John seemed typical of a kind of veteran who feels he needs to pay his dues or render some form of retribution before he can forgive himself. They may establish an individualized pattern of treatment, such as time spent with the therapist in work on their grief and guilt, and time spent literally "in the field."

Veterans with severe character disorders, or disturbed veterans, like Bob, who lack a clear feeling of guilt, usually come to a treatment facility under duress from anti-social symptoms, family, or the police. A supportive assessment of their coping potential and defenses seems indicated rather than an uncovering form of treatment. Their faulty ego-development and control have blunted their sense of guilt, even though they may fear exposure, punishment, or reprisals. These patients tend to "act" rather than "feel," and because of the danger that they may respond with a regressive coping pattern of drugs or criminal behavior, the therapist should capitalize on whatever "motivation", however "imperfect", has brought the veteran to the clinic.

One of the overriding concerns of the combat veterans I have talked to is the extent to which there was individual latitude about who was the enemy and, therefore, who was killed in Vietnam. One veteran, raised in a working-class ghetto, said that before Vietnam "you knew what the limits were." Many of his gang were in prison by the time he left for Vietnam, but there was a logic: "To kill meant to go to jail." In Vietnam he was exposed to situations where men who were known to have killed prisoners, civilians, or fellow soldiers were "walking around scot-free." He looked to his commanders for the old "logic" but claims he found denial, fear, disinterest, or collusion. Accustomed to looking for a harsh outside superego, he describes himself panicking as he realized "anything goes." He feared losing control, but, even worse, that someone might "waste me and never be punished for it."

This group of patients is usually chronically anxious, angry, or frankly paranoid. Appearing "manly" and "tough" are common concerns, and the therapist hears frequently of their striking out at someone who brushed up against them or cut in front of them. They complain in circular fashion that if it were not for Vietnam they would not be so "touchy" but that "if only" they were back in Vietnam they could "waste" someone who "hassled" them. Self-defeating or self-destructive behaviors predominate; they lose jobs, alienate friends/family, provoke arrest/imprisonment, and are in frequent automobile accidents.

Establishment of a therapeutic alliance for this group of patients is the treatment rather than the facilitator of treatment. It is critical that in every sense the therapist be "for real": a "real person" more so than a transference figure, and a "real person" respectful of the veteran's strengths and concerned about but not "put off" by their psychopathology. Countertransference with veterans who do not openly express their guilt stresses the therapist's judgmental tolerance to its limit. In my experience, however, concerns about trust and confidentiality are paramount; and it is the constancy of the "person" of the therapist that enables these patients to confide in another person rather than act on their fears and projections. After three years of a "dropin" form of contact, one Vietnam veteran related a combat experience that had plagued him for four years. He came in on the anniversary of the event and said, "I just got to tell you—I can't hold it inside any longer."

Veterans like Bill suffer from the more traditionally described traumatic war neurosis, albeit with the very special characteristics of Vietnam aggravating their dilemma. He feared both killing and being killed. After Bill had killed his first Vietcong in fact-to-face combat, he felt overwhelmed with guilt and wrote to his father asking for forgiveness and acceptance of what he "was going to have to do for the next year of my life." Wishing to live, while realizing that many will die or be wounded, aggravates the survivor's guilt. To the extent that one's anger during combat may shift to one's own men—as, for example, when Bill blamed the Army commanding officer for the loss of so many Marines—the veteran may feel that his anger or injuries killed the others and enabled him to survive. Out of this guilt the veteran may develop suppressive symptoms or passive-dependent styles of coping, a phenomenon well known in the World War II and Korean

Conflict population. The treatment of traumatic war neurosis involves the unweighting of combat-related guilt in order to aid repression and the treatment of veteran's consecutive depressions.

Therapists within the Veterans Administration have acquired a knowledge of "Nam" (as it is referred to by the veterans), its terrain, villages, types of weaponry and operations, and specific battles. This knowledge and awareness gives an immediacy to the veteran's sense of the therapist's "being there" with him, and is also useful when veterans are downplaying or avoiding certain issues. For example, one veteran who complained of chronic depression, and nightmares (from which he would awake in a profuse sweat with his face feeling "red hot"), casually dismissed Vietnam as a possible factor in his difficulties because "I never saw combat; I only drove supply trucks." I asked him about his route, and then reflected back to him that I had known veterans who had driven the same route (through an exposed mountain pass) and who were under frequent attack. How had it been for him? His eyes filled with tears "remembering", seemingly for the first time in a year, the death of his best friend, who had been incinerated in the cabin of an oil tanker when their supply convoy was attacked. He "remembered" his futile attempts to rescue his friend and his despair and rage when he was driven back by the intense heat that burned his face and clothing. He had come to the clinic within a week of the first anniversary of the friend's death and was successfully able to mourn this loss.

To a greater or lesser degree, many Vietnam combat veterans I have seen feel or complain of the impact or stigma of atrocities. One, an amputee who served only a few months in Vietnam and witnessed no atrocities, was greeted upon his return to college with questions like, "How many babies did you kill?" For many months thereafter he told people he had lost his leg in an auto accident, not wanting to be associated with Vietnam.

Combat veterans may playdown or embellish their "war stories", but initially their reports should be taken at face value. The only report that should not be accepted at face value, although one may choose not to challenge it initially, is the patient's report that combat in Vietnam had no effect on him.

Clearly, many combat veterans have managed a successful readjustment; that is, they have been able to cope with the experience/effects of combat (some feeling it deepened their respect for life) rather than being traumatized by them. For others the effect of combat has been experienced along a continuum of a life pattern of violence. The Vietnam combat veteran who reports atrocities presents a special therapeutic challenge.

The therapist's countertransference and real, natural response to the realities of the patient's experience must be continually monitored and confronted for a therapeutic relationship to be

Drs. Gerald Klerman, Lionelle Wells, and Richard Wolman aided in this study.

References

1 Kerry J: The Vietnam veterans against the war, in *The New Soldier*. New York, Collier Books, 1971, p 92.

2. Hammond WA: *A Treatise on Insanity in Its Medical Relations*. London, HK Lewis, 1883.

3. Glass AU: Psychotherapy in the combat zone. *Am J Psychiatry* 110:725-731, 1954.

4. Bourne PG: *Men, Stress and Vietnam*. Boston, Little Brown & Co. 1970, pp. 7-23.

5. Nordheimer J: Post-Vietnam War Syndrome (series of three articles), *New York Times*, August 1972.

6. Bloch HS: Brief sleep treatment with chlorpromazine. *Compr Psychiatry* 11:346-355, 1970.

7. Bourne PG, Coli WM, Datel WE: Affect levels of special forces soldiers under threat of attack. *Psychol Rep* 22:363-366, 1968.

8. Grinker RR, Spiegel J: *Men Under Stress*. New York, McGraw-Hill Book Co, Inc, 1945.

9. Kardiner A: *The Traumatic Neurosis of War*. New York, Paul B Hoeber & Sons, Inc, 1941.

10. Salmon TW: The war neuroses and their lessons. *NY State J Med* 109:933-944, 1919.

11. Zetzel ER: *The Capacity for Emotional Growth*. New York, International Universities Press Inc, 1970, pp 12-32.

12. Gault WB: Some remarks on slaughter. *Am J Psychiatry* 128:4:82-84, 1971.

13. Borus JF: Reentry: I. Adjustment issues facing the Vietnam veterans. *Arch Gen Psychiatry* 28:501-506, 1973.

14. Lifton RJ: Testimony before the Subcommittee on Veteran's Affairs, November and December 1969, and January 1970, in Oversight of Medical Care of Veterans Wounded in Vietnam. Government Printing Office, 1970, pp. 419-510.

15. Lifton RJ: Home from the war: The psychology of survival. *Atlantic Monthly* 230:56-72, 1972.

16. Lifton RJ: *Home from the War, Vietnam Veterans: Neither Victims nor Executioners*. New York, Simon & Schuster Inc, 1973.

17. Shatan CF: "How do we turn off the guilt?" *Human Behavior* 2:56-61, 1973.

18. Shatan CF: The grief of soldiers: Vietnam combat veterans' self-help movement, *Am J Orthopsychiatry* 43:640-653, 1973.

19. Polner M: No victory parades, in *The Return of the Vietnam Veteran*. New York, Holt Rinehart & Winston Inc, 1971.

20. Levy C: Testimony before the Subcommittee on Veterans' Affairs Nov. 25 and Dec 3, 1970, in *Unemployment and Overall Readjustment Problems of Returning Veterans*. Government Printing Office, pp. 204-218, 1971.

21. Strange RE, Brown DE: Home from the war: A study of psychiatric problems in Vietnam returnees. *Am J Psychiatry* 127:488-492, 1970.

22. Bourne PG: The Vietnam veteran: Department of Medicine and Surgery, Veterans Administration in *The Vietnam Veteran in Contemporary Society, Collected Materials Pertaining to the Young Veterans*. Government Printing Office, pp IV-83, 1972.

XI.

Some Remarks on Slaughter* †

William Barry Gault

During the author's two years as an Army psychiatrist, he learned that many relatively normal young men he interviewed had observed or participated in the slaughter of defenseless Vietnamese people. Six psychological, social, and mechanical principles contributed to the occurrence of such slaughter: The universalization of the enemy; the "cartoonization" of the victim; the dilution of responsibility; the pressure to act; the natural dominance of the psychopath; and the ready availability of firepower.

Bloch[1], Bey[2], and others have reported on the experiences of Army psychiatrists with combat units in Viet Nam. Their reports emphasized what had been learned about effective treatment of psychiatric problems in the field. I did not serve in Viet Nam or in any other combat area, but during two years as a psychiatrist at Fort Knox, particularly during a year in its Mental Hygiene Consultation Service, I evaluated scores of Viet Nam returnees referred for symptoms that often began just before or after their transition to stateside duty.

Goldsmith and Cretekos[3] have commented interestingly on such

*This paper was one of the winners of the Essay Prize on Aggression and Violence awarded at the 124th annual meeting of the American Psychiatric Association, Washington, D. C., May 3-7, 1971.
†Reprinted from the *American Journal of Psychiatry* 128:82-84, 1971. Copyright American Psychiatric Association, 1971.

cases and have been able to recognize several distinct types of soldier vulnerable to such decompensation. It is not my purpose in this paper to further discuss the clinical psychiatric phenomena related to leaving combat. In my conversations with these men, absorbing at length their observations and reflections on the experience of combat and the dramatic contrast between it and routine civilized life, I have developed certain ideas regarding the psychology of slaughter that I wish to explain here.

"Slaughter" is defined in *Webster's Unabridged Dictionary* as "the extensive, violent, bloody or wanton destruction of life; carnage." In using the word I wish to emphasize the connotation of the victim's defenselessness, whether the victim be a disarmed prisoner or an unarmed civilian, and thus to distinguish slaughter from the mutual homicide of the actual combatants in military battle.

The discovery that many of the young Viet Nam returnees whom I was interviewing had in one way or another participated in slaughter was not, in most cases an item of obvious primary relevance in their individual case histories. Hearing a patient mention casually and in passing the brutal acts performed by himself or his fellow soldiers, the psychiatrist—totally unacquainted with the necessarily brutal realities of combat—all too readily reaches the conventional conclusion that his patient is concealing by denial and isolation of affect intense and disturbing feelings. In so doing, he makes the conventional mistake of assuming that his patient sees things more or less as he does and that what is important to him now was important, in another place and time, to his patient. My experience has led me to conclude that when soldiers observe or perpetrate slaughter, they often feel profoundly and enduringly guilty, and often they do not.

I have come to understand a number of devices that I shall try to explain and exemplify through which relatively normal men overcame and eventually neutralized their natural repugnance toward slaughter. In addition I will list some realities of combat on account of which, repugnance notwithstanding, slaughter is permitted to occur.

PRINCIPLES CONTRIBUTING TO SLAUGHTER

1. The enemy is everywhere. The weary, overburdened U.S. infantryman in Viet Nam realistically perceives intense hatred and immediate physical threat from every quarter. He prudently doubts the loyalty of every village-if not, indeed every villager. He knows he cannot distinguish farmer from terrorist, innocent youth from Viet Cong spy. Moreover, in this war of mines and booby traps, in this sweltering land of swamps, dysentery, malaria, and the omnipresent stench of excrement and

decay, he feels that the country itself may murder him at any moment. In so pervasively and implacably hostile a situation, it is not surprising that the young soldier quickly seizes upon a desperate trust in and loyalty to his own immediate unit—company, platoon, perhaps just his squad—and unswervingly identifies everything else, young or old, male or female, animate or inanimate, as his ubiquitous, murderous enemy. He does not have the leisure to individuate and particularize his enemy; he is drowning in a sea of enmity. This perception I call the universalization of the enemy.

2. The enemy is not human. Historically some armies have adopted this conviction officially. It is a mainstay of most religious wars and indispensable in large-scale imperial and colonial operations. I suspect that, unofficially at least, the image of a degraded enemy is essential to the psychology of any robustly homicidal combat team. In any event it is important in the thinking of American soldiers in Viet Nam. Orientals are regularly referred to as "gooks" and "dinks"; are said to be "like children", to experience strong emotions only in a fleeting, evanescent way, soon subsiding to their presumed baseline state of impassive indifference even to matters of life and death. And above all, Orientals are held to be inscrutable, strange, profoundly and irreconcilably different from and incomprehensible to Western man. These attitudes serve to psychologically soften the experience of killing Orientals, so that some soldiers feel that the individual dead enemy was "not like you and me, but more like a Martian or something." I have come to think of this psychological process as the preparatory "cartoonization" of the victim. To observe it one must disregard all official United States statements and policies as well as the guarded, washed-out lingo of officers and other bureaucratically approved spokesmen and listen instead to the everyday language of everyday soldiers.

3. Dilution of responsibility. The individual infantryman often has the sense that responsibility for the specific slaughter of a specific victim is not precisely his but that it is shared. What might be termed "vertical dilution" takes place within the chain of command. For example, battalion command orders the eradication of enemy strongholds in a given area. Company command dispatches a platoon to clean out Viet Cong snipers in a given village. Finally, a squad is directed to wipe out a cluster of suspicious huts. Horizontal dilution then occurs as the entire squad simultaneously directs a torrent of small arms fire, rifle grenades, etc., through the flimsy thatch of the buildings. When the lowly rifleman, picking through the rubble, discovers the corpses of a few mothers and their children, his dismay is not what it might have been had he alone, consciously and deliberately, killed a

single specific woman or child. However ethically or philosophically similar, the roles of executioner and bombardier are psychologically very different.

4. The pressure to act. This factor in the psychology of the combat infantryman can be divided into two general themes: the repudiation of passivity and the desire for vengeance. A soldier is expected to be aggressive. General military prinicples emphasize the need to strike first, act swiftly and decisively, dominate the field of battle, control the lines of fire, keep the enemy on the run, search and destroy, etc. Moreover, in war, inaction is virtually unbearable. Soldiers universally grumble about waiting—that powerful generator of anxiety—and good leaders always keep their troops busy and active. But a rifleman's proper business by definition is the use of his rifle. His role comes to full fruition only in the act of firing his weapon, and a combat unit that does not get a chance to fight become restive. Frequently, however, our infantry units in Viet Nam suffer the gruesome depredations of enemy activity without getting a chance to face the enemy. Mines hideously mutilate the legs, genitals, and lower abdomen, and a bewildering variety of diabolical booby traps kill and maim the rifleman's comrades before his eyes, while no enemy appears for convenient retaliation. The frantic soldier becomes so avid to avenge the suffering of his fellows that eventually any object will suffice to absorb his rage. As one young sergeant told me matter-of-factly, regarding his unit's wanton devastation of a relatively innocuous village, "We took too many casualties; somebody had to pay."

5. The natural dominance of the psychopath. During the actual waging of war, especially a war like that in Viet Nam, standard civilized conventions and prohibitions are widely suspended. Trust, decency, restraint, and gentleness are of little use in the face of relentless pressure to kill or be killed. In such an atmosphere, the man of blunted sensibilities and ready violence, unburdened by empathy or compassion and seeing others merely as objects; the man of restless, aggressively stimulus-seeking disposition; the enthusiastic advocate of wanton destruction—in short, the psychopath—finds himself at last in a world suited to his character. His will thus often prevails; his conduct often is seen as exemplary. He thrives and often leads. War confirms his old conviction that might is right and the rest is nonsense.

6. Firepower. This last consideration is a mechanical, not a psychological one. I refer to the formidable technology of arms whereby a solitary man's destructiveness is preternaturally magnified. Long gone are the days when the sharp-shooting musketeer saved his single precious shot

until the last possible moment of his individuated enemy's clearly visible approach. Today's rifleman carries a lightweight M-16 that spits in one second ten strangely small bullets at bone-shattering velocity. His technique usually is not to aim it but to get it pointed in the enemy's general direction and discharge thither a torrent of destruction. It serves also as a grenade launcher, making every soldier a miniature artileryman. Terrified and furious teenagers by the tens of thousands have only to twitch their index fingers, and what was a quiet village is suddenly a slaughterhouse.

The following typical case is reported because of its representative nature and its illustration of at least four (universalization, cartoonization, dominance of the psychopath, and a pressure to act) of the six factors.

Case Reports

Case 1. This 20-year-old divorced enlisted man was referred to the Mental Hygiene Consultation Service by the commanding officer of the unit to which he had been assigned after his return from Viet Nam. The CO reported that the man was so refractory to discipline that "there must be something wrong with him." Indeed, this patient's history was monotonously that of an antisocial psychopath in whom wanton aggression (vandalism, bullying, fire-setting, animal-torturing) in latency was followed by the usual gamut of truancy, brawling, and increasingly serious crime, until one day in court he was offered the option of a lesser charge and suspended sentence provided he would join the Army at once. There he continued to fare rather badly until he was sent to Viet Nam where, in a combat unit, he incurred no disciplinary action until a change of commanding officers shortly before the end of his tour. In his interview with me, this enlisted man spoke very admiringly of his first combat CO and very contemptuously of the second, under whom he was formally punished on several occasions and whom he likened to his present commander, who had referred him to the Mental Hygiene Consultation Service.

He explained the difference between the despised and the admired officers by the following anecdote.

The first week the new guy is running the company he decides we'll set up an ambush. So we're getting in position and a dink comes down the trail and sees us. So we grab him. New we know that if you try to lay an ambush and a dink sees you, you ain't laying no ambush—you're going to be in one. Unless you shoot the dink. But this new guy says: "No, take him back to camp and put a guard on him." Guard him! Well, I knew right away this guy was going to be trouble.

Further discussion with this enlisted man revealed that the "dink" of his anecdote was a boy of probably about 12 years.

The officer who refused to permit the slaughter of that child did so at a considerable expense. There was real risk of physical jeopardy to himself and his men, whose complete distrust of all Vietnamese civilians was by no means groundless. He could be sure of eliciting at this early critical hour the surliness and distrust of the combat-seasoned men in his new command. In all probability my psychopathic patient was not the only one of them who regarded with disfavor his unwillingness to slaughter.

On diverse occasions I have been told of the following practice by (among others) several mental hygiene patients, an infantry officer who was my neighbor, a corpsman on duty with me in the emergency room, and a medical officer of my acquaintance.

When a group of enemy prisoners is not readily coerced into giving information to their captors, the practice has been devised of questioning them aloft aboard a helicopter. When they are slow to answer, one is pushed to his death. The question is then repeated, and often it is answered.

Every time I heard of this practice the narrator manifested a certain gusto and seemed to regard it as humorous. Regardless of the anecdote's validity, the manner in which these basically.normal men related it gave me a vivid sense of the extent to which the normal affective significance of slaughter is readily circumvented in war. In this case I think the dehumanization of the victim is the chief mechanism.

I mentioned at the outset that the wartime slaughter does not always escape guilt. The following case is a good example.

Case 2. This 24-year-old married enlisted man, a military policeman, consulted me during my regular visits to the stockade, where he was a guard. He complained of headaches, chronic anxiety, restlessness, and insomnia (both difficulty falling asleep and subsequent fitful sleeping). He dated these from the latter portion of a recent tour in Viet Nam, where, he said: "I figure I seen too much crap." Asked to explain what he meant, he gave this example.

We take some RPG (rocket) rounds from a village. So the lieutenant, platoon leader, takes me and about ten other guys into the village and we round everybody up. Then he asks them "Where's the VC?" Nobody says nothing. You know the gooks. So he picks out a couple of old women and stands them over by a well and says: "Tell us where the VC are or we throw them down the well." The gooks still don't talk. So he has a couple of guys push the old women down the well, then throw a grenade in the well. That's the kind of crap I mean.

He further explained that while in Viet Nam "you see something like that—you don't think about it too much," but that since his return he had found his thoughts returning to this and other episodes of carnage and that he had had occasional nightmares on similar themes.

COMMENT

I have not ascertained why similar experiences provoke so much more guilt in one man than in another. I am unwilling to attempt to draw any large lessons from my observations. But I think it safe to say that in Viet Nam a number of fairly ordinary young men have been psychologically ready to engage in slaughter and that moreover this readiness is by no means incomprehensible.

References

1. Bloch HS: Army clinical psychiatry in the combat zone: 1967-1968. *Amer J Psychiat* 126:289-298, 1969.
2. Bey DR: Division psychiatry in Viet Nam. *Amer J Psychiat* 127:288-232, 1970.
3. Goldsmith W, Cretekos C: Unhappy odysseys; psychiatric hospitalizations among Vietnam returnees. *Arch Gen Psychiat* 20:78-83, 1969.

Child Abuse

A 23-year-old college graduate gives birth to her first child. Within three months she finds herself frightened of being alone with the child. Resentful of the helpless infant who has totally altered her relationship with her husband and who seemingly receives more love than she, the mother, receives, the mother becomes hateful. She succumbs to her impulses and pinches the child whenever the child cries. At times she allows the child to go unfed, unchanged in soiled diapers. She feels she is on the verge of drowning the child in the bath. She feels she must "be crazy" to think such thoughts and fears the very treatment she desperately needs. Her family ignores her hints and offers her false reassurances. Will she kill her child?

This is not an idle question. Physical abuse of children, commonly known as "child battery," has received widespread publicity. There are approximately six thousand reported cases of physical abuse of children each year and many more may go unreported or undetected. The exact scope of the problem is unknown. Every instance is of course tragic. Social service agencies have been developed to "protect children." Further research efforts are underway. What types of parents are likely to abuse their children? How can they be recognized. What types of therapeutic interventions are likely to succeed? Dr. Arthur Green reviews the child abuse syndrome and presents data drawn from his experience with child-abusing families in New York. While the phenomena of child abuse does not deserve the exaggerated accounts often given in public media, the child abuse syndrome constitutes a severe social problem and a type of "double jeopardy." For not only do we have battered children but also the increased likelihood that such children will grow up to be brutal and potentially violent adults.

XII.

The Child Abuse Syndrome and the Treatment of Abusing Parents* †

Arthur H. Green

The age old phenomenon of child abuse, a severe dysfunction of parenting, has only recently attracted the attention of mental health professionals. Psychological studies of abusing parents were not carried out until the mid 1960's when the passage of medical reporting laws by all 50 states brought these parents under investigation by the courts and child protective agencies.

The child abuse law in New York State became effective on July 1, 1964. During the first 12-month period, 313 cases of child abuse were reported, with 16 deaths. The statistics for 1972 indicate that 2710 cases were reported, with 58 deaths and in the first 9 months of this year, 76 deaths have already been reported[1]. The ninefold increase in reported abuse over a seven-year period reflects a nationwide trend, and is due to an improvement in reporting procedures as well as an absolute increase in the incidence of child abuse. It is believed by some that child abuse is the *leading cause of death in children* exceeding infectious diseases, leukemia, and accidents[2]. The proliferation of child abuse might bear some re-

*This work was partially supported by Public Health Service Grant MH 18897 from the National Institute of Mental Health, Center for Studies of Suicide Prevention.

† This paper was presented at the Symposium on Violence. Georgetown University Medical Center, October 26, 1973.

lationship to the alarming general increase of violence in our society, demonstrated by the rising incidence of violent crime, delinquency, suicide, and lethal accidents. It is urgent that the prevention and treatment of child abuse be given the highest priority by those concerned with the welfare of children and families, but rational methods of treatment can only be based upon an understanding of the phenomenon of child abuse, of which so little is known. Therefore, it is necessary to explore the roles and motivations of the participants in this tragic process within the context of the family and its immediate environment. This presentation will attempt to develop a logical treatment program for abuse-prone parents from a body of clinical observations and research data recently gathered from a sizable number of abused children and their mothers.

A comprehensive investigation of child abuse was carried out at the Downstate Medical Center from 1970 to 1972 with the aim of studying the impact of physical abuse on the psychological functioning and development of 60 children and exploring the nature of this violent behavior in the parents[3]. The results of the study revealed that the abused children manifested major psychological, neurological, and cognitive deficits when compared to nonabused "normal" controls. The majority of the abused and controlled subjects were black or Puerto Rican ghetto residents from a lower class socio-economic background. The mothers of the abused children were differentiated from the mothers of the nonabused sample by the way they perceived their children[4]. The abused children were reported to be more self-destructive and more aggressive both at home and in school. A larger number of abused children required more attention than their siblings. The mothers of the abused children also described more frequent difficulties with their parents and spouses. These relationships were marred by criticism, rejection, and physical beatings which resulted in the inability of these women to depend on their family for child-rearing assistance. This facilitated their turning toward their children for dependency gratification. The punishment and criticism experienced by these mothers at the hands of their own parents reinforced their feelings of having been burdensome children, and promoted their identification with a hostile, rejecting parental figure. The mother's perception of the abused child as the most aggressive and demanding of her offspring made this child vulnerable to scapegoating.

Outpatient psychiatric treatment of several of the abused children and their mothers provided additional information about the dynamics of child abuse. Child abuse may be construed as the end result of an interaction among three major variables: (a) Parental personality attributes which contribute to their "abuse-proneness" and are incompatible with adequate child rearing, (b) characteristics of the child which increases the likelihood of his being abused, and (c) immediate environmental stresses which maximize the burden of child rearing.

PERSONALITY CHARACTERISTICS OF ABUSE PRONE PARENTS

(1) The parents rely on the child for the gratification of dependency needs unsatisfied in their relationships with their spouses and families. This constitutes role-reversal.

(2) The parents manifest impairment of impulse control based on childhood experience with harsh punishment and identification with violent adult models.

(3) The parents are handicapped by a poor self-concept. They feel worthless and devalued, reflective of the rejection and criticism accorded to them by adults during childhood.

(4) They display disturbances in identity formation. Identifications are shifting and unstable, and are dominated by hostile introjects derived from the internalization of "bad" self and object representations of early childhood.

(5) They respond to assaults to their fragile self-esteem with a compensatory adaptation. Because of their need to maintain a positive facade, they must desperately defend themselves against the awareness of underlying feelings of worthlessness by frequent use of projection and externalization as mechanisms of defense.

(6) The projection of negative parental attributes onto the child causes him to be misperceived and utilized as a scapegoat to bear the brunt of the parent's aggression.

Case 1. Sonia, a 6-year-old Puerto Rican girl, was severely beaten by her mother when she was 4, resulting in a fractured femur. Sonia was the daughter by Mrs. G's first husband, who had left her when Sonia was 1 year of age, after frequent quarrelling, drinking, and "running around." Mrs. G. subsequently entered a common-law relationship with a man who fathered her two young boys.

Mrs. G. initially married in order to escape from her brutal godparents, who had raised her since the age of 18 months after she had been abandoned by her mother. They had been extremely punitive and restrictive. Mrs. G. remembered one occasion in which her stepfather had broken a flowerpot over her head. Mrs. G's marriage was arranged by the godparents. She went to work in a factory and was virtually ignored by her husband. She soon became pregnant, but did not want a child, as her husband spent no time with her. He deserted when she was six weeks pregnant, and Mrs. G moved in with her sister-in-law to have the baby. She hoped for a boy, stating, "I don't like girls, boys are more interesting." In addition to displacing her rage toward her ex-husband and godparents onto Sonia, Mrs. G obviously identifies with her little girl and brutalizes her in the same manner as her own experience at the hands of her godparents. She described the following feelings toward Sonia. "Since she was born, I let out all the anger and frustration that I had in myself on her. Whenever she came to me, I sent her away with a beating." It is worth noting that Mrs. G's relationship with her male children is better.

CHARACTERISTICS OF THE CHILD WHICH CONTRIBUTE TO HIS ABUSE-PRONENESS AND SCAPEGOATING

(1) *Pathological traits,* which might create an extra burden for "average" parents.

(a) Extreme physical or psychological deviancy of the child. Children with major physical defects and congenital anomalies, as well as psychotic, retarded, or brain-damaged youngsters are tolerated poorly by narcissistic parents who regard them as new editions of their own defective self-image. These children are also extremely burdensome and increase the task of child rearing.

Case 2. Martin, a 7-year-old white boy, was referred to the Bureau of Child Welfare by school personnel who noticed numerous marks on his body. Mrs. C., his mother, admitted hitting him daily, often with a broomstick because of his disruptive behavior, which included restlessness, excessive demands for attention, silliness, and his failure to learn. She felt that Martin's misbehaving was an effort to punish her. Mrs. C. complained about her alcoholic husband's failure to involve himself with Martin, and her three other young children.

Mrs. C. reported an unhappy childhood marked by a frustrating relationship with her mother, who consistently criticized and punished her, while showing affection to her four brothers. Her mother forced her out of the house when she was 16.

Psychiatric examination of Martin revealed a clumsy, awkward child who was agitated and hyperactive. Speech was grossly impaired, and he was preoccupied with uncontrollable aggressive and destructive fantasies. There was a pronounced lag in his acquisition of speech and motor functions. The neurological examination indicated impaired motor coordination and perceptual motor functioning, with an abnormal EEG. His full scale IQ on the WISC was 72. Mrs. C. admitted disliking Martin from birth, because he was "difficult," and demanded so much attention.

(b) Children who respond poorly to nurtutance. These may be colicky, irritable, and hypertonic infants who are difficult to satisfy and comfort. The mothers perceive their unresponsiveness as a rejection reminiscent of experiences with their own parents, intensifying their sense of inadequacy.

(c) Older children who display difficulties with impulse comtrol. They manifest such behavior problems as lying, stealing, assaultiveness, and are often disruptive in school. They relate to significant objects in a provocative, sado-masochistic fashion. They clearly find some gratification in their ability to elicit punishment from the abusive parent.

(2) *Normal or "Accidental" Traits*, which are misperceived or only attain special significance for abuse-prone parents.

(a) The child identified with a hated person or situation: For example, a mother will beat a child whose conception forced her into a premature and unhappy marriage. Another mother will abuse a child who resembles a despised ex-husband or boyfriend.

Case 3. **Sam, a 9-year-old Jamaican boy, was severely beaten with a** broomstick by his mother for distributing the family's food stamps at school. This event transpired shortly after his return from Jamaica where he had been cared for by several "babysitters" since the age of 2 when his mother left him and his year old brother in order to come to New York. Mrs. R. had beaten Sam frequently as an infant before she left him, and he and his brother were given regular severe beatings by the woman who was responsible for most of their care. Mrs. P. subsequently had three out-of-wedlock children in New York. She readily agreed to allow Sam to live with her own mother after she was reported to the Bureau of Child Welfare.

Mrs. R. had conceived Sam when she was 16 and had broken off with had the baby. Another son was born 16 months later, and Mrs. R left for New York shortly thereafter. Mrs. R. recently married the father of her youngest child and has not visited Sam since he was placed with the grandmother. Mrs. R. could only cope with this unfortunate child, whom she unconsciously blamed for her mother's abuse and abandonment of her, by subjecting him to the same punishment.

9(b) The child whose parent remarries and is subsequently regarded as an unwelcome and burdensome "stepchild" by the stepparent: the stepchild is often treated as a sibling rival who threatens the stepparent's dependency on the mate. The stepchild also becomes a convenient target for the stepparent's hostility originally directed toward the spouse.

Case 4. **Don, an 11-year-old black child, was severely beaten by his step-**father resulting in multiple contusions and lacerations of his back and buttocks necessitating his hospitalization. Don is an only child who had lived with his mother and maternal grandparents on a farm in the South. Don remained with his grandparents when his mother came to New York to find employment. Wven his mother married Mr. R., Don, then 7, came to New York to live with them. Since his arrival, Don has been a source of wife of spoiling Don and failing to curb his "meaness." Mr. P. complained constant friction between his mother and stepfather. the latter accused his that Don was a financial burden and, especially when drinking, subjected him to frequent and excessive beatings. When Don's mother would intervene to protect him, Mr. P. threatened to leave if the boy was not sent back to the grandparents.

9(c) A young child who exhibits age-appropriate sexual or aggressive behavior which is considered to be abnormal; This behavior cannot be tolerated because it evokes the parent's own unacceptable impulses which are excluded from consciousness, and ascribed to the child by means of denial and projection. Sexual acting out in older children will often elicit physical abuse from a parent who identifies with these unacceptable impulses.

Case 5. **Debby P., a 7-year-old black girl, had been subjected to recurrent** abuse by her mother for alleged mutual masturbation with her five-year-old sister. Mrs. P. habitually examined Debby's panties for stains or some other evidence pointing toward masturbation. She would then accuse her and punish her with beating. The abuse was accompanied by threats of abandonment.

Mrs. P.'s childhood had been marred by abandonment by her mother and a punitive relationship with her grandmother, who used to beat Mrs. P. and her twin sister while they slept. At the age of 14, Mrs. P. was placed in a training school, where she had engaged in some homosexual activity. Debby's masturbation undoubtedly evoked her mother's long-standing guilt and anxiety over homosexuality, which she managed by attacking Debby with the full fury of her punitive superego.

CURRENT ENVIRONMENTAL STRESS

Environmental stress includes current events which widen the discrepancy between the limited availability and quality of parenting and increased child rearing pressures. The stress may consist of:

(1) A diminishing of child-rearing resources, which might be due to a spouse's illness or desertion, or the unavailability of a previous caretaker, such as a neighbor, or some other member of the family.

Case 6. Calvin, age 10, was referred to the Bureau of Child Welfare by the school guidance counselor because bruises, scars, and cuts were observed all over his body. This resulted from beatings inflicted by his father, Mr. A. Mr. A., an alcoholic, began to beat Calvin and his two younger children regularly with a knotted ironing cord two years ago after he assumed full-time child care responsibility when his wife became incapacitated following a stroke. Mr. A. decided to leave his job and seek public assistance in order to take care of the three children. These arrangements broke down, however, when the pressures of child care caused an increase in Mr. A.'s drinking which was accompanied by a progressive loss of impulse control.

(2) The actual or threatened loss of a key relationship which provides the parent with emotional security and dependency gratification. This may occur when the spouse becomes physically or emotionally unavailable, or when ties with parents or important relatives are severed due to estrangement, illness, or death.

(3) Additional child-rearing pressures, such as the birth of another child, children becoming ill, or assuming the temporary care of other children occasioned by illness or death of friends or relatives.

At this point, one may summarize the psychodynamic pattern operating in the abusive mother during her interaction with the scapegoated child.

The increased demand for nurturing by the child intensifies the mother's own unsatisfied dependency longings. Since the mother is usually unable to receive gratification and support from her spouse and family, she turns to the child for the satisfaction of these needs. These claims on the child are inevitably frustrated, as they are incompatible with the satisfaction of his own urgent demands. At this point the mother unconsciously equates the child with her own critical, rejecting mother who never could satisfy her.

The mother passively reenacts with the abused child the rejection and humiliation she originally experienced with her own mother. The resulting anxiety, guilt, and loss of self-esteem threatens the mother's fragile, narcissistic equilibrium. Her "bad" self-image and unacceptable feelings become intolerable and are displaced onto the child with the aid of defense mechanisms such as denial, projection, and externalization. With this shift, the mother assumes the identification with her "bad" mother, representing her punitive superego, and attacks her child who now symoblizes her past and current inadequacies. This identification with the aggressive mother allows her to actively master the traumatic rejection she had passively experienced as a child at the hands of her own mother. Signs of poor responsiveness, failure to thrive, or deviancy on the child's part may facilitate the role reversal and the transfer of unacceptable maternal traits onto the child.

In addition to representing the "bad mother" and "bad childhood self" in the mother's unconscious, the abused child may become linked to other individuals who have been associated with ambivalence and/or rejection. He may symbolize a despised former mate or lover, a hated sibling rival, or a disappointing parental substitute; but all of these additional objects retain a tie to the original "bad," rejecting mother.

Nonabusive mothers whose children have been battered by husbands or boyfriends exhibit a slight variation in the psychodynamic pattern. The interaction between mother and child begins in a similar fashion as the mother endows the child with the attributes of her own rejecting mother. However, the resulting "bad" childhood self image derived from her mother is partly maintained and partly transferred to the child, while the internalized "bad mother" is projected onto the abusive mate. The mother identifies primarily with the "child-victim" rather than with the "mother-aggressor."

These women submit to the physical cruelty of their mates as a masochistic repetition of their childhood victimization by rejecting, aggressive parents. The pain-dependent attachment to the spouse serves as a defense against their hostility toward the child. This is confirmed by the tenacity with which these women cling to brutal and humiliating relationships and by their tendency to assume the abusive role if the spouse leaves.

TREATMENT OF ABUSING PARENTS

The treatment of child-abusing parents poses specialized difficulties beyond those usually associated with an impoverished, poorly motivated, psychologically unsophisticated, multiproblem population. These difficulties impinge on the treatment team as well as on the family of the abused child. The following problems are superimposed on the treatment situation by the characteristics of the abusing parents.

(1) The effects of ongoing investigative and punitive procedures inhibit the establishment of a confidential and supportive relationship with the therapist. The problem of confidentiality may be met by divorcing the child protective services and court-related activities from the therapeutic team. Psychiatric evaluations required by the agencies or the court should be performed independently by their own personnel.

(2) The suspiciousness and basic mistrust of authority exhibited by these parents also interfere with the formation of a trusting relationship with the treatment staff. This is a result of their life-long experience of humiliation and criticism at the hands of their own parents.

(3) The fragile self-esteem of these parents makes it difficult for them to accept advice and help from the therapeutic team. Crucial advice concerning child rearing and home management might be rebuffed if it is construed as criticism. The parents require continual reassurance and support, especially during the initial stages of treatment. Their own basic dependency needs must be gratified before "demands" can be placed on them.

(4) Therapeutic focus on the abused child must be approached gradually and with caution, as the parents feel threatened by a change in their special relationship with this child. They feel a great deal of jealousy and competitiveness with adults who would preempt their parental role. This has been observed in cases in which the abused child has been treated simultaneously with the parent. The parent often attempts to interrupt treatment as soon as the child develops a warm attachment toward his therapist.

(5) The abusive parents are masochistic and provocative, and they possess a strong unconscious need to turn the treatment situation into a repetition of their frustrating and humiliating interaction with their parents and spouses. The treatment staff must be trained to handle such provocative behavior without counterreacting.

The next group of treatment obstacles is primarily determined by those personal attitudes and feelings elicited on the part of therapists by abusive parents and the act of child abuse itself.

(1) The phenomenon of negative countertransference is such an obstacle. This involves the tendency of the therapist to instinctively condemn

and dislike a parent who would cruelly subject an innocent infant or child to physical abuse. The primary therapist of the abusive parent, as well as the whole treatment staff, must learn to control feelings of anger and self-righteous indignation toward the guilty parent. Such expressed attitudes, needless to say, are incompatible with a therapeutic program.

(2) The therapist tends to overidentify with a "good" parent, by rescuing the child from a threatening situation. These rescue fantasies are often accompanied by an attempt to "reform" the abusive parent by transforming her into a model parent. The abusive parents are obviously unable to tolerate such zealous competitiveness on the part of the therapist.

(3) The infantile, demanding qualities of the abusing parent are often threatening to the therapist, especially when they are accompanied by hostility and lack of cooperation and commitment to the treatment process. These parents frequently arrive late or miss their appointments and seem unappreciative of the therapist's investment of time and energy. Their behavior is certainly a threat to the narcissistic gratification of the therapist.

In view of these formidable obstacles to treatment, many have questioned the value of involving the abusing parents in a therapeutic program. Some workers in the field consider the parents to be untreatable and recommend that abused children be routinely taken from their parents and referred for placement in foster homes or institutions. This solution, however, is not without its limitations and disadvantages. Abused children, who usually manifest serious psychiatric impairment, may adjust poorly to placement. In addition, the quality of children's shelters and institutions leaves much to be desired and, in fact, might be even more damaging to the child. Foster parents vary immensely as to their child-rearing capabilities, and it is not uncommon for abused children to receive additional abuse at the hands of foster parents. In addition, foster and institutional care is expensive, and constitutes an enormous economic burden for the city. (The annual cost to maintain a child in a foster home or institutional setting in New York City ranges between $4,000 and $13,000)[5].

Others familiar with child-abusing parents feel that many of them can be rehabilitated. Pollock and Steele[6] estimate that 80 % of these parents can be treated with satisfactory results under optimal conditions. Our own treatment program at the Downstate Medical Center, operating with limited resources, has helped the majority of the families involved. The Downstate program supplies psychiatric treatment to both abusing parents and the abused children. Approximately 16 families have been involved in the program during the past year, and 11 of them are still receiving treatment. An effective program for the prevention and treatment of child abuse should be directed toward the modification of the major variables previously implicated in its etiology. Some of our treatment goals for the parents are as follows:

(1) Helping the parent establish a trusting, supportive, and gratifying relationship with the therapist and with other adults.

(2) By assisting the parent to receive gratification from others, he will no longer depend on the child to bolster his self-esteem.

(3) Helping the parent improve his chronically devalued self-image.

(4) Providing the parent with a positive model to identify with regarding child-rearing techniques.

(5) Enabling the parent to derive pleasure from the child, and to develop the parent's ability to give to the child (undoing the role reversal).

(6) Helping the parent to understand the relationship between the painful experiences of his own childhood and current misperception and mistreatment of the child.

Needless to say, the traditional psychiatric treatment process must be greatly modified if these goals are to be attained. The therapist must be active, supportive, and flexible and must eventually provide the type of dependency gratification which these parents were previously unable to obtain. "Giving" to the parent may be expressed in the form of providing child-rearing advice, being available on an emergency basis, making visits to the home, securing necessary medical services for the family, establishing liason with the schools and with the numerous social agencies as an advocate of the parent. Group therapy has also been extremely helpful to abusing mothers for ventilation and mutual support and as a bridge to the establishment of social contacts.

The major ingredient of any treatment program is the involvement of the parent in a corrective emotional experience with an accepting, gratifying, and uncritical adult. The helping person need not be a psychiatrist or physician. Social workers, nurses, and mature volunteers who have mothered successfully may be trained to help abusing parents.

The basic focus of intervention with the children should be on preventing abuse in "high risk" cases whose physical or behavioral defects might prove to be too burdensome to an immature "abuse prone" mother. These children could be identified by pediatricians in a clinic setting or in private practice. These parents should be helped to understand the nature of the child's impairment and the appropriate changes in management that might be required.

The basic aims of psychiatric intervention with the children are the reversal of psychological and cognitive damage already inflicted and the prevention of future maladaptation.

The environmental stress may be reduced by providing day care facilities for infants and preschool children and homemaking assistance for the parents when appropriate. Some family crises might be helped by family consultation and treatment and by emergency home visits.

The attainment of these difficult goals requires the imaginative deployment of the many services and techniques available to those whose professional concern is the welfare of children and families.

References

1. New York City Central Registry for Child Abuse, 1972-1973.
2. Fontana V: The Maltreatment Syndrome of Children, presentation at American Medical Association Convention, New York, June 26, 1973.
3. Green A, Gaines R, Sandgrund A, and Haberfeld H: Psychological sequellae of child abuse and neglect. (Submitted for publication.)
4. Green A: Child abuse: Pathological syndrome of family interaction. (Submitted for publication.)
5. Schedule of rates paid to voluntary child and maternity care agencies. Form M-2836—Special Services for Children, Bureau of Child Welfare, New York City.
6. Pollock C, and Steel B: A therapeutic approach to parents, in *Helping the Battered Child and his Family*. Kempe C, and Helfer R (eds): Philadelphia and Toronto, JB Lipincott Co, pp 3-21, 1972.

Societal Perspective

It is clear that the violence abroad in our land interferes with the pursuit of happiness and is undermining the domestic tranquility. As Dr. Charles Aring has written: "The trend is toward direct action with many a basal ganglion tuned for combat."

In this context social factors which diminish interpersonal aggression need to be identified. Are there new patterns of societal relationships which might reduce violence? Dr. Roderick Gorney, author of the Human Adgenda, explores the determinants of interpersonal intensity, aggression, and mental illness. He focuses on competition and social synergy. Last, Dr. Albert Rotherberg comments upon anger, a frequent emotion but one often confused with aggression, hostility, and violence.

XIII.

Interpersonal Intensity, Competition, and Synergy: Determinants of Achievement Aggression, and Mental Illness*

Roderic Gorney

On the basis of his investigations of some aspects of interpersonal bonding in several widely different species and human cultures, the author suggests that high-intensity interpersonal bonding may be a prerequisite for various human behaviors, including cultural achievement, aggression, and mental illness. He further suggests that by increasing the degree of synergy in our society we may be able to reduce aggression and mental illness while maintaining a high level of cultural achievement.

Action to reduce violent human aggression and mental illness without exorbitant social sacrifice must be based on a very broad range of understanding. The purpose of this paper is to integrate important hypoth-

* Reprinted from the *American Journal of Psychiatry* 128:68-76, 1971. Copyright American Psychiatric Association, 1971.

eses drawn from Lorenz, Freud, and Benedict both with hypotheses of my own and with data from disparate fields.

Lorenz reported[1] that in species that do not form individual bonds but associate in an anonymous crowd, there is little interaction, let alone fighting, between individuals. The greatest amount of fighting is found in species whose social organization includes a definite bond between individuals. He explained that most of the hostile combative element in the behavior of such pairs is displaced onto an outsider through actual or symbolic threat. The rest is discharged in rituals shared by the bonded mates or friends, and it is this "ritualized aggression" that forms and maintains the bond. Moreover, a mated male cichled fish cannot maintain the peaceful bond to his female unless his excess spontaneous aggression can be displaced onto an outsider. If this "scapegoat" fish is removed, the male is likely to kill his mate. Analogizing to man, Lorenz concluded that the human bond (love) that unites individuals is also formed out of "phylogenetically programmed"[2] spontaneous aggression.

Among primates, however, the bond between individuals derives not from ritualized aggression but from the early experiences of comforting interaction during infancy. This conclusion, supported by psychiatric and psychoanalytic findings, is also substantiated by Harlow's results in his primate laboratory[35]. Although a monkey's potential for affectional bonds may be permanently stifled by early social deprivation, removing a sociable adult monkey from the objects of his aggression does not by itself disrupt his affectional bonds to other monkeys.

Comparison of various primates under natural conditions corroborates these judgments. Baboons show little more individual bonding than arboreal monkeys, but a great deal more fighting. On the other hand, apes show much more individual bonding than baboons and much less fighting. Thus it is not possible to account for the intensity of primate affectional bonding by the level of intraspecific aggression.

TABLE 1
Primate Lifespan and Close Infant Dependency*

SPECIES	AVERAGE LIFESPAN (YEARS)	PERIOD OF INFANT DEPENDENCY	
		YEARS	PERCENTAGE OF LIFESPAN
Rhesus monkey	15	1	6.7
Baboon	15	1.13	7.5
Chimpanzee/gorilla	35	3	8.6
Man	70	8	11.4

* Based on various sources (4–12).

However, I believe there is another factor that correlates well with the intensity of affectional bonding in primates: the percentage of the lifespan spent in the state of marked closeness that is characteristic of the period of infant dependency on the mother (see table 1). When more data become available, the correlation between the intensity of affectional bonding and the proportion of the lifespan spent in gradually decreasing dependency until full maturity is reached may be even more convincing.

HUMAN AGGRESSION AND LOVE, FREUD AND LORENZ, INTERPERSONAL INTENSITY

Man's interpersonal relationships are in general much more intense that those of other primates. Yet human beings too can maintain established affectional bonds for long periods without discharging aggression onto others.

Freud's discouraging view of aggression was that it welled up from within spontaneously. Although directed inward, primarily against the self, it could be deflected outward upon other people or things. It would act to the detriment of the self or its external objects unless under special circumstances it could be blended artfully with, and diluted by, the loving impulses. These loving impulses arose from a separate source, were beneficial to the self or object, and were in fact indispensable protections from the destructive effects of undiluted aggression.[13]

This formulation allowed for the possibility that if one could shut off aggression (and violence) at the source, love would still exist. Lorenz' supposition carried the instinctual conception of aggression a dismal step further toward hopelessness. Because love was to him nothing but made-over aggression, elimination of aggression would also eradicate love.

In comparing human social organizations with one another, I have been struck by a different relationship from that described by Lorenz in animals and I herewith propose it in the form of three hypotheses: 1) In just those societies that give rise to the most intense interpersonal relationships, people often display not only the highest level of general cultural achievement but also the highest level of intrapsychic conflict. 2) Excessively high intensity of interpersonal relationships is a cause of both the high level of achievement and the high level of intrapsychic conflict. 3) Violent aggression and mental disorder are the results of intrapsychic conflict (largely so engendered) that exceeds the individual's power to resolve conflict in better ways. What I am suggesting is that rather than the high intensity of aggression being a prerequisite for interpersonal bonding, it is the other way around: high-intensity interpersonal bonding may be a prerequisite for various human behaviors, one of which is aggression.

Since some frustration is inevitable, everyone must experience some intrapsychic conflict. If my hypotheses prove correct, it behooves us to assure that the level of intrapsychic conflict does not exceed that which the individual can sublimate into achievement without overflow into aggression or mental disorder. One obvious way might be to reduce interpersonal intensity.

Interpersonal intensity derives from two principal factors. One is urgency, the degree to which the fire of the drives is fanned or dampened by the patterns of emotional conditioning prevalent within the culture. The other is exclusivity, the degree to which the drives are focused upon one or a very few persons.

Interpersonal intensity denotes a sort of cultural style that seems to regulate the impact of the communication transmitted in interpersonal relationships while leaving the content relatively unaffected. For example, feeding a child is ordinarily a loving act of conferring survival needs. The content, but not the impact, of the communication may be the same whether the child is offered a variety of natural foods by any of a group of adults (low intensity) or overly tempting foods that the mother insists must be presented only by herself (high intensity). By heightening drive and concentrating dependency exclusively upon herself, the mother could be laying the groundwork for severe intrapsychic conflict when later plain foods and other adults might have to be substituted.

Likewise, there is a momentous difference between the impacts of the same hostile content when a handful of .22 cartridges is irritably flung at one's noisy companions during target practice (low intensity) and when a pistol is turned and one bullet is fired into one man's chest (high intensity).

Love arises as the joint product of the basic drives and the interpersonal relationships in which they must be expressed. Love can be satisfactorily transmitted and aroused through interpersonal relationships of a wide range of intensity.

If correct, the above hypotheses would lead to more hopeful conclusions. First, contrary to Lorenz, we could afford to diminish aggression without jeopardizing love. Second, contrary to Freud, we may conclude that aggression has a stimulated rather than a spontaneous origin. We could therefore afford to reduce interpersonal intensity because, while retaining any protective effects of love, we would thus be minimizing aggression. To my knowledge no one has previously suggested that interpersonal intensity might be one controllable determinant of the incidence of achievement, aggression, and mental disorder.

INTERPERSONAL INTENSITY: Cultures Compared

Verification with human beings requires comparison of a culture that generates high intensity interpersonal relationships with one that generates low intensity interpersonal relationships. Ideally all other factors should be the same. Human societies are not controlled laboratory experiments, but the cultures of the peoples of the United States and the Pacific Islands, particularly that of Tahitians, imperfectly illustrate these contrasts.*

In this connection, it should be emphasized that ethnographic interpretation, always a blend of simplified fact and speculation, herein becomes a doubly speculative foundation for my hypotheses. Lack of harder data is regettable,

THE FAMILY ROMANCE: American versus Tahitian

Current American family life includes high intensity in all interpersonal relationships, e.g., the hostile rivalry between a little boy and his father, the tender attachment of a girl to her father, the bitter competition between siblings, the possessive jealousy of parents toward one another or of a mother toward her growing son. In America we tend to isolate individuals from all but their families. Close relatives may live thousands of miles away. Even next-door neighbors often remain strangers for years. Within separated families the intense attachments, dependencies, and rivalries that infants everywhere tend to develop are fanned into infernos and focused sharply only on immediate family members.

Inflamed emotional attachments at home continue into childhood as "best" friendships, crushes on teachers, and passionate infatuations during adolescence, all of which we accept as normal, fixing a pattern that persists throughout life of maximum emotional intensity in interpersonal relationships. The efforts of today's adolescents to be "cool" seem largely an attempt to deny or conceal those inner fires, since it is too late to either prevent or extinguish them.

As a consequence we value, these relationships induce the child to incorporate the exacting standards of self-discipline, sacrifice, and attachment that he (rightly or wrongly) attributes to his parents. Thus he

---

*In this paper, "Tahitian" refers to the Society Islands in general. But it must not dissuade us from proceeding nevertheless to study urgent matters. We must conclude that what we have, to paraphrase Freud's wry appraisal of the conscious mind, isn't so good but it's all we've got.

"identifies" even today with such residual elements of the Puritan ethic as work, thrift, and frugality.

Throughout childhood and adolescence he must continue in the unrelenting emotional closeness of the family. At the same time he must stifle within himself, rather than act upon, the most insistent sexual, hostile, or dependent urges thus stirred up in him. Consequences for his personality are often critical, leading to renunciation not only of the expression of his most urgent but unacceptable feelings and impulses, but of his awareness of them as well. We require that the child deflect and sublimate such impulses into achievement and "success." When any unmanageable excess bursts out in the disguised compromise of intrapsychic conflict we call a neurosis, psychosis, or personality disorder, we promptly undertake to "cure" it and send the child right back to his intense family closeness, hoping naively—and often vainly—that this time the cauldron will sit calmly on the flame without allowing the steam to blow its lid.

Particularly illustrative is our reaction to the child's immature sexual impulses, which inevitably focus on those who nurture him. Incest taboos still firmly block the child from the gratifications toward which our culture's extreme family closeness constantly entices him. Sex education no more does away with sexual urges than a course in gourmet cooking does away with hunger. Sexual play with other children in general is also forbidden in our culture.

Considering the exaggerated dependencies and conflicts engendered, it is no wonder that in our society the death of a parent, child, or spouse, or the breakup of a marriage or love affair, constitutes emotional catastrophe that can blight the rest of a person's life.

While we do everything possible to heat up interpersonal relations, Tahitians do a great deal to cool them down. Tahitians, although occupying separate households, live mostly in villages of no more than a few hundred people, all of whom are at least acquainted with each other, thus diffusing rather than concentrating emotional attachments. Also, the stable kinship system maintains ties between relatives outside the immediate family. Land is owned and worked jointly by related families, and children can visit back and forth between related households much more freely than they can here.[14]

Most important for the development of interpersonal intensity is the different way a Tahitian child is treated within his family. For the first two or three years he is indulged affectionately by his mother and everyone else. Then a sudden transition is forced on him as his mother decides abruptly that the time has come to "cool" the child (in Tahiti the word does not signify a denial or pretense). From that moment on his demands are increasingly ignored, ridiculed, or punished, and the child is given what he wants only when his wish is expressed mildly and moderately.

Exclusive attachments to persons, things, or activities are also discouraged. The child is conditioned to be casual and never again to become too involved or passionate about anyone or anything. Hostile aggression, whether in terms of feeling or action, is particularly deterred. Fighting ordinarily involves nothing but shouted imprecations.

Whereas our world is dangerous, in the nonperilous surroundings of rural Tahiti, a child may roam about safely alone or only with other children. Most of his supervision is carried out by newly cooled brothers, sisters, or cousins, which dilutes resentment against no longer indulgent parents.

Whereas an American child is constantly stimulated to go on having intense wishes and attachments, which he himself must then sublimate or stifle, a Tahitian child is decisively trained by adults to renounce both permanently.

Tahitian Adoption

The most significant institution that favors reduced interpersonal intensity is the Tahitian style of adoption. In the United States only about 25 percent of children are adopted. In a Tahitian village the rate may be 40 percent. A large proportion are given to foster parents who demand them against the wishes of the biological parents. A child someone has asked to adopt is generally yielded because the community exerts strong pressure against a parent's desire to keep his own child.[15]

The degree of transfer is not complete, varying from mere knowledge of the identity of his original parents to a continuing warm relationship with them. The adopted child may be taken back by the biological parents if he is mistreated or if his foster parents die. And on his own initiative an adopted child may return to live with his biological parents following punishment or disturbance in the adoptive home. Also, a child living in his biological home may still follow the old custom and go to live with another relative if he feels mistreated[14], making the differences in experiences of adoptive and biological children seem minor.

These social patterns constitute a message about how to be a Tahitian that has profound impact. It reads:

. . . relationships between all parents and children are fragile and conditional . . .

One should not care enough, or be engaged enough to be vulnerable if anything goes wrong . . . relationships . . . must not be taken too seriously . . . (including) adolescent romantic love relationships . . . mourning and intense desires . . . attract dangerous spirits, which lose their power if one is casual enough . . . loneliness and feelings of deprivation involving broken intense relationahips are interpreted as illness, or supernatural uncanny states.[15]

Thus Tahitian society scarecely satisfies fantasies of psychological utopia. But it does offer other elements useful for our comparison. If a child's biological mother dies or goes off with another man, there are other women who will stand in for her. If a young woman's husband leaves her and she sheds more than a tear or two, friends chide her, saying that men are plentiful, all much alike, and so not worth making a fuss about.[14]

Before the missionary invasion there was little secrecy or constraint about sex. Children were given instruction in sexual intercourse and possibly even adult demonstration[16] [17] the objective being suppression of the personal aspect of sex, or its transformation "from a passion into a craft"[14]. Especially foreign was any notion of guilt in connection with sex. Tahitian women thought it amusing that English sailors should want to go off to hide in the bushes when it was so pleasant to make love in the open.[17] Even today, despite 200 years of Western influence, ordinary and nonincestual sexual curiosity and activity of children are considered by adults to be natural and of no particular concern.[14]

The Tahitian child grows up with fewer inner and outer restraints against casual pleasure-seeking and with less intense interpersonal relationships. The adult personality thus formed accords well with the island's abundant resources. Energetic striving is unnecessary and is considered dangerous to the harmony and balance of man and nature. The emphasis is on getting along with rather than ahead of everyone, on living harmoniously rather than accomplishing devotedly, on enjoying mildly rather than stifling righteously.

General Cultural Achievement

The Incas, Aztecs, East Indians, Chinese, and Japanese produced relatively complex cultural achievements. But the admirable adaptation of Tahitians to a generous clime did not include a written language, extensive arts, elaborately organized religion, or an imposing political structure.[18] There was practically no goad of scarcity to push them into preoccupation with material wealth. For the Tahitians there was never a wolf at the door until the missionaries and mercenaries imported him in mercantile sheep's clothing. Given their style of nonintense interpersonal relationships, one can readily grasp why they did not evolve high productivity or ambition. Tahitians, like other Pacific island peoples, also show marked limitations in the related characteristics of spontaneity and creativity.[14] [19]

Such adults may seem "irresponsible" by our standards. For example, if a man is fiu ("fed up") he may just not show up at his job. He is likely to be astonished that his employer would consider his own inconvenience of any consequence to an employee.

So it seems reasonable to surmise that there may be an association in Tahiti between the low levels of interpersonal intensity and the low levels of general cultural achievement.

Aggression

The evidence seems equally suggestive as to aggression. Early descriptions of Tahitians depict a people who were remarkably peaceable and gentle. Descriptive words included: humane, courteous, affable, friendly, unruffled, slow to anger, soon appeased, benevolent.[20] Early observers recognized that their infanticide was mainly a technique of population control, their stone-throwing attack on Captain Cook primarily a provoked attempt to subdue a foreign invader, and their warfare little more than ceremonial feuds between rival upper castes. Fundamental Tahitian non-aggressiveness is illustrated by their response to Cook's punishment by flogging of an Englishman who had threatened a Tahitian woman with a knife. They wept copiously after the first blow and begged Cook to halt the punishment.[17]

Two centuries of Western intrusion have modified much in Tahitian culture. But even today the Tahitian style of child-rearing results in adult personalities lacking in any troublesome amount of aggression. Suicide and homicide rates are both low; interestingly among the Chinese living in Tahiti the suicide rate is considerably higher.[21]

Mental Disorder

Before the European invasion, there were words for shy, strange, and morose, as well as shamans who undertook to exorcise the intrusive spirits assumed to be the cause[22], all indicating ordinary psychological disturbances in living. Nevertheless accounts agree that early Tahitians were extraordinarily healthy and happy. Observers maintain that true neuroses were unknown until missionaries reached them with their guilt-edged insecurities. Mental disorders seemed to follow in the wake of "modest" clothes and strictly circumscribed sexual behavior. Europeans also intensified interpersonal relationships, stressing the importance of devotion, fidelity, duty, and family closeness. Many stories are told of formerly well-adjusted adults (or their offspring) who responded to these new pressures with a variety of emotional disturbances.[17][18]

Although cultural change enforced from the outside disrupts psychological functioning in various other ways also, there may be some causal relationship between increased interpersonal intensity and the increased amount of frank mental disorder apparently now found in Tahiti. We may conclude provisionally that:

It may be possible to reduce aggression and mental illness by reducing the intensity of interpersonal relationships. The catch is that the price may be a decrease in devotion to the persons and beliefs of the parents, as well as to much-prized general cultural achievement.

ECONOMY, COMPETITION, AND INTRASOCIAL AGGRESSION

Interpersonal relationships are the vehicle of the love so crucial to human beings. Why should high interpersonal intensity be associated with undesirable consequences? Does some other element in human life render toxic what is otherwise tonic?

We must remember that interpersonal relationships are also the vehicle for hostile human attitudes and emotions. Marmor showed that high interpersonal intensity, even within an American family, does not often become destructive unless these relationships are also excessively competitive, controlling, or exploitative;[23] this is often the case in our society, but seldom so in Tahiti.

Any culture must generate personalities adapted to its realities, the foremost being that of economic structure. The level of ambitious striving, prominent in the United States and inconspicuous in Tahiti, fits its possessors for economic survival in a particular culture. But basic personality structure is not determined solely by material scarcity versus abundance. Among the Zuni and the Kwakiutl, for example, subsistence, if not always truly abundant, is readily available to all. Yet Zuni culture is characterized by the virtual absence and Kwakiutl culture by the exaggeration of ambitious striving of the competitive, controlling, and exploitative sort. Likewise, the Chuckchee and the Eskimos both live in severe subsistence scarcity, yet the former manifest these traits while the latter do not.[24]

But economic adaptation, in addition to acquiring the prestige, esteem, and status (the so-called security systems) valued in the culture. In instances mentioned where interpersonal relationships tend to be competitive, controlling, or exploitative, the economy is characterized by the emergence of "have" and "have-not" groups. The data do not always tell us whether or not these societies develop intense·interpersonal relationships, but the basic personality structures of such societies show marked ambitious striving and associated intrapsychic conflict manifested as aggression and mental disorder. Moreover, different as they are in terms of subsistence availability, the basic personality structures of Tahitians, Zuni, and Eskimos, who do not prominently develop "have" and "have-not" groups, tend to be cooperative, noncontrolling, and nonexploitative, whereas those of Americans, Kwakiutl, and Chuckchee, who do prominently develop such groups, tend to be the reverse.[24]

A striking instance of the transformation of one sort of society into the other is found in the cultures of Tanala and Betsileo.[24-27]Both had become wet rice cultivators, but the Tanala had gradually shifted from dry rice to wet rice more recently than the Betsileo. When studied, therefore, the Tanala had not yet experienced fully the psychocultural derivatives of wet rice economy that had long since crystallized among the Betsileo. Dry rice cultivation requires regular shifts to fertile new land, with resultant moves of the village in which its workers live. Wet rice cultivation, because the crop can grow almost continuously on the same terrace, makes a permanent village feasible and, what is more, makes individual permanent ownership of nearby land valuable for the first time.

With a dry rice economy, the Tanala had been a transient, classless, democratic society in which recurrently abandoned land was owned communally by the village and worked jointly by family groups who all remained more or less equal in wealth.[27] In both the Betsileo and Tanala-in-transition the family organization and basic disciplines remained similar to those of the old Tanala, comprising a pattern likely to generate relatively high levels of interpersonal intensity.[24]

Like the Betsileo, the Tanala developed a landowning caste, with the eventual establishment of a hereditary nobility and a king. When studied, resultant changes in its culture already included the replacement of tribal democracy by feudalism, the development of complex upkeep and warfare in defense of the village, and the evolution of economic importance in the institution of slavery.

Clearly Tanala culture was en route to the more exaggerated changes found in Betsileo: establishment of great differences in wealth, rank, and deference (including absolute power of the king over everyone's life, property, and status); belief in retaliation for aggression; more common possession by evil spirits; suspicion that everyone was a malignant sorcerer; more apprehension expressed in dreams, omens, and superstitions; higher incidence of crime (such as stealing and murder); and fears of retaliatory misfortune, a reflection of the hostile envy of others.[24, 26, 27] All these findings indicate increased tension within the society of a sort that tends to restrict the healthy development of the individual.

Most social scientists agree that, in general, intrasocial aggression is greater in societies in which the structure of the economy depends on intrasocial competition, and vice versa. The evolution of Tanala culture into Betsileo culture itself, a marked increase in aggression and mental illness that is attributable to a change in the economic system and in the absence of any evident change in the level of interpersonal intensity. So perhaps our tentative formulation should be modified to include something like this:

If the level of interpersonal intensity in a society is high, the amount of intrapsychic conflict (manifested as aggression and mental illness) will be directly related to the degree of competition within the subsistence of security sector of the economy.

This addition allows for the possibility that, by reducing the amount of institutionalized intrasocial competition, a cultural factor within our control, we can perhaps create conditions in which 1) relatively high interpersonal intensity need not lead to undesirable results, and 2) relatively high interpersonal intensity can safely be maintained to foster general cultural achievement.

In the United States especially we need to know whether this possibility can be realized, for in both the subsistence and security sectors of the economy we engage in severe intrasocial competition. One has only to think of the intense competitiveness and high interpersonal intensity found among ghetto dwellers to realize how urgently we need to know if we can reduce the former while maintaining the possibly redeeming effects of the latter.

SYNERGY AND INTRASOCIAL AGGRESSION

Among baboons the rigid social dominance hierarchy relieves the individual from the strain of being perpetually on guard alone against predators. Among chimpanzees, who are almost never endangered by predators, the much looser hierarchical structure serves mainly as etiquette, facilitating companionship and the opportunity to learn from others without running afoul of excitable and occasionally irritable members of the band.[9] In these two quite different species, orders of social dominance simultaneously serve, far more than they frustrate, the needs of both the individual and the group. In human social dominance orders the needs of the individual often run directly counter to those of the group as, for example, in the practice among some peoples of enforced sale of oneself into semistarved slavery to pay debts or the collection of gold dental inlays in Nazi concentration camps.

What makes this difference possible? First, among other primates each forages for his own subsistence amid ample vegetation. Second, no individual benefits from another's work. Third, the group does not benefit by the death of any of its members. Finally, with respect to needs other than those for survival, nonhuman primate individuals simply do not have the enormous potential of human individuals, and so there is in them neither as much to stifle nor as much to cultivate. Having arrived at this perspective, I found clarification of its relation to culturally determined patterns of interpersonal relationships in a brilliant concept of anthropologist Ruth Benedict and in its elaboration by Maslow and others.[28] [20]

Benedict strove to develop a comparative sociology that would account for the differences in societies that she grasped intuitively and that, as I read her, she felt were related to the overall human fulfillment they could afford their inhabitants. Benedict prepared brief descriptions of four pairs of cultures. One of each pair was anxious, surly, and nasty and showed low morale, much hatred, and much aggression. She spoke of these cultures as "insecure." The other four contrasting cultures were "nice", showed affection, and seemed to be "secure." The secure ones were the Zuni, the Arapesh, the Dakota, and an Eskimo group. The insecure ones were the Chuckchee, the Ojibwa, the Dobu, and the Kwakiutl. I was struck by the resemblance between her lists and those I presented earlier of societies that do or do not develop "have" and "have-not" groups, with their associated distinguishing characteristics of competitive, controlling, and exploitative interpersonal relations.

Benedict tried to find distinctive features that separated her two groups of cultures, but none of the standard generalizations then known were present or absent in all four secure and insecure cultures. What finally worked was what Maslow calls " . . . the function of behavior rather than the overt behavior itself . . ."[28]. Benedict's concept was that of "synergy," a term taken from medicine signifying the combined action of separate factors that work in the same direction, such as the effect of aspirin and codeine, which mutually strengthen one another's pain-relieving effects:

   . . . societies where nonaggression is conspicuous have social orders in which . . . the individual by the same act and at the same time serves his own advantage and that of the group . . .. Nonaggression occurs not because people are unselfish and put social obligations above personal desires but because social arrangements make these two identical . . .

I shall speak of cultures with low synergy, where the social structure provides for acts that are mutually opposed and counteractive, and of cultures with high synergy, where it provides for acts that are mutually reinforcing.[28]

As I indicated earlier, in nonhuman primate societies synergy prevails, though it is established more by biological than by cultural means. Benedict showed that human societies with low synergy arrange that "the advantage of one individual becomes a victory over another," whereas in societies with high synergy the advantage of one individual becomes a victory also for the group:

. . . raising yams is a general benefit, and if no man-made institution distorts the fact that every harvest . . . adds to the village food supply, a man can be a good gardener and be also a social benefactor. He is advantaged, and his fellows are advantaged.[28]

The absolute amount of wealth in a society is not the determining factor in the quality of life it affords, a conclusion also reached earlier from a different viewpoint. What counts is whether the economic system, in both its subsistence and security sectors, tends to concentrate a society's riches among a contracting "have" group or to disperse them widely to all. In the former society, with low synergy,

. . . no man can reach a security from which he cannot be dislodged . . .. He is insecure. His only security lies in having not merely much property, but more property than his neighbor.

He is driven into rivalry with his peers and he must outdo them, better yet, if he can, undo them. He is driven into rivalry because the system works that way.[29]

By contrast, in the society with high synergy:

. . . Since everyone is provided for . . . poverty is not a word to fear, and anxiety is absent to a degree that seems to us incredible . . . murder and suicide are rare or actually unknown . . . (In) periods of great scarcity, all members of the community cooperate to get through these periods as best they can . . . (Each man knows that) desertion or humiliation will not fall to his lot unless he defaults; he does not have to snatch and grab to maintain himself.[29]

It is important to remember that Benedict referred not to our own industrialized society but to an assortment of so-called "primitive" societies—some are benign paradises in comparison with ours and some are so malignant as to cast ours by contrast in a rosy utopian glow.

As Benedict went on to show, gods, ghosts, or magic tend to be benevolent and helpful in the high synergy societies, whereas they tend to be cruel and hurtful in the low synergy societies. The transformation of Tanala into Betsileo culture is amply illustrative.

So now I must add to my modified formulation one more idea:

The level of intrasocial competition in a society is determined inversely by the degree of synergy between acts required to benefit the individual and acts required to benefit the group. Therefore, in order to create conditions in which the benefits to human well-being of intense interpersonal relationships can be maintained and the hazards avoided, the degree of synergy fostered by the institutions of a society must be increased.

Some children in the Soviet Union and Israel have been raised largely by experts rather than individually by their parents. Among adults raised on a kibbutz, a culture characterized by relatively high synergy and relatively modest individual creativity, interpersonal relationships tend to be cool, but also highly cooperative. Little aggression is shown and neuroses and perversions are extremely rare.[31] [32] On the other hand, when they were grown a small but disturbing proportion of such children (in both countries) showed a remarkable lack of interest in or dedication to the ideals of the collective farm or kibbutz on which they were raised, ideals that were important to their parents, wandering away idly to languish in big cities.[33] [34] These youngsters were, in effect, precociously fiu.

CONCLUSIONS

What use can we make of this perspective? I assume that the values the majority of mankind selects consciously and undogmatically to guide our future evolution will reconcile us neither to an indefinite increase in intrapsychic conflict, aggression, and mental disorder, nor to adopting a lifestyle as relatively simple, static, and nonachieving as that of Tahitians. No doubt there is some room for compromise between the two cultural patterns, with some lessening of intensity in our interpersonal relationships and some increase in closeness between our families. Provided we simultaneously reduce intrasocial competition and increase synergy, we might thereby be able to minimize aggression and mental disorder without impairing the zestful investment of self in learning and doing that makes life and unending adventure.

198   *VIOLENCE AND VICTIMS*

References

1. Lorenz K: *On Aggression,* Translated by Wilson MK, New York, Bantam, 1967.
2. Lorenz K: *Studies in Animal and Human Behavior,* vol. 1. Translated by Martin R. London, Methuen and Co., 1970.
3. Harlow H: Basic social capacity of primates. *Hum Biol* 31:40-53, 1959.
4. Harlow H, Harlow M: A study of animal affection. *Natural History* 70:48-55, 1961.
5. Harlow H, Horlow M: Social deprivation in monkeys. *Sci Amer* 207:136-146, 1962.
6. Asdell SA: Gestation period, in *Encyclopaedia Britannica,* vol. 10, Chicago, William Benton, 1967, pp. 372-373.
7. *1970 New York Times Encyclopedic Alumanac.* New York, New York Times. 1969.
8. Spector W (ed): *Handbook of Biological Data.* Philadelphia, WB Saun-ers Co, 1956.
9. Eimerl S, De Vore I: *The Primates.* New York, Time-Life, 1965.
10. Lawick-Goodall J: *My Friends the Wild Chimpanzees.* Washington, D.C., National Geographic Society, 1967.
11. Montagu A: *The Human Revolution.* New York, Bantam, 1967.
12. Moore R: *Evolution,* rev ed. New York. Time-Life, 1968.
13. Freud S: The ego and the id, in *Complete Psychological Works,* standard edition, vol. 19. Edited 14. Levy R: Personal Communication, 1969.
15. Levy R: Tahitian adoption as a psychological message, in *Adoption in Eastern Oceania.* Edited by Carroll V. Honolulu, University of Hawaii Press, 1969, pp. 71-87.
16. Ford C, Beach F: *Patterns of Sexual Behavior.* New York, Harper. 1951.
17. Morehead A: *The Fatal Impact.* New York. Harper & Row. 1966.
18. Danielsson B: *Love in the South Seas.* Translated by Lyon FH, New York, Reynal and Co, 1956.
19. Levy R: Personality studies in Polynesia and Micronesia; stability and change (Working Paper no. 8), Honolulu, University of Hawaii Social Science Research Institute, 1969.
20. Levy R: Tahiti observed. *Journal of the Polynesian Society* 77:33-42, March 1968.
21. Levy R: On getting angry in the Society Islands, in *Mental Health Research in Asia and the Pacific.* Edited by Caudill W, Lin T-Y. Honolulu, East-West Center Press, 1969, pp. 358-380.
22. Levy R: Tahitian folk psychotherapy. *International Mental Health Research Newsletter* 9:2-15, Winter 1967.
23. Marmor J: Personal Communication, 1970.
24. Kardiner A: *The Individual and His Society: The Psychodynamics of Primitive Social Organizations.* New
25. Linton R: *The Study of Man.* New York, Appleton-Century-Crofts. 1936.
26. Linton R: The Tanala: *A Hill Tribe of Madagascar* (Anthropological Series Vol. 22). Chicago, Field Museum of Natural History, 1933.
27. Marmor J: Some observations on superstition in contemporary life. *Amer J Orthopsychiat* 26:119-130, 1956.
28. Maslow A: Synergy in the society and in the individual. *J Individ Psychol* 20:153-164, 1964.
29. Maslow A, Honigmann J: Synergy: some notes of Ruth Benedict. *American Anthropologist* 72:320-333, 1970.
30. Slater P: Social bases of personality, in *Sociology: An Introduction.* Edited by Smelser N. New York, John Wiley and Sons, 1967, pp. 566-570.
31. Bettelheim B: *The Children of the Dream.* New York, Macmillan Co. 1969.

32. Spiro M: *Children of the Kibbutz*. Cambridge, Mass, Harvard University Press, 1958.
33. Israeli sources (anonymous by request): Personal communications, 1962, 1964.
34. Soviet sources (anonymous by request): Personal communications, 1963, 1964, 1966.

XIV.

On Anger*

Albert Rothenberg

It is enormously strange that so little attention has been paid in psychiatric and psychological literature to the phenomenon of anger. Problems of violence, destructiveness, and hate are so much with us in the current scene, and there seems to be a crying need for clarification and understanding of such processes and any process related to them. Furthermore, as clinicians we devote a considerable portion of our thinking and practice to unearthing, clarifying, and tracing the permutations of anger in our patients. In depression we look for evidence of anger behind the saddened aspect: in hysteria we experience angry seductiveness: in homosexuality and sexual disorders we see angry dependency: in marital problems we unearth distorted patterns of communication, particularly involving anger. We interpret the presence of anger, we confront anger, we draw anger, we tranquilize anger, and we help the working through of anger.

Yet not a single modern psychiatric or psychological volume deals with this topic, and an extensive search of periodical literature reveals only a sprinkling of experimental articles and fewer theoretical ones. Almost invariably, anger has not been considered an independent topic worthy of

*Reprinted from the *American Journal of Psychiatry* 128:454-460, October 1971. Copyright American Psychiatric Association, 1971.

direct investigation but has been subsumed under a general category such as aggression, emotion, or affect. Such categorization has not only deprived anger of its rightful importance in the understanding of human behavior, but it has also led to a morass of confused definitions, misconceptions, and simplistic theories. Little consideration has been given to the reasons for lumping anger together with aggression, for example, and systematic distinctions are seldom made between anger and other affects or emotions. Consequently, a clear picture of the anger phenomenon itself has not emerged.

When we are confronted with the phenomenon of anger as it occurs in our patients we seem to know what we are about. For one thing, we seldom behave as though anger were simply a manifestation of aggression, and we make other implicit distinctions as well. We operate on the basis of a whole series of assumptions, none of which has been clearly spelled out. It is the purpose of this paper to clarify some of these assumptions and distinctions and, in doing so, to present a clearer picture of anger as it is clinically understood. No systematic theory of affects will be attempted, nor will a theory of aggression per se be adopted. Anger will be discussed in relation to other issues generally categorized with it: aggression, hostility, anxiety, and violence.

ANGER AND AGGRESSION

Anger is generally considered to be a manifestation of the broader phenomenon of aggression. Theories of aggression, therefore, are considered to be theories of anger as well. "To be angry" is considered to be an aggressive act, and "to feel angry" is considered the subjective awareness of aggressive impulses. Aggression also includes violence, hatred, hostility, and all manifestations of destructiveness. Much controversy has existed about the genesis of aggression in human affairs.

Freud and his followers eventually took the position that aggression was an instinct and therefore an inborn aspect of the human endowment.[13] Recently, this position has been supported in modified form by the noted ethologist Konrad Lorenz[4] and by a group of diverse specialists following him.[5] [7] Learning theorists, following an early assertion of Freud's, have taken the position that aggression is basically a response to frustration, pain, or threat and therefore is not inborn but learned in the course of human development.[8] [9] A third position, taken implicitly or explicitly by various authors[10] [11] and first set down in general terms by Sullivan[12] asserts that aggression is a derivative of anxiety that may assume constancy and drive qualities depending on cultural factors and other circumstances.

Rather than entering into a detailed discussion of the relative validity of these three theoretical positions, I will emphasize as my main point that all three positions take for granted that anger is a manifestation of aggression. This assumption, uncritically adopted in scores of clinical and social analyses, in theoretical discussions about analogies between the behavior of animals and humans, and in the formulation of myriad laboratory experiments, has crucially influenced all aggression theories. Careful study of Berkowtiz' excellent review[9] of experimental work based on the important frustration-aggression hypothesis, for example, indicates that a large proportion of the data pertaining to this hypothesis is based on observations about manifestations of anger or fantasied aggression, a closely related phenomenon.

Controlled psychological experiments cannot very readily be based on manifestations of violence or other forms of destructiveness since it would be highly impractical or even dangerous to try to induce violence in the psychological laboratory. Other difficulties relating to time factors and observational technique arise with respect to the laboratory induction of hate, rage, and hostility as well as other types of feelings and acts thought to be manifestations of aggression. Anger is relatively easily observed and reported both inside the laboratory and out, since it has definite physiologic concomitants and it is often clearly experienced subjectively. Nonlaboratory observations of naturally arising behavior labeled as aggressive, such as those found in anthropological studies, are also frequently observations of anger or else they are descriptions of complicated sequences of behavior whose relationship to frustration must be highly inferred.

In short, empirical exploration of the so-called frustration-aggression hypothesis has most clearly demonstrated a link between frustration and anger. However, the relationship between anger and other forms of behavior labeled as aggressive, such as hate, violence, and hostility, has not been clearly worked out. There is reason to believe, in fact, that anger is critically different from these other manifestations. As will be clarified further, anger does not necessarily involve destructiveness, whereas hate, violence and hostility do.

The instinct theory of aggression has also been influenced by the assumption that anger is a direct manifestation of aggression, although in a somewhat opposite direction from the frustration-aggression theory. Many psychoanalytic theorists have rejected or ignored Freud's final formulation about aggression and the death instinct[1][2] and have considered that he postulated two possibilities: an aggressive instinct that they accept and a death instinct about which they are dubious. Regardless of whether one or both of these possibilities are espoused, confusion exists about the essential characteristics of this instinct. Freud clearly labeled the instinct as intrinsically destructive, but his followers have variously referred to assertiveness, mastery, and even simple motor activity as direct or modified manifestations of aggression. Although many of these formulations are accompanied by complicated expositions of energy dynamics (including the notion of neutralized aggression) as well as extensive observations about child development, the clinical and behavioral examples of aggression cited are often examples of anger alone.

The underlying confusion, and some of the complicated theoretical superstructure as well, seems to result in part from such automatic equating of anger with aggression. Since anger is considered to be invariably a manifestation of aggression, but since it is well known (but never spelled out) that anger is not invariably destructive, it is thought that aggression itself is not necessarily destructive. From this chain of reasoning, it seems a small extension to consider such intrinsically nondestructive behavior as assertiveness, mastery, or motor movement as other derivatives of aggression. It should be noted that these distinctions are more than semantic ones, unless one insists that the theory itself is based totally on semantic manipulations. As for instinct theories of aggression based on animal studies, more will be said later. As a theory of aggression intermediate between the frustration-aggression hypothesis and the instinct theory, the theory loosely associated with Sullivan suffers from the problems of both of the others with respect to anger. Since anger rather than aggression per se has been most reliably linked with frustration, anger could logically, and perhaps preferentially, be considered a drive. If anger is considered a drive, however, we must ask: What then is its status with respect to other acknowledged drives such as hunger, thirst, or sexuality? The problems raised by such questions and the essential nature of anger itself can best be resolved through a specific consideration of anger and hostility.

ANGER AND HOSTILITY

Hostility, like anger, is either an affect or a behavioral manifestation or both—one can feel hostile or be hostile. The critical distinction between anger and hostility is that hostility always has a destructive component, whereas anger does not. "Feeling hostile" always involves the wish or intent to inflict harm, pain, or actual destruction on another person or object. "Being hostile" always involves inflicting or trying to inflict some type of destruction, psychological or physical, upon another.

Anger is often equated with hostility because we observe the two phenomena occurring together fairly frequently. However, constant association between anger and hostility is more true of animals than it is of man. In animals, the physical manifestations we associate with anger always appear prior to an attack. Hair stands on end, pupils dilate, muscles tense, and loud piercing or deep voice sounds are made, continually or in repetitive pattern. In some species, destructive attack always follows these physical manifestations, whereas in others, attack may be delayed, deferred, or even aborted at times. In humans, however, careful statistical documentation of innumerable instances of everyday anger[13], as well as general clinical and everyday experience, indicates that anger is seldom followed by destructive attack. Furthermore, destructive attack often occurs without preceding anger.

Before we rush too quickly to attribute this fact to learning and the effects of civilization, let us consider whether anger in humans is in any way essentially distinct from hostility and destructiveness. For one thing, human anger occurs most frequently under conditions of need, love, and involvement. During the course of development, we feel anger most consistently toward our parents and in our later years, we feel intense and frequent anger toward those we love, those we need, or toward situations in which we are involved. Furthermore, the physiological events associated with anger, events that the noted physiologist W. B. Cannon called the "fight-or-flight" syndrome[14], are integrated into behavior differently in humans than they are in animals.

In animals, flight and fight are the only alternatives in the face of threat or significant obstruction, but humans can employ complicated communications. Anger is particularly suited for communication. The physiologic concomitants of anger and the state of motoric readiness they produce are involuntary and discernible phenomena. Muscle tension, vascular changes, and involuntary voice change (although this may be consciously controlled) are minimally present. This is true even when a person is unaware that he is angry, so that an observer can infer it. *For humans, therefore, anger is an alerting phenomenon for the individual and for others that provides a basis for communication.*

The angry individual experiences an involuntary increase in muscle tension almost simultaneously with a perception of threat or obstruction, and he is alerted to a need for motor discharge. Rather than discharge this tension through flight or fight, however, the angry individual can employ verbal discharge and a whole series of specific communications to others designed to promote removal of the threat or obstruction. Others around the angry person are also alerted to his state of motor readiness, and if his verbal communications are clear they can help remove the threat or obstruction. Furthermore, verbal discharge itself serves to reduce muscle tension.

To be sure, both the angry individual and those around him perceive that attack or destruction is a possible outcome of the angry state, and this is one of the reasons others act. Attack is far from inevitable, however, and it occurs only when verbal communication is not specific to the source of threat or obstruction, is not sufficient as a motor discharge, does not effect removal of the threat, or is not permitted in the first place because of external or internal restraints. In other words, human beings can and do separate anger from attack. Because anger affords possibilities for communication, it is potentially constructive rather than destructive, given the inevitable threats and obstructions that occur in human experience.

But aren't hostile thoughts and verbal hostility invariable accompaniments of anger? The actual incidence of such phenomena in the angry state has never been documented, but it is clear that anger is commonly manifested solely in an altered voice tone and a communication to desist from some action or other. When supposedly hostile words or thoughts such as "Go to hell" or God damn him" are associated with anger, they often serve to be primarily alerting phenomena. Such words and thoughts are not in themselves physical attacks, of course, but they are symbolic designators of the state of motor readiness and perceived threat. They serve as stereotyped communication cues designed to avoid attack. We all know that the words in themselves do not necessarily seem destructive if the tone of voice is right. And don't we all accept it as a clinical maxim that the tone of voice that says "Go to hell" unthreateningly is an angry one, not a truly hostile one?

In essence, *hostility does not allow the object of the feeling or action to remove particular threats or obstructions but it tends to destroy the object itself.* Thus attack, violence, and revenge are manifestations of hostility, but so are sarcasm, teasing, gossip, and passive obstructiveness. These manifestations in thought or action are not simply the result of intense or increased anger, as is commonly thought. They are related to the angry state, but they occur primarily when the angry individual resigns in advance. He feels that direct communication will be ineffective or else he feels that anger itself must be suppressed or avoided.

In other words, it is hidden or unexpressed anger that leads to destructiveness. Unexpressed anger does not become a clear communication, but it still requires motor discharge or symbolic expression allowing for muscle relaxation. The sense of threat or obstruction and the internal communication of arousal persist and often lead to diffuse and indirect expression or discharge. Indirect avenues of discharge such as gossip, teasing, and obstruction are destructive because they are aimed at the integrity of the individual rather than the specific threat or obstruction he produces. Violence and revenge are destructive direct discharges, but they are not expressions of anger per se; they are in part expressions of failed or unattempted communication.

On many occasions anger is unexpressed because the threat or obstruction disappears almost immediately or else the angry individual questions the correctness of his perception of threat or obstruction and quickly finds himself mistaken. Little or no residual effect occurs. Frequently, however, anger expression is inhibited because it is considered unacceptable under any circumstances. An exposition of the many reasons for unexpressed anger in human affairs would involve an analysis of the psychopathology of anger, a task that is beyond the scope of this paper. One point, however, bears mentioning. One of the reasons anger is avoided or suppressed in advance is that it indicates arousal and need. Anger, in distinction from other forms of communication, is an immediate and sudden response and arises primarily when need is so intense that threats and obstructions are readily perceived. Such vulnerability, it appears, has long been considered unacceptable in human affairs. It is on this basis, rather than on the basis of a fear of destructiveness alone, that anger is often inhibited.

Actually, anger is highly related to love, both because of its connection to need and involvement and because of its constructive communication aspects. When anger is accompanied by a clear communication, it is a sign of basic respect for a loved person.

ANGER AND ANXIETY

It would be a serious mistake to present anger as a totally constructive and adaptive process and to neglect its noxious aspects, particularly the state of insecurity and defensiveness from which it arises. In fact, the hint from clinical practice that gave rise to some of the preceding deliberations about the distinctions between anger, aggression, and hostility was the well-substantiated two-step therapeutic approach to patient anger: recognition and acceptance of the anger; and exploration of the underlying reasons for it. When this second step is undertaken and the roots of anger are adequately explored, another more basic phenomenon almost invariably appears: anxiety.

Lest it be argued that this finding only pertains to persons manifesting psychopathology, it must be hastily affirmed that experimental work with normal subjects following Cannon's work tends to confirm the strong connection between anger and anxiety (cited by Ax[1][5]). This assertion is also true of more recent experiments, notably those of Ax,[15] Schachter and Singer,[16] and Funkenstein and associates[17], which demonstrate some differentiation in the physiological accompaniments of fear and anger. Although the operational definitions of anger and anxiety differ in these studies, Ax's conclusion from his own careful work could clearly apply to the results of the others: "These results do not refute Cannon's hypothesis of a unitary visceral excitement reaction but merely reveal a further differentiation in physiological reaction pattern" (p. 442).

On the basis of all that is currently known about anger and anxiety, both clinically and experimentally, it seems likely that both of these phenomena are aspects of a diffuse alerted and aroused state. Anger becomes the predominant manifestation of this state when the motoric arousal begins to be directed at the source of threat or obstruction or at an imagined source. Anxiety is the predominant manifestation when the motoric arousal is undirected or is directed toward avoidance or escape. However, neither of these manifestations ever seems to occur exclusive of the other. Anger, especially, is always accompanied by anxiety.

The presence of anxiety associated with anger is apparent in those instances where action is inhibited and anger is unexpressed. The state of arousal and motoric readiness continues and subtle involuntary reactions occur such as trembling, overall tension, and hyperalertness. A vicious cycle ensues where further arousal occurs readily and anxiety increases until there is disruption of thought processes, the irrationality associated with outbursts of temper or acute anxiety.

The presence of anxiety helps clarify further the threatening quality of anger and the hostile destructive thoughts and words that accompany it. In addition to the previously discussed alerting function of these hostile words and thoughts, this quality of anger is an immediate, ingrained response that defends against the anxious aspect of the state of arousal with its associated sense of helplessness. As Sullivan[12] has pointed out, the destructive thoughts and words that occur to us give us a sense of strength and power. If we think of hitting someone or even killing someone, we feel far more powerful and in control of the situation than if we think of fleeing or doing nothing. Indeed, such thoughts are often accompanied by forceful motor acts, such as pounding the table and stamping the foot. Although anxiety may also instigate the motor discharge of running away, pacing back and forth, or other aimless movements, such acts create a vicious cycle. They reinforce a sense of helplessness and may lead to even greater anxiety.

Destructive thoughts and words, of course, are themselves associated with anxiety and guilt because of social prohibitions, fear of loss of control, and other factors. Furthermore, since anger itself is socially unacceptable in varying degrees, experiencing anger produces anxiety in its own right. The relationship between anger and anxiety is quite complex, involving many vicious cycles and dynamic interactions that cannot be spelled out here. For the present discussion, suffice it to say that both anger and anxiety arise out of a diffuse state of arousal in the face of perceived threat, pain, or obstruction. Since anxiety is more disruptive and more uncomfortable than anger, it seems reasonable to assume that anger is a defense against anxiety or, at the very least, a preferred reaction. If we direct our attention to the sense of threat, fear, and insecurity when confronted with an irrationally angry person, his rationality usually returns quite rapidly and his anger subsides.

ANGER AND VIOLENCE

Finally, what about violence? We all know that violence does occur in conjunction with anger and that actual destruction can be associated with the angry state. According to the formulations presented here, the relationship between anger and violence is as follows: First, violence occurs when anger cannot serve as a sufficient alerting process for the angry person himself or for other persons who can remove the threat or obstruction, largely because of poor intrapsychic and interpersonal communication. Second, violence occurs when anger is unexpressed and threats cannot be removed; motoric readiness is not discharged and the presence of the threat continues either in memory or actuality. Subsequent threats and the motoric response to them are enhanced and destructiveness follows. Human beings can and do remember experiences of threat, anxiety, and anger, and these memories influence the perception of threat throughout life. Therefore, there are predispositions to anxiety and anger in relation to particular situations and persons or classes of situations and persons. Such predispositions are so constant and predictable that they may be considered to be structural features of the personality that tend to instigate violence. Since no such special structural features are necessary to account for anger, it is clear that anger is both qualitatively and quantitatively different from violence.

Finally, violence occurs, to a significant degree, when there is too much anxiety associated with the angry state itself regardless of previous experience with particular threats. This may be due to the intensity of the perceived threat (it may be immediately life threatening, for example), and it may also be due to excessive guilt about the experience of feeling angry or excessive fear of destructive thoughts or words. Excessive guilt induces anxiety in its own right when anger is in the offing. The added burden of this anxiety coalesces with the initial anxiety associated with anger and can result in violence.

It is necessary in closing to say a few words about hate, rage, and guilt in order to clarify anger further. Hate and rage are products of ongoing states of anxiety, truly destructive predispositions, and concomitant guilt about the destructiveness. Neither hate nor rage is simply a manifestation of an intense degree of anger, as is commonly stated, but is predominantly a manifestation of prolonged or intense anxiety. Such prolonged or intense anxiety is usually related to guilt, shame, or extreme deprivation. Violence is frequently associated with hate and rage, and violence is often a means of overcoming an extreme sense of helplessness and worthlessness.

Clinical discussions pertaining to anger often fail to make a distinction between anger and rage. Consequently, psychodynamic formulations about obsessive-compulsive behavior, schizophrenia, and other syndromes often refer inappropriately to anger rather than to rage. Although rage sometimes has the communicative potential of anger and can sometimes serve as a constructive response to threat or obstruction, it is commonly directed at the integrity of others rather than their specific behavior, and, therefore, like hostility, it tends to be destructive. As such it is a more constant psychodynamic factor than anger in many organized psychopathological syndromes.

Guilt about angry feelings is a puzzling phenomenon. It has been considered to be a result of fear of destructive impulses, a manifestation of aggression turned against the self, and a result of social prohibitions. Also, as suggested, it is produced by a fear of exposing one's involvement and vulnerability. Regardless of the explanation, it is a consistent observation that the most truly violent people are those who have difficulty dealing with angry feelings. Clinically, we meet such problems every day. In trying to help people deal more effectively with angry feelings we operate implicity on the basis of the definition of anger presented here: Anger is an assertive, alerted communicative state that arises as an alternative to and defense against anxiety and is not the same as aggression or true destructiveness.

References

1. Freud S: Beyond the pleasure principle (1920), in *Complete Psychologica. Works,* standard edition, vol 18. Translated and edited by Strachey J. London, Hogarth Press, 1955, pp 3-64.
2. Freud S: Civilization and its discontents (1930), in *Complete Psychological Works,* standard edition, vol 21. Translated and edited by Strachey J. London, Hogarth Press, 1961, pp 59-145.
3. Hartmann H, Kris E, Loewenstein R M: Notes on the theory of aggression. *Psychoanal Stud Child* 3-4:9-36, 1949.
4. Lorenz K: *On Aggression.* New York, Harcourt, Brace & World, 1966.
5. Ardrey R: *The Territorial Imperative.* New York, Atheneum, 1966.
6. Storr A: *Human Aggression.* New York, Atheneum, 1968.
7. Morris D: *The Naked Ape.* New York, McGraw-Hill Book Co, 1968.
8. Dollard J, Doob L, Miller N, et al: *Frustration and Aggression.* New Haven, Conn, Yale University Press, 1967.
9. Berkowitz L: Aggression: *A Social Psychological Analysis.* New York, McGraw-Hill Book Co, 1962.
10. Becker E: Anthropological notes on the concept of aggression. *Psychiatry* 25:328-338, 1962.
11. Lidz T: *The Person.* New York, Basic Books, 1968. 12. Sullivan HS: *Clinical Studies in Psychiatry.* New York, WW Norton & Co, 1956.
13. McKellar P: The emotion of anger in the expression of human aggressiveness. *Brit J Psychol* 39:148-155, 1949.
14. Cannon WB: *Bodily Changes in Pain, Hunger, Fear and Rage.* New York, Appleton & Co, 1929.
15. Ax A: The physiological differentiation of fear and anger. *Psychosom Med* 15:433-442, 1953.
16. Schachter S, Singer JE: Cognitive, social, and physiological determinants of emotional states. *Psychol Rev* 69:379-399, 1962.
17. Funkenstein DH, King SH, Drolette ME: *Mastery of Stress.* Cambridge, Mass, Harvard University Press, 1957.

INDEX

213